# The Investor Relations Guidebook

Second Edition

Steven M. Bragg

For more information about AccountingTools® products, visit our Web site at www.accountingtools.com.

ISBN-13: 978-1-938910-33-3

Printed in the United States of America

# Table of Contents

**Chapter 1 - Introduction to Investor Relations**................................................................1

*What is Investor Relations?* ............................................................*1*

*The Investor Relations Officer*............................................................*2*

*The Investor Relations Staff*............................................................*5*

*Investor Relations Funding*............................................................*5*

*Specific Advantages of Investor Relations*............................................*7*

*Interactions with Public Relations*............................................................*8*

*The Securities and Exchange Commission* ............................................*9*

**Chapter 2 - The Value Proposition** ............................................................**10**

*The Value Proposition Concept*............................................................*10*

*Background Research*............................................................*11*

*Formulation of the Value Proposition*............................................*12*

*The Problem of Too Much Market Share* ............................................*18*

*The Problem of Seasonality*............................................................*19*

*Communication of Risk Mitigation*............................................*19*

*The Impact of a Negative Reputation*............................................*20*

*Communication of the Value Proposition*............................................*21*

*The Value Proposition and Corporate Strategy* ............................*23*

**Chapter 3 - Communicating the Message** ............................................**25**

*The Press Release*............................................................*25*

*The Earnings Press Release* ............................................................*28*

*The Annual Report*............................................................*29*

*The Fact Sheet* ............................................................*31*

*Conference Presentations and Discussions* ............................*34*

*Newspapers and Related Media* ............................................*34*

*Other Forms of Communication*............................................*36*

*The Communications Review Process* ............................................*37*

*The Communications Calendar* ............................................*38*

*The Communications Mailing List*............................................*38*

*Handling Negative News* ............................................................*39*

The Negative News Response System ....................................................39
The Negative News Early Warning System ...........................................40
The Contagion Effect ..........................................................................41
The Nature of the Response ................................................................41
Risk Mitigation by the Investor Relations Officer ...............................42

**Chapter 4 - Regulation FD** .....................................................................**44**

*The Essentials of Regulation FD* ..........................................................*44*

*Compliance with Regulation FD* ..........................................................*45*

**Chapter 5 - The Earnings Call** ................................................................**49**

*Earnings Call Attendees* ......................................................................*49*

*Earnings Call Logistics* .......................................................................*49*

*Structure of the Earnings Call* .............................................................*50*

*The Question and Answer Session* ........................................................*51*

*Earnings Call Variations* .....................................................................*53*

*Earnings Call Bad Behavior* ................................................................*53*

**Chapter 6 - Guidance** ..............................................................................**55**

*The Case for Guidance* ........................................................................*55*

*Guidance Guidelines* ...........................................................................*56*
    Timing .............................................................................................57
    Type of Information .........................................................................58
    Guidance Range ..............................................................................59
    Consistency .....................................................................................60

*How Guidance is Communicated* ..........................................................*61*

*The Preannouncement* .........................................................................*61*

*The Guidance Schedule* ........................................................................*62*

*Aggressive Guidance* ...........................................................................*62*

*The Consensus Earnings Estimate* ........................................................*64*

*When Not to Issue Guidance* ................................................................*64*

**Chapter 7 - The Forward-Looking Statement** .........................................**66**

*The Legal Basis of the Forward-Looking Statement* ..............................*66*

*The Private Securities Litigation Reform Act* .......................................*68*

*The Safe Harbor for Forward-Looking Statements* ...............................*69*

*The Cautionary Statement* ...................................................................*70*

**Chapter 8 - The Investor Relations Website** ...........................................**73**

*Contents of the Investor Relations Website*..............................................................*73*

*Functionality of the Investor Relations Website* ..........................................*76*

*Multimedia*.................................................................................................*77*

*Using the Website for Regulation FD Disclosure*..........................................*77*

*Hyperlinks to Third-Party Information*..........................................................*80*

*Interactive Website Features* .......................................................................*82*

*Website Information Removal*.......................................................................*83*

*The Website and the IPO* ............................................................................*84*

*Third Party Providers*..................................................................................*85*

**Chapter 9 - The Sell Side and the Buy Side**..................................................**86**

*The Sell Side* ...............................................................................................*86*

    The Analyst...........................................................................................86

    The Stockbroker....................................................................................94

    The Investment Banker .........................................................................95

*The Buy Side* ...............................................................................................*96*

    The Institutional Investor .....................................................................96

    The Buy Side Analyst ...........................................................................98

    The Hedge Fund....................................................................................99

    Sovereign Wealth Funds .......................................................................99

    The Individual Investor .........................................................................99

    The Foreign Investor ...........................................................................101

    Investment Clubs ................................................................................102

**Chapter 10 - Investing Strategies** ................................................................**104**

*Investing Strategies*.....................................................................................*104*

*Implications for Investor Relations*..............................................................*107*

**Chapter 11 - Short Sellers**............................................................................**109**

*The Short Selling Strategy* ...........................................................................*109*

*The Short Seller Target*................................................................................*112*

*Short Interest* .............................................................................................*112*

*Dealing with Short Sellers* ..........................................................................*113*

*The Passive Approach* .................................................................................*115*

**Chapter 12 - Stock Exchanges** ....................................................................**117**

*Stock Exchange Overview*............................................................................*117*

*The New York Stock Exchange* ....................................................................*119*

*The NYSE Amex*...........................................................................................*120*

*The NASDAQ*..................................................................................................*120*
    The NASDAQ Global Select Market.....................................................120
    The NASDAQ Global Market ...............................................................121
    The NASDAQ Capital Market................................................................122

*The Toronto Stock Exchange* ........................................................................*122*

*Delisting from an Exchange* ..........................................................................*124*

*The Over the Counter Bulletin Board*............................................................*124*

*The Pink Sheets*.............................................................................................*125*

**Chapter 13 - Share Management** ....................................................................**126**

*Float Management*..........................................................................................*126*
    Activities to Increase the Float.............................................................126
    Activities to Delay Stock Sales .............................................................127

*The Direct Stock Purchase Plan*....................................................................*128*

*The Employee Stock Purchase Plan* ..............................................................*128*

*Dividend Reinvestment Plans* ........................................................................*129*

*Stock Splits*....................................................................................................*129*

*Dividend Payments* ........................................................................................*130*

*The Stock Buyback Option*.............................................................................*132*

*The Stock Repurchase Safe Harbor Provision*..............................................*133*

*Odd Lot Shareholders* ...................................................................................*134*

*Treatment of Abandoned Property* ................................................................*135*

**Chapter 14 - SEC Filings** ...............................................................................**137**

*The Income Statement*....................................................................................*137*

*The Balance Sheet*.........................................................................................*140*

*The Statement of Cash Flows*.........................................................................*144*
    The Direct Method................................................................................144
    The Indirect Method ............................................................................146

*The Statement of Retained Earnings*..............................................................*147*

*The Form 10-Q*...............................................................................................*148*

*The Form 10-K* ...............................................................................................*149*

*The Form 8-K* .................................................................................................*152*

*Forms 3, 4, and 5*...........................................................................................*156*

*The Disclosure of Non-GAAP Information*.....................................................*157*

**Chapter 15 - Annual Meeting Planning and Voting**.......................................**160**

*Registered and Beneficial Shareholders*...................................................................*160*

*The Annual Shareholder Meeting*............................................................................*161*

*The Electronic Shareholder Meeting*.......................................................................*164*

*The Shareholder Voting Process* ..............................................................................*165*

*The Notice and Access Rule*.....................................................................................*168*

*The Householding Concept*.......................................................................................*169*

*NYSE Rule 452*.........................................................................................................*169*

**Chapter 16 - The Initial Public Offering** ...............................................................**172**

*Reasons for and Against an IPO*...............................................................................*172*

*The Initial Public Offering*.......................................................................................*173*

*The Reverse Merger*..................................................................................................*177*

*Blue Sky Laws*...........................................................................................................*179*

*The Role of Investor Relations in an IPO* ...............................................................*180*

**Chapter 17 - The Sale of Restricted Stock**.............................................................**183**

*Restricted and Unrestricted Stock* ...........................................................................*183*

*The Accredited Investor*............................................................................................*183*

*Regulation D Stock Sales*.........................................................................................*184*

*Regulation A Stock Sales* .........................................................................................*186*

*Rule 144 Stock Sales*................................................................................................*187*

**Chapter 18 - The Road Show**...................................................................................**189**

*The Fund Raising Road Show*...................................................................................*189*

    Road Show Routing ..............................................................................................189

    The Presentation Team ........................................................................................190

    Presentation Format .............................................................................................190

*The Non-Deal Road Show* ........................................................................................*191*

    Road Show Timing ..............................................................................................191

    Road Show Routing ..............................................................................................192

    Sell Side Participation..........................................................................................193

    The Presentation Team ........................................................................................193

    Road Show Attendees ..........................................................................................194

    Presentation Format .............................................................................................195

    Presentation Follow Up........................................................................................195

*The Reverse Road Show*............................................................................................*196*

*The Presentation*.......................................................................................................*196*

*Road Show Preparation*............................................................................................*198*

*Road Show Logistics and Other Meeting Issues* ..................................................................*199*

*Road Show Boredom*..................................................................................................................*202*

**Chapter 19 - Third Party Investor Relations Services** ...............................................**204**

*The Investor Relations Consultant*............................................................................................*204*

*The Stock Transfer Agent*.........................................................................................................*206*

*The Proxy Solicitor*...................................................................................................................*207*

*Annual Meeting Voting*............................................................................................................*208*

*The Company-Paid Researcher* ...............................................................................................*208*

*The Public Relations Firm* ......................................................................................................*209*

*Press Release Distribution Services* ........................................................................................*209*

*NOBO Reporting* .....................................................................................................................*210*

*Coordination of Third Party Services*......................................................................................*211*

*The National Investor Relations Institute* ..............................................................................*212*

**Chapter 20 - Share Performance Measurements**.........................................................**213**

*Overview of Share Performance Measurements*.......................................................................*213*

*Price / Earnings Ratio* ............................................................................................................*214*

*Capitalization Rate*..................................................................................................................*215*

*Total Shareholder Return* ........................................................................................................*216*

*Market Value Added*.................................................................................................................*216*

*Market to Book Ratio*...............................................................................................................*218*

*Insider Buy/Sell Ratio*.............................................................................................................*219*

*Options and Warrants to Common Stock Ratio* .......................................................................*220*

*Short Interest Ratio*..................................................................................................................*222*

*Institutional Holdings Ratio*....................................................................................................*222*

*Management of Performance Measurements* ...........................................................................*223*

**Glossary**.............................................................................................................................**226**

**Index** ................................................................................................................................**234**

# Preface

When a company is publicly held, it has an obligation to communicate with the investment community on a regular basis. Doing so raises general awareness of the business and creates an understanding by investors of how a company generates value. *The Investor Relations Guidebook* reveals how a business should structure its investor relations function to enhance communications with the outside world.

In Chapters 1 and 2, we provide an overview of investor relations and how to construct the value proposition that forms the basis for communicating a company's message. In Chapters 3 through 8, we describe many forms of communication, as well as the impact of Regulation FD on how information is disseminated, and whether to issue guidance. In Chapters 9 through 11, we discuss the investment community, including the roles of the buy side and sell side, the investment strategies most commonly employed by investors, and the world of short sellers. In Chapters 12 through 15, we explore the mechanics of how a publicly held company operates, including stock exchanges, share management, the various types of SEC filings, and how to organize an annual shareholder meeting. We then move on to a discussion of fund raising activities in Chapters 16 through 18, with emphasis on the initial public offering and the road show. We conclude with discussions of third party investor relations services and share performance measurements in Chapters 19 and 20, respectively.

You can find the answers to many questions about investor relations in the following chapters, including:

- How do I derive a value proposition for a business?
- How do I deal with members of the media?
- How does Regulation FD impact the investor relations function?
- How is an earnings call structured?
- Under what conditions should a company provide guidance?
- What information should be included in an investor relations web site?
- What are the listing requirements for the major stock exchanges?
- What is float management?
- What are my options for dealing with short sellers?
- What information is included in SEC filings?

*The Investor Relations Guidebook* is designed for both professionals and students. Professionals can use it as a reference tool for conducting investor relations activities, while it provides students with an overview of how the department should operate. Given its complete coverage of investor relations, *The Investor Relations Guidebook* may earn a permanent place on your book shelf.

Centennial, Colorado
June 2014

# About the Author

**Steven Bragg, CPA,** has been the chief financial officer or controller of four companies, as well as a consulting manager at Ernst & Young. He received a master's degree in finance from Bentley College, an MBA from Babson College, and a Bachelor's degree in Economics from the University of Maine. He has been a two-time president of the Colorado Mountain Club, and is an avid alpine skier, mountain biker, and certified master diver. Mr. Bragg resides in Centennial, Colorado. He has written the following books and courses:

| | |
|---|---|
| Accountants' Guidebook | Financial Analysis |
| Accounting Controls Guidebook | Fixed Asset Accounting |
| Accounting for Inventory | GAAP Guidebook |
| Accounting for Investments | Human Resources Guidebook |
| Accounting for Managers | IFRS Guidebook |
| Accounting Procedures Guidebook | Inventory Management |
| Budgeting | Investor Relations Guidebook |
| Business Ratios | Lean Accounting Guidebook |
| CFO Guidebook | Mergers & Acquisitions |
| Closing the Books | New Controller Guidebook |
| Corporate Cash Management | Nonprofit Accounting |
| Cost Accounting Fundamentals | Payroll Management |
| Cost Management Guidebook | Revenue Recognition |
| Credit & Collection Guidebook | |

# On-Line Resources by Steven Bragg

Steven maintains the accountingtools.com web site, which contains continuing professional education courses, the Accounting Best Practices podcast, and hundreds of articles on accounting subjects.

# Chapter 1
# Introduction to Investor Relations

## Introduction

The investor relations function is a unique area within a business, because it does not design, manufacture, sell, or account for products or services to the outside world, as other departments do. Instead, it communicates the value of an entire company to a certain segment of the outside world that is interested in owning a share of the business.

In this chapter, we describe the goals of investor relations, the job of the investor relations officer, how much funding the department should receive, how it interacts with the public relations function, and similar matters.

## What is Investor Relations?

Investor relations is a function almost exclusively found within publicly held companies. It provides information about the financial and operational performance of a company to members of the investment community. In addition, it maintains relations with those investors who may be interested in making additional investments in the company in the future. Thus, the function maintains a two-way line of communications with the investment community. These capabilities can be translated into the following investor relations goals:

- *To maintain an active market in the company's stock.* Investors want to have confidence that they can easily move in and out of stock positions, which is only possible if there is a large and active market for a company's stock.
- *To obtain a fair valuation.* By adopting an understandable story for a business and managing expectations around that story, a company should achieve a reasonable stock price valuation.
- *To enhance the company's ability to cost-effectively raise capital as needed.* There should be investors who are sufficiently cognizant of a company's capabilities and results to be willing to invest in it at a reasonable share price.

The investor relations function disseminates a mix of information that is required under financial regulations, or which it voluntarily issues. The information released is intended to give recipients a detailed knowledge of how a company operates, its financial performance, governance, and future prospects. The intent is to give someone enough information to make an informed decision to invest (or not) in a business.

There are many forms in which investor relations information can be distributed, including road shows, press releases, required filings with the SEC, annual reports, and an investor relations section within the company website. The investor relations staff uses all of these tools to ensure that information about the company is distributed to every corner of the investment community.

Investor relations should be an ongoing activity, rather than something that a business only engages in when it goes public or needs to raise additional funds. There are thousands of publicly held companies, and they are all clamoring for the attention of investors and the business media. If a company does not allocate sufficient resources to ensure that it is heard, it will attract little investor interest, and its stock price and trading volume will both likely linger at a low level.

To a lesser degree, the investor relations staff can act as a gateway between the investment community and management. The staff can decide when managers should interact with outsiders to convey the company's goals and strategic direction. In particular, institutional investors may insist upon meeting senior managers before agreeing to invest in a company. The investor relations staff must take its gatekeeper role seriously, to ensure that the management team still has the time to run the business. Thus, a certain amount of prudence is needed to keep managers from being overwhelmed with investor relations activities.

---

**Tip:** Schedule investor relations activities for the chief executive officer and chief financial officer well in advance, since the investment community will probably want to meet with them on an ongoing basis.

---

Creating and adequately funding an investor relations department does not mean that the goals outlined in this section will actually be achieved. It is entirely possible that an economic downturn, poor financial results, or the rise of a strong competitor will keep those goals from being realized. If so, it is still important to have an investor relations function, if only to ensure that the investment community is fully informed about the business.

## The Investor Relations Officer

The investor relations officer is responsible for the entire investor relations function. In general, this means establishing a message about the company as an investment opportunity, and presenting it consistently to the investment community. This task is easiest to accomplish when the investor relations officer has been with the company for a number of years, and so has an in-depth knowledge of its operations and where to go within the company to obtain additional information. In more detail, the investor relations officer's job description is:

Investment Message

- Oversee the development and maintenance of a consistent company story
- Monitor company operational changes and financial results, and be prepared to integrate these results into any communications concerning the company story

- Monitor the actions of competitors, their reported results, and how they react to changes instituted by the company, with the intent of differentiating the company from them
- Advise management regarding the initial use of or changes to the corporate dividend policy

## Communications

- Research databases to determine which prospective investors and analysts to contact
- Serve as the primary point of contact for the investment community
- Organize and participate in road shows and earnings calls
- Serve as the liaison to the stock exchanges on which the company's securities are traded
- Work with the CEO and CFO to formulate guidance regarding expected future results, and communicate guidance at regular intervals

## Feedback

- Analyze the statements made in analyst reports, and forward this information to management, along with recommendations for adjustments to company strategy
- Listen to the views of investors about the strategic direction and financial results of the business, and forward these comments to management
- Monitor the mix of current investors, and comment on changes in this mix to management
- Advise the CEO on how to deal with short sellers

## Disclosure

- Provide training in the requirements of Regulation FD to all employees likely to deal directly with the investment community (see the Regulation FD chapter)
- Participate in the creation of the annual report, proxy statement, and other SEC filings (see the SEC Filings chapter)
- Oversee the development and updating of the investor relations portion of the company website
- Create press releases to cover such topics as financial results, the declaration of dividends, the results of shareholder elections, acquisitions, and operational changes
- Supervise the creation of investor relations materials, such as fact sheets, the annual report, and road show presentations

Management

- Be responsible for the prudent use of funds in accomplishing investor relations goals
- Develop and monitor performance measurements for the investor relations function

This job description makes it appear as though the investor relations officer is a senior member of the management team. In reality, that depends upon the amount of funding for the department. If there is only sufficient funding for the investor relations officer, then this person will handle all clerical chores, as well; anyone hired into such a position needs to be capable of personally handling *every* aspect of investor relations.

Note the extent to which the job description involves interactions – there are sections for communications, feedback, and disclosure. An investor relations officer (IRO) can only succeed in this job if he or she constantly meets with people throughout the company, which means attendance at a broad range of company meetings. An IRO who does not have an excellent knowledge of how a company operates is worse than useless to the investment community, since the IRO is supposed to be funneling this information to the outside world.

The extent to which the IRO is allowed to become the "face" of a company depends to a large extent on the CEO. Many CEOs (especially of the celebrity variety) believe that they should be the focus of attention, and so are inclined to relegate the IRO to a more administrative role. However, if the CEO is willing to delegate speaking engagements, and if the IRO has proven public speaking abilities, it is entirely possible that the IRO may make a number of solo presentations.

The ideal IRO does not necessarily come from the accounting or finance side of a business, though those areas certainly impart a strong knowledge of the financial aspects of investor relations reporting. An IRO also needs extremely strong communication skills for dealing with the investment community, either with press releases, phone calls, or formal presentations. Further, the IRO acts as the liaison between the outside world and management, and so must be able to tactfully deal with parties both inside and outside of the company. Also, the investor base of a larger company may be so wide-spread that an IRO must commit to a heavy travel schedule to meet with investors, analysts, and stockbrokers. In addition, the IRO should have worked within the industry long enough to have a firm footing in its fundamentals, and to be conversant with any special terminology. And finally, the IRO should have a deep knowledge of how the equity markets function, in order to properly position the company's investor message to best show its inherent value. Thus, the ideal IRO has strong technical knowledge, coupled with an extroverted personality and the willingness to travel.

---

**Tip:** The IRO reports to the CEO or CFO, since either of these positions has sufficient authority to back up the IRO in any requests for information or interviews.

---

## The Investor Relations Staff

In a larger public company, the investor relations department could employ as many as two dozen people. In these larger organizations, the many demands of the function make it more efficient to specialize either by task or by target audience.

If the investor relations officer elects to have the staff specialize by task, there are a number of possible areas in which employees could specialize. For example:

- *Writing.* Have someone with an excellent financial background and writing skills work with the accounting and legal departments to construct SEC filings and press releases, as well as the content for presentations.
- *Logistics.* Some of the staff could specialize in staging events or managing the logistics required for road shows and other meetings.
- *Website.* Hire website specialists to design the investor relations site, update it with new material, and monitor it for problems.
- *Research.* Have an analyst research the latest results among the company's competitors, as well as attend their earnings calls and read their public filings, to gain a sense for the overall direction of the industry and the concerns of the investment community about it.

If the investor relations officer elects to instead have the staff specialize by target audience, the department can be split into three pieces, with groups serving:

- *Institutional investors.* This group handles meetings with and information requests from institutional investors, as well as earnings calls.
- *Individual investors.* This group handles road shows to meet with groups of investors, and is most likely to handle interactions with the company's stock transfer agent.
- *Brokers and analysts.* This group handles meetings with and information requests from stockbrokers and analysts.

A possible consolidation of these responsibilities is to merge the groups that deal with institutional investors, brokers, and analysts.

It is also possible to combine these two organizational structures. For example, there may be logistics specialists who manage the road shows, meetings and presentations for anyone in the department, no matter which target audience they deal with. This combined approach works best in well-funded departments that can afford to employ specialist positions.

## Investor Relations Funding

How much money should a company spend on its investor relations activities and staffing? To a considerable extent, the proper level of funding is based on what management wants to do with the company. If a business can best be described as "sleepy," with no particular funding requirements and a long-term shareholder base that does not appear to be interested in trading its stock, there may be no need for an investor relations function at all. Instead, the business just makes its required SEC filings in a timely manner, and does nothing to intrude on the collective consciousness of the investment community.

If, however, a business has an exciting investment story to tell, with strong growth prospects, and a voracious need for cash, it should hire a fully-staffed investor relations department at once. The key functions for which funding should be provided are:

- *Institutional investor relations*. If a business wants to raise large amounts of money, it has to maintain relations with those institutional investors most likely to invest in its investment profile.
- *Non-deal road shows*. There must be an active market in a company's stock before institutional investors will have any interest in buying shares from the company, so there should be sufficient staffing and a travel budget for a large number of ongoing road show presentations.
- *Analyst and media relations*. Someone must act as the interface between analysts and management, while also scouting for possible story opportunities with the business media.
- *Press releases*. The company should release an ongoing stream of press releases about company activities and financial results, which requires a budget for a writer, legal counsel for press release reviews, and for paying a press release distributor.
- *Web site*. A company that is determined to have a sophisticated investor relations presence must maintain a high quality investor relations website, which requires both in-house staffing and a budget for several types of news feeds (see the Investor Relations Website chapter).
- *International*. It may eventually be useful to look for new investors in more distant locations, which requires staffing for all of the preceding activities, but in other countries.

These activities may translate into the following budgeted line items for the department:

- *Salaries*. Includes compensation and benefits for the investor relations officer and supporting staff.
- *Road show expenses*. Includes travel expenses, which may be among the higher per-person travel expenses of any department in a company.
- *Press release charges*. Includes the charge per press release issued by the company's press release distributor.
- *Data feeds*. Includes the cost of the ongoing data feeds listed in the investor relations section of the company website.
- *Conference call fees*. The company is charged a usage fee by the conference call company that handles its quarterly earnings calls.
- *Printing*. Includes the cost of any mailings, printed presentations, and reports issued by the department.

It may not be possible to initially budget for all of the activities just described. If so, begin with an investor relations officer who can spend time on all of these activities, and then add more specialized staff as the company is able to afford more functionality. The level of functionality purchased should be based on a detailed review of the company's investor relations strategy, and whether it is meeting the goals established under that strategy.

Once funding is allocated to investor relations, it is of considerable importance to consistently continue the funding for a long period of time. The impact of this area on the investment community builds gradually, as the department arranges more events and meets with investors on a repetitive basis to build its presence. If a company were to shut down the department during difficult budget periods, the investment community's collective knowledge of the company would decline rapidly.

## Specific Advantages of Investor Relations

Based on the preceding discussions, a penurious CEO might come to the (correct) conclusion that there is no specific legal requirement to have an investor relations department; if the CEO has no immediate need to raise funds, he might then decide to eliminate the entire function. What quantitative drawbacks might this have?

If a company does not go out of its way to communicate its value proposition to investors, there are likely to be two outcomes, which will occur at the same time:

- Some investors refuse to invest, due to the lack of information
- Other investors estimate an excessively high or low stock price, based on the limited amount of information available through SEC filings

The result is likely to be a less active trading market, because there are fewer participants, coupled with a highly variable stock price. This scenario can lead to three possible outcomes, none of which a CEO would welcome:

- *Short sellers.* A highly variable stock price is much more likely to attract short sellers (see the Short Sellers chapter), who will attempt to drive down the price of the stock.
- *Fund raising.* If the company wants to sell stock, the limited number of willing buyers and the presence of short sellers will probably keep the price low, so the company must give up more shares than it would like in order to raise a certain amount of cash.
- *Hostile buyers.* If a company's share price is persistently low, the company may attract a hostile bidder who is willing to snap up the company at a low price.

Thus, the absence of an investor relations function makes it more likely that the share price will be depressed, which has several negative ramifications.

## Interactions with Public Relations

The public relations department fulfills a function that is distinctly different from that of the investor relations staff. Public relations is tasked with creating a strongly positive image of a company in the areas where the company currently is, or where it plans to do business in the future. The intended result of these activities is to give outsiders a favorable view of the company in the communities where it has facilities, and where it offers its goods and services for sale. Public relations is designed to have the same impact on those government entities that can influence the company through their regulatory oversight and permitting roles. In short, the public relations department is in the business of generating goodwill.

The investor relations function is not in the business of generating goodwill; instead, it provides a complete set of information about a business, so that investors can make informed decisions about whether to invest in it. These differences in orientation create several concrete differences between the two functions, which are noted in the following table.

| Issue | Investor Relations | Public Relations |
|---|---|---|
| Audience | The investment community | Varies depending on the message |
| Core message | Creates a story regarding the type of investment opportunity that a company represents | Persuades recipients to adopt a certain point of view |
| Message duration | Reinforces a single message over the long term | May support a variety of messages that have different durations, depending on the audience |
| Legal ramifications | Statements made are more likely to be examined by the SEC for factual basis | Statements made are less likely to be perused for factual basis |
| Spin | More concerned with issuing material information quickly and accurately | Generally intended to create the most positive image of the company |
| Tools | Heavy reliance on individual meetings, road shows, SEC filings, and press releases | Works with traditional and Internet media to spread information |

The table shows that there are not necessarily glaring differences between the two functions, but there are a sufficient number of differences to keep them separate and under different management. Otherwise, the investor relations staff might find itself confusing the investment community with too many conflicting statements about what a company does, and not paying enough attention to the factual basis of the information issued.

If the investor relations officer has a small budget and too many uses for it, one option is to selectively hand off certain tasks to the public relations department. This usually involves media relations, which has the potential to be quite time-consuming if the investor relations officer would otherwise find it necessary to participate in interviews and other meetings.

## The Securities and Exchange Commission

Much of the information issued by or commented upon by the investor relations department is required under the regulations of the Securities and Exchange Commission (SEC). The SEC is a federal government entity whose mandate is a combination of regulating the securities markets and protecting investors.

From the perspective of the investor relations department, the SEC's primarily role is to require that vast amounts of information be filed with the SEC in exhaustive detail. The SEC then makes the information available to the public, which helps it to fulfill the mandate of protecting investors by flooding them with information.

The investor relations staff is not directly responsible for SEC filings, which are handled by the accounting department and the company's attorneys. However, it must be fully aware of the contents of each filing, since the investment community will go straight to the investor relations staff to obtain clarification of statements made in the filings. Consequently, someone in the investor relations department could inspect outgoing filings to suggest greater levels of clarity, thereby heading off requests for additional information from the outside world. Another option is to issue a press release that expands upon the information listed in selected SEC filings.

## Summary

If one central task can be ascribed to the investor relations function, it is to ensure that the investor relations community has an in-depth understanding of the company. The value of this task is extremely difficult to measure, which results in highly variable treatment of the function within different public companies. Those with sufficient funding tend to invest heavily in investor relations, while those in financial straits tend to treat it as a discretionary expense.

Though the amount of available cash certainly plays a role in deciding upon the extent to which a business should engage in investor relations, a more broad-based view is to accept that a publicly held company needs to have an investor relations function, and that function must engage in a certain set of activities. Thus, if the management team wants the company to be publicly held, they must accept that there will be investor relations; if they are not willing to have investor relations, then the company should instead be privately held.

In the following chapters, we will address how a company creates a coherent message for the investment community, discuss the investment community, address the communication tools of the investor relations function, describe the administrative mechanics of operating a public company, and note the fund raising functions that a public company may become involved in.

# Chapter 2
# The Value Proposition

## Introduction

A key role of the investor relations function is to ensure that the full value of a business is recognized by the investment community. To do this, the investor relations officer coordinates the building of a central theme, or *value proposition*, that investors use as the basis for assigning a value to a company. If a business routinely follows its stated value proposition and reinforces the message with the investment community, this can be a powerful tool for driving investor perceptions of what the correct stock price should be.

In this chapter, we describe the value proposition concept, how to create it, and how to communicate it to the investment community. We also address a number of issues related to the value proposition.

## The Value Proposition Concept

To the greatest extent possible, discussions with the investment community should incorporate the value proposition of a business – that is, the underlying intrinsic value that the company represents. Intrinsic value is the worth of a company's assets, which may be much more than its *physical* assets. The following intangible assets can add a great deal to the value of a business:

- Branding
- Patents and copyrights
- Research and development / Product pipeline
- Store locations
- Value of real estate
- Government licenses
- Partnerships
- Employees

Offsetting these assets are a number of subtractions, both for recorded liabilities and those that are not yet probable or material enough to appear on a company's balance sheet. Examples of these liabilities are:

- Lawsuit settlements
- Regulatory penalties
- Impact of revoked government permits
- Environmental remediation costs
- Declining market share
- Declining overall market

- New competitors
- Product obsolescence

It is difficult to assign specific values to the preceding lists of intangible assets and liabilities, but it is certainly possible to assign a *range* of plausible values. When a company's intrinsic value is presented as falling somewhere within a likely range, investors can be encouraged to pick a value somewhere within this high-low continuum, which they use as the basis for whether they should buy, continue to hold, or sell the company's stock at its current market price. No matter what value they may pick, it is still within boundaries established by the company, and so achieves the goal of arriving at a reasonable market value.

## Background Research

Before formulating a value proposition, conduct a detailed review of how the company's competitors have positioned themselves with their own value propositions. You should know each value proposition, and how it is supported over time by the investor relations messages being issued by the various competitors. If possible, peruse each company's earlier statements to see if their stated value propositions have changed over time; this can yield clues about which variations on value propositions have been found by others to be untenable.

The second research step is to see how the value propositions compare to each other. There is likely to be some variation between the messages being issued by each competitor, so that they can achieve some differentiation in the eyes of the investment community. Evaluate how well each value proposition appears to be working, based on the valuations being awarded by investors. This can be determined by comparing such metrics as market value to sales or market value to net profits for each competitor.

The third step is to review how the investment community reacts to the various value propositions. Have they commented about it during earnings calls, or as part of the question and answer sessions at annual meetings? Are any of the value propositions viewed with such skepticism that it would be unwise to emulate them? Are others viewed as being believable? This is a very qualitative analysis, but may yield impressions about certain variations on the basic story that are not going to be accepted.

Finally, conduct a search of adjacent industries to see if there are any companies using value propositions that might be transferable to the company. This is especially useful if these other industries are ones being awarded higher valuations by the investment community. If so, give strong consideration to positioning the company's value proposition to more closely align with the adjacent industry.

In summary, the background research begins with the value proposition advanced by each competitor, proceeds to a comparison of the various propositions and how each one is perceived by the investment community, and ends with a review of adjacent industries. With this information in hand, you can now create a value proposition for the company, knowing the context in which it will be perceived by outsiders.

## Formulation of the Value Proposition

The formulation of a value proposition is a group effort that is usually coordinated by the investor relations officer. The ultimate decision as to what the stated proposition will be is confirmed by the CEO, but the entire management team should be involved in its formulation, in order to gain a variety of perspectives on the issue.

The process begins with the background research noted in the last section; this gives the management team a good idea of the types of value propositions being used, and how they are viewed by the investment community. The group then discusses the strengths and weaknesses of the business, and what they want investors and analysts to focus on when they view the results and prospects of the company. Based on this information, the group develops a number of one-sentence statements about the value proposition that the company represents. Examples of value propositions are:

- "The company provides a Tuscan-style dining experience for families." This statement implies a high-volume chain restaurant that is value-priced. Investors would be attracted to the implication of high volume sales at a themed restaurant.
- "The company manufactures premium hardwood office furniture." This statement implies a high price, and therefore high margins in a large market.
- "The company provides strategic consulting to Fortune 500 companies." This statement implies high-priced services to customers who can afford to pay. Investors would be attracted to the prospect of strong profit margins.

A value proposition does not have to be entirely based on the current capabilities of a business. Instead, it can reflect the *reasonable* aspirations of the management team. For example, it is entirely reasonable for a company that supplies tires to state in its value proposition that it will be *a* worldwide supplier of racing tires. It is probably *not* reasonable for the same company to state that it will be the *dominant* worldwide supplier of racing tires, especially if it currently occupies only a small part of the market. The latter statement would be essentially impossible in many industries, where market dominance is based on large investments in manufacturing capacity, significant capital requirements, patent portfolios, and long-term incremental gains in sales volume. In these cases, investors will be more likely to assume that such an ambitious company will squander its resources in a bid to gain market share, and so may assign it a *lower* market value than would otherwise have been the case. In short, always confine the value proposition to what investors will consider to be credible ambitions.

It is extremely important to arrive at a concise value proposition that associates the company with a segment of the market that is perceived as being particularly valuable. By doing so, investors may link the company to the targeted market segment, and give it a correspondingly higher market valuation. For example, the management team of an apartment management company might begin with the value proposition of being the largest operator of apartments in the southwestern United States. However, the statement of the geographic region conveys no value to an investor. Instead, the management team re-examines the operations of the company to derive a more targeted message, and finds that its renters tend to be older than the industry median, and to rent for longer periods of time. This leads to a revised value proposition, which is that the company operates long-term rental housing for retired people. Investors interpret this group to be more reliable payers of rent than the average renter, and so give the company a higher valuation.

The preceding example greatly increases the precision of a value proposition, but it does not necessarily place the company in a category that will convince investors to award it a higher valuation. There are several possible ways to improve the perceived valuation, such as:

- *Niche restatement.* Many companies service some kind of niche market, rather than selling on a strictly low-cost basis against the largest competitors. It is important to avoid making it appear as though a company is locked in a death struggle with a large low-cost provider. Instead, restate the value proposition to focus on the niche in which the company really operates, such as "produces racing tires," "handcrafts fine men's suits," or "manufactures the world's best motor yachts."

- *Refocus the company.* A company may have more than one line of business, which makes it difficult to craft a value proposition. For instance, to cite a real example, how do you summarize the value proposition for a company that engages in consulting for the federal government *and* compiles land ownership databases for the oil and gas industry? In such cases, it may be best to sell off whichever part of the business has the least potential, so that the remainder of the business can focus on fulfilling the promise of a concise value proposition statement.

- *Reposition the company.* What if a company competes in an industry that is generally not given much of a valuation by the investment community? Perhaps it is one in which there is little growth, plenty of competition, and low margins. It would appear that any value proposition that a company might propose would be doomed, since investors will pin the same industry-wide valuation multiples on the company. However, if a business were to operate in a particularly profitable and well-protected niche within this larger industry, perhaps it would be possible to craft a value proposition that really places the company in an adjacent industry where valuations are higher. For example, companies located in the auto parts supply business have microscopic profits and so have been accorded minimal valuations for years; but what if a company produced automated vehicle guidance software that could also be applied to manufacturing robots, airplanes, and satellites? This company would be able to present a strong case for being part of an entirely different industry, such as manufacturing equipment, software, or even aerospace. In short, there may be an opportunity to reposition the company into a different peer group to which investors assign higher valuations.

---

**Tip:** It may be worthwhile to discuss possible value propositions with investors or analysts who cover the company's industry. They may advise management to avoid value propositions that would be considered by the investment community to be significantly different from the company's current market positioning.

---

If a business is functionally an amalgamation of several disparate lines of business, management may want to retain all of it because the company as a whole generates a significant profit. However, there is a danger that the investment community will assign a valuation to the entire business based on just one or two of its more prominent subsidiaries. If those subsidiaries are in industries to which low valuations are being assigned, the valuation of the company as a whole will suffer, especially if other parts of the business would otherwise have been assigned higher valuations. Thus, management should be careful about taking a company public that appears to be heading in several different directions at once.

The initial formulation of a company's value proposition typically occurs during the period leading up to its initial public offering (IPO). At this time, the company's investment banker provides advice about the types of value propositions that the market tends to favor. This does not mean that the investment banker should be allowed to control the basic message – instead, the management team formulates its own value proposition within the framework of the investment banker's advice and its own background research (as noted in the last section).

The following bullet points contain examples of value propositions that a company might use, based on different sets of circumstances. These examples can be used as general guidelines for companies that are faced with similar situations.

- *Low cost proposition.* A company may have built such a large market position that it can routinely offer products for sale that have lower costs than those of its competitors. This story line should only be used by large market-share companies, though a business that has access to unusually low-cost raw materials may also be able to employ it. If this approach is used, state the reason for the company's ability to sustain low costs. For example:

  The company achieves low-cost dominance in its markets by constructing automated factories close to its customers, thereby driving down both labor and distribution costs.

- *Steady income proposition.* A company that is well-positioned to reap strong cash flows in a relatively stagnant market could formulate a value proposition that emphasizes its reliable issuance of dividends. Under the stated circumstances, this may be the only viable value proposition, since there is little evidence of growth in the core business. For example:

> The company has generated steady cash flow from its power generation facilities to fund a consistent and reliable dividend for its investors for the past half-century.

- *Intellectual property proposition.* A company may be essentially funded as a research and development laboratory, and has an array of approved patents and/or patent applications. It may not yet sell any products. These circumstances allow for several possible value propositions, including licensing of intellectual property, the eventual establishment of the company's own product lines, or the sale of the patent portfolio to a larger company. For example:

  > The company has a deep patent portfolio covering all aspects of the production of the new copper-chromium battery, which stores electricity much longer than lithium-ion batteries. The company intends to license the use of its patents to several larger battery manufacturers.

- *Pacing proposition.* A company may have developed a strong capability to open a large number of retail stores with supporting distribution systems. This is a significant value proposition, since a business can use it to rapidly expand into new geographic regions. For example:

  > The company sells home improvement supplies from trucks that rove through older neighborhoods where homes are more likely to be in need of repair. The concept has successfully been applied to a franchise model, for which the company is accepting applicants for franchises throughout the country.

- *Green or ethical proposition.* A company wants to include an ethical component into its business plan, such as only sourcing in countries that prohibit child labor laws. Or, it may commit to only buying from suppliers who practice environmentally friendly manufacturing methods. Focusing solely on these elements does not constitute a value proposition, since it does not reveal how the company will generate profits for its investors. Instead, it only introduces a concept of how the business will be run. This proposition may be of interest to those funds that only invest in ethical or green companies, but it will not be the core reason for any investments they may make. The following example expands upon the concept to create an actual value proposition that might interest an investor:

  > The company manufacturers a new type of solar-powered fabric that is derived from organically-grown cotton plants. The company intends to adapt this fabric to power portable electronic devices.

- *Customer credibility proposition.* A company may have deep penetration into the largest and most high-profile customers serviced by an industry, which indicates a combination of high-quality sales efforts, customer service, and product quality. The value proposition can state how the company finds and retains these customers, and may even name some of the customers. For example:

> The company provides emergency air conditioning maintenance services to over 300 of the Fortune 500 companies by guaranteeing rapid response times from its network of regional service centers.

- *Employee quality proposition.* A company may have an unusually strong management team, or a system for building managers or training employees that is unique in its industry. Be careful in using this approach as a differentiating factor, since a few key hires by a competitor could eliminate any competitive advantage. An example of this approach is:

> The company uses its in-house management college to train all employees in the concepts of lean production on a repetitive basis, which has been the key reason for the company's consistent, high level of manufacturing efficiency.

- *Branding proposition.* A company may have invested substantial amounts in a brand name, which allows it to generated outsized profits. The value proposition should focus on the duration and amount of the company's investment in the brand, and how this translates into additional profits. For example:

> The company has invested 10% of its cash flow in the DuraSoft brand of multi-use diapers for the last decade, resulting in a secure customer niche that generates profits twice as high as the industry average.

- *Unique product proposition.* A company may have a unique and well-known product that the investment community closely identifies with the business. The company can use an association with this particular product to build a story line around the entire business, even if the remainder of the company provides relatively generic products and services. For example:

> Hegemony Toy Company, maker of the industry-leading Napoleon Wars board game, is a provider of military-oriented toys and games to the under-20 age group.

- *Sales channel proposition.* A company may make use of a unique sales channel that is difficult for rivals to duplicate, and from which the company generates unusually high profits. If so, state the nature of the sales channel and how the company defends its turf. For example:

> The company sells its power tools through home-based salespeople who use sports-television viewing parties to gather neighborhood men to view

power tool demonstrations. This sales channel requires a great deal of time to build, and so cannot be easily duplicated by a competitor.

Consider the initial formulation of a value proposition as only a first draft. It is worthwhile to discuss this draft with key investors and analysts to see how they react to it. If they are not in favor, ask questions about how their perceptions of the company invalidate the proposed value proposition. In many cases, you can reasonably extrapolate their opinions to the market at large, which may call for a re-evaluation of the value proposition. In other cases, the problem may be that the company has failed to properly communicate some aspect of its operations or plans that would have altered the opinions of those consulted. If the latter is the case, consider a focused and repetitive release of information to the investment community that emphasizes the missing information.

**Tip:** The value proposition must be short and easy to understand, since it will likely be used by stockbrokers in their sales pitches to clients.

Once the value proposition has been formulated, create a set of value drivers that are the key determinants of the value of the business. Examples of value drivers in various industries are:

**Value Driver Examples**

| Industry | Value Driver |
| --- | --- |
| Airlines | Price of jet fuel |
| Consumer electronics | Contents of product pipeline, time to market |
| Home building | Mortgage interest rate, cost of lumber |
| Retail chain | Efficiency of product distribution system, store locations, real estate value |
| Destination resort | Price of transportation to the resort, perception of travel safety |
| Mining | Environmental remediation regulations, labor costs, commodity demand |

It is useful to survey key investors and analysts about what they perceive a company's value drivers to be, and to consider incorporating these drivers into the company's "official" set of value drivers. Investors like to focus on value drivers, since changes in these drivers typically alter the overall value of a business.

**Tip:** Consider working with investors and analysts to derive a *ranked* set of value drivers. Knowing the perceived relative ranking of each driver may force management to focus on those drivers that can be controlled by the company.

Once established, the investor relations staff can routinely quantify identified value drivers, which investors then use to adjust their views of what the most appropriate stock price should be for the company.

It is impossible to over-emphasize the need to keep a company's value proposition as short and easy to understand as possible. Doing so presents investors with the image of a business that has a laser focus on how to generate value. Conversely, a large and difficult to understand story implies that either management does not understand its own company, or the entity is active in so many disparate areas that it is impossible to tie everything together under a single story line. In the latter case, investors will see no reason why a business can achieve its goals, since it is so difficult to define what those goals should be. If so, spinning off unrelated subsidiaries to focus on a single value proposition may be the best way to proceed, even if doing so results in a significant shrinkage in the size of the company.

## The Problem of Too Much Market Share

The valuation of a company may actually suffer if it has too much market share. The problem is that investors will not see much upside for the stock, since it is increasingly difficult to earn those last few points of market share percentage that the company does not already have. In addition, any company with massive market share is the automatic target of every other company in the industry, so there is a high likelihood that its market share will be gradually whittled away. Further, government oversight makes it difficult to buy competitors if the result is an excessive amount of industry consolidation. The following steps can overcome this investor perception:

1. Communicate a plan for how the company plans to defend its existing market share, and follow this up with any number of press releases to prove that the company is vigorously defending its turf. These communications not only impress the investment community, but may also drive away possible competitors.

2. Show how the company plans to expand the size of its primary markets through such measures as expansion of the existing product line and entry into new geographic regions. It is nearly always less risky to expand within the current market than to expand into a new market, so this is a high priority item.

3. Describe how the company plans to move into adjacent markets. There is an increased risk of failure if the company moves too far from its core competencies, so adjacent moves are perceived as being riskier, and are therefore discounted by investors.

In many markets, there is no industry group that tracks market share, so there may not even be a way for the investor relations officer to derive the amount of market share that a company has. If so, it may be better to avoid making *any* market share claims. After all, a successful company may eventually run up against the issues noted in this section if its stated market share reaches a level that investors consider to be too high. Instead, let investors and analysts make their own estimates of market share.

## The Problem of Seasonality

A business may sell the bulk of its products or services during certain seasons of the year. Since a public company is required by the SEC to release its quarterly results in a Form 10-Q, readers of these reports may be startled to find that the business is recording substantial losses in some quarters, which are (hopefully) offset by the profits earned during other parts of the year.

Seasonality should not be a problem, as long as investors are properly educated about it. The investor relations officer can do so in many ways, such as:

- During earnings calls
- During road show presentations
- In press releases
- In the management discussion and analysis section of quarterly and annual SEC filings

Whenever *any* presentation is made to the investment community, point out the level of seasonality to which the company is subjected, and how this has historically impacted the company's profits. By doing so, there should be a reduced risk that investors will sell their shares at the first sign of bad news in a quarterly SEC filing.

> **Tip:** If a company is subject to seasonal earnings fluctuations, this is a particularly good reason to provide earnings guidance (see the Guidance chapter), so that investors will know what to expect in each of the upcoming reporting periods.

## Communication of Risk Mitigation

The preceding discussion has been about giving the best possible viewpoint on how a company provides value to an investor. But what about the downside risk to an investor? Every company is subject to an array of risks, which investors are also concerned about. Examples of these risks are:

- Products that are coming off of patent protection
- Products that are nearing the end of their life cycles
- The entry of new competitors into the market from adjacent markets
- The possibility of new government regulations requiring the purchase of expensive pollution control equipment
- The sudden restriction of key raw materials due to supply chain disruptions

A company is required by SEC regulations to state its key risks in various filings, which are available to the public. If investors cannot place a value on these risks, there will be uncertainty in the marketplace about the most appropriate price at which the company's stock should sell. The investor relations officer can take steps to reduce this uncertainty by stating how the management team plans to mitigate them. For example:

- *Patent risk.* If key products are coming off of patent protection, state how the company is working on extending the duration of key patents, which patents are being applied for, and which patents it has recently purchased from other parties.
- *Old product risk.* If key products are old, describe the company's product development process and its pipeline of new products.
- *New competitors.* If there is a risk of entry into the market by new competitors, describe how the company has altered the competitive environment to increase the amount of capital required to start a business, its lobbying to require government licensing for new competitors, and so forth.
- *Government regulation.* If there is a risk of government controls that will increase costs, describe the ability of the company to pass these costs through to customers.
- *Raw material restrictions.* If there is a risk of supply chain disruption, describe how the company is stockpiling key supplies, or how it is shifting to suppliers who are located closer to the company's facilities.

As long as the investor relations officer clearly shows the extent of risk mitigation efforts, investors will be more comfortable holding a company's stock, and will be able to price the stock within a narrower range, thereby reducing variability in the stock price.

If a business operates in a market that is subject to occasional severe downturns, it is quite useful to prepare a presentation about what the company plans to do if another such downturn occurs. This preparation indicates to investors that the company is ready for even the most severe eventualities. For example:

The company always maintains an outsized cash reserve, which it plans to use during industry downturns to buy competitors who are not so well prepared.

The company operates in multiple agricultural regions, so a weather-related problem in one area is unlikely to have a large impact on the company's agricultural supplies business as a whole.

These disaster plans do not have to be trotted out at every investor presentation, but should be available if a more investigation-minded audience asks about catastrophic risk issues.

## The Impact of a Negative Reputation

A company could do an excellent job of establishing and communicating a reasonable value proposition, and yet still see its stock price languishing at an inordinately low level. If so, the problem may be the reputation of the business. Some companies have become embroiled in any number of public relations snafus over the years, and the cloud associated with those events may continue to hover over them for years. The baneful effects of these events may be particularly pernicious if investors believe that the same events could occur again. Consider the impact of any of the following reputational issues on the value proposition of a business:

- An uncapped oil well that causes a massive environmental disaster
- A series of vicious labor strikes that result in protestor deaths
- An explosion at a chemical facility that kills neighboring people
- Any plane crash

All of the examples are, in effect, the negative outcome of risk issues. In all cases, greater attention to risk mitigation issues might have prevented them, and might therefore have saved the reputations of the companies involved in them. However, there are also outlier events that will occur, despite every reasonable risk mitigation issue that a business might implement.

If there is a prospect of an outlier event that can cause significant reputational damage to a company, it may be useful to build the groundwork for an offsetting amount of existing favorable reputation. For example, a company that has a long history of supporting local community activities with funding and the paid time of its employees might find that local support will counteract the effects of a one-time negative event. Similarly, a business might invest an inordinate amount in green environmental controls, corporate governance issues, and/or attention to labor relations to build its reputation against the effects of a reputation-damaging event.

It can be expensive to build a high-end reputation, especially given how difficult it is to ascertain the correct amount to invest in this effort. Nonetheless, the investor relations officer should work with the public relations staff to create a budget for reputation-enhancing activities. From the perspective of the investor relations officer, the point of this exercise is to keep the negative effects of reputational issues from damaging the value proposition perceived by investors.

## Communication of the Value Proposition

The value proposition should be repetitively enforced with the outside world by weaving it into every investor relations presentation. There should be a brief statement of the value proposition and value drivers at the beginning and end of each presentation, with occasional references to it elsewhere, if doing so can be accomplished without interfering with the flow of a presentation.

> **Tip:** Where possible, have a staff person specialize in creating investor relations presentations. Centralizing this task ensures that the value proposition is consistently presented in all communications.

Though the investor relations officer may have a handy concept of the value proposition that a business represents, this does not mean that precisely the same message must be communicated to *all* investors. Instead, consider that the more quantitatively-minded investors will have their own investment models that they use to derive the price of a share. For example, a model may be primarily based on earnings, or sales, or cash flow, or at least incorporate these items. They may also incorporate one or more of the value drivers described in the last section. This can result in slightly different messages that are tailored to the audience. For example:

- *Basic message*. The company has invested 10% of its cash flow in the DuraSoft brand of multi-use diapers for the last decade, resulting in a secure customer niche that generates profits twice as high as the industry average.
- *Message for growth-oriented investor*. The company expects revenues from its DuraSoft products to increase at a rate at least twice as high as the industry growth rate for the next three years.
- *Message for analysts*. The company expects its DuraSoft-related revenues to increase by at least 20% per year, while related cash flows should increase at a 25% rate.

The value proposition can be translated into whatever information investors need as inputs to their valuation models. To do this, ask prospective investors which types of information they use in their valuation models. Then adjust the standard presentation to emphasize the required elements.

In those cases where an investor does not want to divulge the inputs to his valuation model, present the company's valuation model instead. Explain how the model works, the inputs to it, and the likely range of inputs to the model (e.g., cash flows are expected to be between $1 million and $1.2 million next year). This approach at least gives an investor the company's viewpoint on the intrinsic value of the business.

In short, the basic underlying message stays the same from presentation to presentation, but there can be a varying emphasis on the inputs that listeners need for their valuation models.

> **Tip:** Enforce a central review of all presentations, press releases, and SEC filings to ensure that extraneous information is not issued. Instead, there should be a tight focus on the value proposition and value drivers, which is not muddied by superfluous information.

A company can also use its value proposition to present an expanded story about the business, so that investors can see how its value proposition is driving its business decisions and results. For example:

Hegemony Toy Company makes military-oriented toys and games for the under-20 age group. It has entered into licensing agreements with several military-oriented high school programs, which will use the Hegemony name as the basis for their military strategy classes. The company expects that these licensing agreements will lead to additional brand recognition within its target market.

In the example, the company shows how a new licensing deal fits directly into its value proposition by expanding the number of potential users of its product line.

## The Value Proposition and Corporate Strategy

Once a company has devised a reasonable value proposition and it has been communicated to the investment community, there must be a commitment to maintaining that proposition for a long time. The worst thing that a company can do is to constantly change its message about why it is in business. Instead, investors want to hear a consistent story that a company reinforces with solid results that adhere closely to its value proposition.

This level of consistent, long-term performance is difficult for some companies to achieve, for one or more of the following reasons:

- Change in company leadership
- Inconsistent or nonexistent planning systems
- Inadequate financial results

A new CEO frequently wants to make his or her mark on a business by altering its direction. While this is excellent news for the CEO's ego, it forces the company to project a new value proposition to the investment community, which may look askance at the new approach and drive down the company's stock price. The following suggestions can mitigate the impact of a change in company leadership:

- Promote someone into the CEO position from within, since insiders understand the company's current direction and are less likely to change it.
- Have a long-term employee development system in place, so that there are several employees capable of taking over the CEO position.

If there are inconsistent or nonexistent planning systems in place, the obvious solution is to install those systems. However, this is not quite so simple. There must be a solid system of accountability in place to ensure that plans are followed, which is remarkably rare. Also, the investor relations officer must continually impress upon the planning staff the need to adhere to the value proposition that the business has been communicating to the outside world. If there is a divergence between where management wants to take the company and the stated value proposition, there must be an excellent reason for doing so that can be clearly stated to the investment community.

What if a company simply cannot achieve a reasonable level of profitability within the boundaries of its stated value proposition? It would be foolish to continue down the same path if doing so will lead to a paltry stock price or bankruptcy. Thus, in cases where a substantial pivot in strategy must be made, a company should certainly do so. However, it is worthwhile to first reach out to key investors and analysts for their opinions about what this pivot will do to the perception of the company's intrinsic value. It is entirely possible that heading off in a certain direction will be viewed poorly by investors, who will sell their shares in droves. If the management team were to instead incorporate the views of the market into any necessary change in direction, and then explain its new value proposition thoroughly, the result may be accepted with much less fuss.

The level of self-examination that goes into creating a value proposition may result in an actual change in strategic direction. A company may find that it does not, in fact, exactly fit the operational profile that its preferred value proposition implies. If so, it may make considerable sense to shed some operations and invest in other areas in order to arrive at a repositioned business that *does* fit the value proposition.

A special situation arises when management has a vision for the direction of the company, but the business is not currently positioned properly to communicate a matching value proposition. In this case, it may not be useful from a competitive standpoint to divulge the company's long-term plans. Instead, consider a gradual, long-term series of incremental changes to the stated value proposition, until the company actually reaches the point where it can justify the value proposition that it has been striving for all along. If investors see that the company efficiently meets the expectations set by each incremental change in value proposition, they will be more likely to accept subsequent changes in the proposition.

In short, the value proposition should be maintained over a long period of time, whenever the financial results of doing so are sustainable. This requires consistent support from the CEO, as well as a well-founded system of accountability for implementing plans. When a value proposition does not prove to be financially sustainable, obtain the input of the investment community before heading off in a new direction. The worst possible situation is for a company to continually swap out its value proposition, to the point where investors and analysts dismiss them as being "the flavor of the week," and derive their own valuations of the business, irrespective of what the company says about itself.

---

**Tip:** If the investor relations officer is hired into a situation where the value proposition has changed constantly, expect to spend several years of intensive communications with investors to convince them that the company's most recent announced path is one that it intends to follow.

---

## Summary

The investor relations officer can use the concept of a value proposition to create a central theme about why a company exists. The investor relations department then uses this value proposition to show the investment community how to formulate a stock price that relates to the underlying intrinsic value of the business. A company should construct a value proposition that shows how a business has the potential to maximize the return to investors of their shareholdings, without making such outrageous claims that it is clearly evident that the company is making claims beyond its ability to fulfill them. Thus, the value proposition represents a balance between the realities of a company's current capabilities and the prospects to which it aspires.

The concept of the value proposition forms the foundation of the communications that a company generates for the outside world. In the following chapters, we describe the different types of communications that a business can employ.

# Chapter 3
# Communicating the Message

## Introduction

A critical role for the investor relations department is to convey information about a company to the investment community. There are a large number of tools available for doing so. In this chapter, we discuss some of those tools, including the press release, annual report, fact sheet, conference presentation, and other forms of communication. We also describe how to set up relations with members of the media and how to deal with negative news. The investor relations staff should be well-versed in all of the tools discussed in this chapter.

## The Press Release

A press release is a brief statement about a company event that is released for outside consumption. It is one of the most important tools of the investor relations officer, since it can be constructed almost entirely within the investor relations department (subject to the approval of corporate counsel); this is not the case for many other forms of corporate communication, such as mandatory filings with the SEC.

> **Tip:** Restrict a company's attorneys to reviewing press releases for compliance with disclosure regulations. If they were to write press releases, they would minimize the amount of information conveyed in order to reduce the company's liability.

The investor relations officer can use press releases to issue many kinds of information that may be of interest to the investment community, such as:

- New hires into senior management, along with their resumes. Investors can use this information to estimate the impact of a new hire on a company's operations.
- The receipt of a contract award, along with the amount of associated revenue and the period over which the revenue is to be earned. Investors can incorporate this information into their valuation models for the business.
- New facility openings, which is of particular importance when the facility is a new store location. Investors can then estimate the likely revenue to be generated by the new location.
- New product launches, including enough specifics for investors to estimate likely revenue levels that will result, and the extent to which the new product sales may cannibalize the sales of existing products.

In a press release, the event being described is placed within the first one or two sentences, followed by a management statement about the event, followed by general information about the company. This level of brevity is needed to reduce the distribution cost of a press release, which is typically priced by word count. A sample press release is:

---

**Date**                                                    **FOR IMMEDIATE RELEASE**

### Hegemony Awarded Gaming Contract

Boston, Massachusetts – Hegemony Toy Company has been awarded a contract by the U.S. Naval War College to develop a gaming platform that can be used to train members of the U.S. Navy and other members of NATO in how to deal with open ocean threat situations. The contract is for $5 million, and is to be completed within 24 months.

"Hegemony is bringing its expertise in developing military-oriented games to the professional military," states Hegemony president Douglas Bradley. "We will use our Nelson seaborne gaming software to provide a unique solution for the War College. This patented system is uniquely designed for the multi-player distributed environment that the War College envisions for this critical tool."

**About Hegemony Toy Company**

Hegemony is a provider of military-oriented toys and games to the under-20 age group. Its primary offerings are in the areas of board games and multi-player on-line games.

**Forward-Looking Statements**

[See the Forward-Looking Statement chapter for more information]

**Contact Information**

Gerry Patton
123 Bastogne Way
Boston, Massachusetts 02203
Phone: 617-330-8900
E-mail: gpatton@hegemonytoy.com

---

In the sample press release, the event summarization states the name of the customer, the amount of revenue expected, and the time period over which the revenue is to be earned. Investors can use this information to alter their estimates of company financial performance. In addition, the press release points out the existence and use of intellectual property, which improves investor perceptions of the company's intangible assets.

Additional examples of the primary content of a press release are:

(1) Hegemony Toy Company has just licensed its Napoleon Wars board game to a distributor in the United Kingdom. As a result of this agreement, Hegemony

expects to build recognition for its other products in its target age group in the United Kingdom market.

(2) Hegemony Toy Company has just hired Mr. Dale Trotsky as its vice president of manufacturing. Mr. Trotsky has deep experience in lean manufacturing practices, which Hegemony expects him to use to drive down costs within the Hegemony manufacturing facilities.

(3) Hegemony Toy Company has just released its new Thirty Years War multiplayer online gaming platform. The game is available to users worldwide, and is paid for with a $15 per month subscription fee.

In the first example, the press release is used to announce a potential increase in the company's target market. In the second example, the press release tells investors that the company intends to reduce costs through the revision of its manufacturing practices. The third example reveals that the company intends to create a recurring revenue stream with a subscription-based sales model. Thus, each press release conveys a specific message that the investment community would likely consider to be valuable.

Where possible, quantify the information conveyed in a press release. A greater level of detail is more useful to investors, since they can use it to more accurately estimate the timing and amount of a company's earnings. Examples of the requisite level of detail are:

(1) The contract has maximum funding of $5 million. The customer has the option to extend the contract for an additional five years, with maximum funding of $3 million in each of the additional years.

(2) The outsourcing agreement provides that the company will pay the supplier $15 million per year for the next ten years for outsourced IT services, with a built-in inflation adjustment that is capped at 5% per year.

(3) The company recognized a charge of $25 million associated with the facility shutdown for employee terminations and environmental remediation. These payments should be completed within the next six months.

It is most efficient to distribute press releases through a press release distribution service. Though relatively expensive, they have massive distribution networks that can issue press releases to thousands of newspapers, radio stations, television stations, and any number of Internet-based services. Also, their in-house proofreaders examine every press release prior to distribution, which can result in minor improvements to the presentation and content of a release. See the Third Party Investor Relations Services chapter for more information.

---

**Tip:** Since the distribution fee for a press release is based on its word count, consider storing the bulk of the press release information on the company website, and simply linking to it from the press release. This has the added advantage of driving investors to the company website.

---

## The Earnings Press Release

The earnings press release summarizes a company's financial results, usually for the preceding quarter. It is typically released immediately after filing a Form 10-Q with the SEC. An earnings release usually mentions key financial items, such as revenues, net profit, and earnings per share, sometimes in comparison to the results for the same period in the preceding year. The format of the earnings release is typically copied forward from the last such release, and so leaves little room for expansion on any topics. A sample earnings press release is:

> Hegemony Toy Company (NYSE: HETC), a provider of military-oriented toys and games, today announced its financial results for the third quarter ended September 30, 20x2:
> - Revenue of $120,000,000, up from $112,000,000 in the third quarter of 20x1
> - Net income of $13,500,000, up from $8,200,000 in the third quarter of 20x1
> - Basic and diluted net profit per share of $0.12 and $0.11, respectively, as compared to $0.09 and $0.08 in the third quarter of 20x1

At a more informative level, the earnings press release can be expanded to include a company's summarized financial statements, as well as management's discussion of those results. If this latter approach is used, additional information may include:
- Changes in accounting standards that impacted results
- Explanations of extraordinary items and other unusual revenue and expense items
- Seasonal or industry trends impacting results

A limited example of this expanded format follows.

> Hegemony Toy Company (NYSE: HETC), a provider of military-oriented toys and games, today announced its financial results for the third quarter ended September 30, 20x2:
> - Revenue of $120,000,000, up from $112,000,000 in the third quarter of 20x1. The primary cause of the change was a 7% across-the-board increase in product prices at the beginning of the quarter.
> - Net income of $13,500,000, up from $8,200,000 in the third quarter of 20x1. The aforementioned price increase was the primary cause of the net income change, though it was partially offset by a one-time $3,000,000 charge caused by a change in accounting standards related to the company's pension plan.
> - Basic and diluted net profit per common share of $0.12 and $0.11, respectively, as compared to $0.09 and $0.08 in the third quarter of 20x1. There were no changes in the company's shares outstanding during the two comparison periods.

Hegemony is hosting an earnings call today, October 31, 20x2, at 5:15 p.m. EST to expand upon the results described in this press release. Once completed, a transcript of the call will be posted on the Hegemony website at www.hegemonytoys.com/IR/earningscalls.

The earnings press release is constructed by the accounting department, since this group has the most knowledge of financial information. The investor relations staff should review earnings releases before they are issued, to be aware of any issues that investors or analysts may inquire about. The investor relations officer may also suggest that additional explanatory information be included in an earnings release, especially if there are unusual items that impacted the reported results.

## The Annual Report

The annual report has traditionally been a hefty, multi-colored assemblage of information about the operations and financial results of a business, which is sent to its shareholders once a year. The report used to be a massive production that was considered one of the key methods used by the investor relations officer to communicate with the investment community. It was carefully constructed, with input from many parts of the company, and stylishly presented. However, the flood of on-line information that is now available makes the annual report a much less critical source of information for the investment community.

Given the decline in importance of the annual report, companies have tended to deal with it in one of two ways:

- *As a marketing tool.* A company may continue to invest a considerable amount of time and money in its annual report, with the intent of using the report as a marketing tool that can be handed out to anyone interested in the company. It can also be posted as a PDF file or even a series of full HTML web pages on the company website.
- *As a regulatory requirement.* Public companies are required to issue an annual report, so some organizations treat the requirement as an annoyance that must be dealt with by the least expensive means. This is most easily accomplished by issuing a *wrap report*. A wrap report is the annual Form 10-K that a company is already required to issue, accompanied by a small amount of commentary and an annual report cover. This option provides no new information about the company to the recipient.

Of these two options, we recommend the first one. An active investor relations officer should be meeting with investors and analysts constantly, and needs a handout that explains the company. A well-designed annual report is one of the better methods for conveying this information.

Assuming that the investor relations department wants to produce a complete annual report and has the budget to do so, what should it contain? The following list addresses the more common components of the annual report:

- *CEO letter*. There should be a letter to investors at the beginning of the report, signed by the CEO, in which are briefly described the results of the business, issues encountered during the year, milestones achieved, and plans for the future. If this letter is actually written by the CEO, be sure to advise him regarding its contents, so that it is properly integrated into the rest of the information provided in the report.
- *Description of the business*. This is a key section that differentiates the annual report from the Form 10-K. The investor relations staff should succinctly describe the nature of the business, the markets in which it competes, and the types of products and services that it provides.
- *Value proposition*. This is the underlying intrinsic value that a company represents. See the Value Proposition chapter.
- *Key performance indicators*. This is a table of key performance indicators (KPIs) for the business, usually presented for the most recent and several prior years. There should be a thorough description of the KPIs and why they are important indicators of company performance.
- *Strategy*. Management may not want to make specific forecasts about the future results of the business in the annual report, so it instead states the general corporate strategy. Readers can then make their own assumptions about how the company is likely to perform, based on a combination of the historical results of the business and its stated strategy.
- *Risks and uncertainties*. The value proposition and strategy must be balanced by a discussion of the downside – those risks and uncertainties that may impact the company.
- *Governance*. The governance section describes the qualifications of the board of directors, and the nature of the committees working for the board.
- *Financial statements*. This is the complete set of financial statements, as well as accompanying disclosures.

If there is any question about what to include in an annual report, examine the reports issued by competitors. These other reports are setting the standard for what the investment community expects to see, so assume that you must at least match the content of competing annual reports.

---

**Tip:** Hire a specialist to design the layout and graphics of the annual report. This is the one product of the investor relations department that is expected to be stylish, so budget an adequate amount for this work every year.

---

A well-constructed annual report may also contain information about the industry as a whole, so that investors can place a company in the context of its competitive environment. Industry information is considered more valid if it comes from a respected outside source, such as an industry trade group.

An organization may include so many topics in its annual report that the result is a bloated document that is impossible to peruse. As part of the annual report construction process, include a task to examine the relevance of the presented information, and be willing to strip out anything that is overly detailed, or which only pertains to a limited audience. Adopt the same stance when considering whether to include new information; in many cases, it is easier to keep ancillary information out of the annual report and instead post it on the company website.

It may be possible to post an enhanced version of the annual report on the company website. The report could be enhanced with links to video clips showing company facilities, products, the annual meeting, and so forth.

When constructing the latest annual report, be cognizant of how the information stated in the preceding edition should roll forward into the next report. For example, if the CEO projected in the preceding report that certain milestones would be achieved in the following year, be sure to describe what happened to those milestones in the next report. This is of particular importance if the company posts all of its annual reports on-line, where someone would be more likely to read them in sequence and note disparities from year to year.

The creation and printing costs associated with an annual report can be significant in relation to the entire budget for the investor relations department. It should certainly be budgeted for as a separate line item in the investor relations budget. Doing so makes it easier to ascertain the total cost of the report, so the investor relations officer can judge whether the company is incurring too great a cost for this item.

---

**Tip:** Rather than issuing the annual report in multiple languages for distribution in other countries, consider posting it in HTML format on the company website, where readers can use the foreign language conversion feature in their web browsers to automatically convert the text to another language.

---

In essence, a well-constructed annual report should contain sufficient information for a reader to obtain a reasonably in-depth understanding of the company, the value proposition that it holds for an investor, and its financial performance.

## The Fact Sheet

What if a company has created an elaborate and expensive-to-produce annual report, and so does not want to incur the cost of distributing it in bulk? Or it only uses a wrap report, which is a dense compendium of information that may turn away a casual reader? In these situations, a reasonable alternative is the *fact sheet*. A fact sheet is a few pages of information describing the key points about a company's market positioning, operations, financial results, and financial position. It can be posted as a PDF file on the company website, and is also useful as a handout for presentations and other meetings. Suggestions for the content of a fact sheet are:

- The name of the company, the name of the exchange on which its stock is traded, and its ticker symbol
- The number of shares of common stock outstanding, the recent stock price or stock price range, and the market capitalization

- Overview of what the company does, and its value proposition
- Financial highlights
- Summary of recent press releases
- Key management personnel
- Key products, customers, and sales regions
- Investor relations contact information

An extremely abbreviated fact sheet appears in the following example.

---

**FACT SHEET**

**Hegemony Toy Company**

**NYSE: HETC**

| | |
|---|---|
| Common shares outstanding: 50,000,000 | Recent price: $15.25 |
| Management ownership: 9,200,000 shares | Market capitalization: $762,500,000 |

| **Hegemony Overview** | **Financial Highlights** |
|---|---|
| Hegemony was founded shortly after World War II by a group of retired army and navy officers, with the intent of replicating famous battles in a series of war-related games for children. The business expanded from board games to multi-player online games, and now also sells games configured for the top three most popular gaming platforms.<br><br>Hegemony went public on the New York Stock Exchange in June 20x1, and now trades there under the HETC symbol. | • Exceeded $250 million in revenues in the most recent fiscal year<br>• Has consistently earned more than 15% after tax for the past decade<br>• Commands 35% of the market for military-related games<br>• Has had a 25% rate of revenue growth since going public<br>• Has obtained multiple contracts to provide on-line gaming environments for all of the country's military colleges |
| **Key Products** | **Management Team** |
| The Saar Offensive – Released in 20x1, $50 million revenues to date.<br>Attack on Narvik – Released in 20x2, $35 million revenues to date.<br>WW II On-line – Released in 20x3, $175 million revenues to date.<br>Battle of Leyte Gulf On-line – Released in 20x4, $320 million revenues to date. | The senior management team includes five people with doctorates in military history, as well as three award-winning programmers and game designers. This combination of management talent allows the company to repeatedly produce highly-successful games that integrate accurate historical portrayals of battles with the latest gaming technologies. |

| **Recent Press Releases** |
|---|
| March 11, 20x4 – Hegemony Acquires MacArthur Software. This acquisition gave the company control over a key on-line gaming platform. |

January 25, 20x4 – Hegemony Announces new Pacific Theatre Gaming Platform. This new platform allows gamers to develop their own battles anywhere within a 64 million square mile gaming grid for the Pacific Ocean.

November 3, 20x3 – Hegemony Announces Record Number of Gaming Subscribers. The number of subscribers to Hegemony's WW II On-line gaming platform exceeds five million for the first time.

**Contact Information**

| CFO<br>Bernard Montgomery<br>617-320-9809 | Investor Relations<br>Hugh Dowding<br>617-320-9842 | Corporate Counsel<br>Henry Arnold<br>617-320-9814 |
|---|---|---|

Consider formatting the fact sheet so that it can be folded, stamped on the back, and mailed without using an envelope. This requires the integration of a blank space into the document where mailing information and a stamp are to be located.

**Tip:** Update the fact sheet following the release of every set of quarterly financial statements. Such frequent releases make it more cost-effective to avoid expensive graphics or layouts in a fact sheet.

Of particular interest to investors is the financial highlights section of the fact sheet. This section should highlight key performance achievements for the company that might trigger an investment. Examples of financial highlights are:

(1) "Organic cash flow has increased by at least 20% per year for the past ten years." [useful for attracting investors concerned about stability]

(2) "The company has no debt and maintains a $1/2 billion cash reserve after dividend deductions." [useful for presenting the conservative nature of management]

(3) "Year-over-year revenue growth exceeded 40% in the past two years." [useful for attracting investors seeking rapid growth situations]

(4) "The company invests at least 10% of cash flow in its research, development, and branding activities." [highlights the commitment to increase new product sales]

(5) "The company has successfully acquired 20 companies in the past five years, which have cumulatively added $1.50 to earnings per share." [reveals a company's ability to integrate acquisitions, which attracts growth investors]

(6) "The company's backlog now exceeds $1 billion, which represents a two-year backlog." [useful for attracting investors who want stable or growing earnings]

(7) "The company has increased its dividend for the 20th consecutive year." [tends to attract investors who want recurring income]

It is essential not to confuse readers with a plethora of financial highlights. Instead, focus on those few items that most closely support the value proposition of the business. For example, if management wants to emphasize the growth aspects of a company, it would be more inclined to use the third, fourth, and fifth of the preceding example statements.

> **Tip:** The fact sheet is the most-frequently updated document that the investor relations department uses. To ensure that only the most recent version is distributed, always include the version number somewhere on the document.

## Conference Presentations and Discussions

Investment bankers and analysts sometimes sponsor industry conferences. These conferences can result in a considerable amount of networking with key members of the buy side and sell side, which can be a major source of contacts for the investor relations officer.

These conferences are always looking for people to make presentations on pertinent topics, as well as to participate in round table discussions. If invited, either the investor relations officer or someone from the senior management group should certainly attend, and make presentations. This is a golden opportunity to discuss the company with the investment community, and spread awareness of the company's value proposition. The result may well be excellent contacts on the sell side that can produce a multitude of investor contacts to populate a future road show. Also, members of the buy side may express interest in investing in the company, which the investor relations staff should cultivate for future funding rounds.

> **Tip:** It is particularly important to accept conference invitations from new investment bankers, since they are more likely to have investor contacts that the investor relations staff has never met.

## Newspapers and Related Media

With the reduction in advertising experienced by newspapers, there has been a massive cutback in the amount of space available in newspapers. This means that few newspapers are willing to provide extensive coverage of company activities or their routine earnings announcements. Thus, many investor relations officers no longer consider it cost-effective to spend time dealing with newspapers. Nonetheless, in the rare situations where an article is printed, it can generate local interest about a company, which can enhance its reputation (see the Value Proposition chapter).

In those rare cases where a newspaper reporter contacts the company about a story, be sure to call back immediately. Reporters operate under extremely tight deadlines, so a leisurely callback a day or two later will probably eliminate any possibility of a story.

A larger company may have more luck obtaining coverage from an industry-specific magazine or a more general business magazine. If the investor relations officer wants to pursue this option, it makes sense to build relations with the staff writers that work for these magazines. Doing so requires that you understand the needs of the targeted journalists, rather than burying them with mounds of unwanted information. To gain this level of understanding, it is best to travel to them, which can be most cost-effectively accomplished by scheduling road show presentations to be near their cities, and then combining meetings with road show presentations. The discussion would likely include:

- *Journalist needs*. As just noted, it is of paramount importance to understand the types of stories that a journalist is interested in producing. In particular, find out if the magazine has a certain theme for each issue, into which the investor relations officer might be able to insert a compatible story about the company.
- *Industry overview*. Be willing to provide an overview of the industry in which the company operates. This is valuable background information that a journalist can use to create multiple stories concerning that industry.
- *Company story*. Only after discussing the preceding two topics should the discussion turn to the company itself, and probably only to sketch an over-view of what it does. The journalist may not have an immediate interest in doing a story about the company, so treat this as a getting-acquainted dis-cussion.

**Tip:** Prior to meeting with a journalist, compile a list of information items that have not yet been released to the public, and which therefore cannot be discussed. Release of this information would violate Regulation FD (see the Regulation FD chapter).

Once this initial contact has been made, the investor relations officer can follow up by phone or e-mail with other information. These contacts may be concerning information specifically requested by the journalist, or about general industry issues that the journalist has stated may be of interest.

**Tip:** Only put a journalist on the department's mailing list for press releases if the journalist agrees to it in advance. It is generally better to more carefully curate information going to journalists, so that they only receive that information most useful to their needs.

At a minimum, these types of one-on-one discussions with journalists position the investor relations officer as an industry expert. As such, the investor relations officer will likely be contacted for comments on other stories being researched by journalists, which allows the investor relations officer to insert his view of markets and competitors into general-distribution stories.

Stories that are more likely to be printed by a business magazine are those that address a unique aspect of a product or an unusual problem. Here are several examples of different "spins" on a business that would be more likely to be printed:

- *Governance angle.* Note how the company used an all-electronic format to conduct an annual meeting.
- *Green angle.* Describe how the company has hired a "green" architectural firm to design a company headquarters that requires no outside source of power.
- *Community service angle.* Tell a story about how the company contributed to a local construction project, emergency rescue, or other community issue.
- *Supply chain angle.* Describe how the company overcame supply chain issues, or used certain techniques to manage overseas suppliers, or how it used just-in-time deliveries to enhance its production system.
- *Technology angle.* Describe how the company has used technology in a unique way to enhance its operations.

It will be evident from the examples that magazine and newspaper stories are more likely to address very small slivers of a company's total activities. These stories will probably be reputation enhancers, rather than ones that reinforce a company's value proposition. Nonetheless, they are useful for increasing general awareness of a business, and so should be pursued.

A variation on the magazine journalist is the financial journalist. This person may write in a blog, newspaper, or magazine, and may have a large following of investors. The journalist may give opinions on earnings reports, mention rumors about a company, and/or specialize in interpreting information at an industry level. Given their outsized impact on the market, treat them essentially the same as analysts. For more information, see the Sell Side and Buy Side chapter.

It is best to make some attempt to build relations with members of the media. If you were to instead stonewall them, they would have to report based on generally-available information or the opinions of outsiders who may not have a kind view of the business; the results would be more likely to characterize the company in a more negative or neutral light than would be the case if the company had discussed its views with members of the media. In addition, the reporting of outsiders is considered more reputable than a typical company press release, since the information is coming from a presumably independent third party. In short, dealing with the media may appear to consume a considerable amount of time, but any resulting news stories about a company can strongly leverage its reputation.

## Other Forms of Communication

There are a number of other forms of communication that the investor relations staff can use to convey its message to the investment community. Some require so much in-depth discussion that we have addressed them in separate chapters. These other forms of communication include:

- *Annual meeting.* Every public company is required to have an annual shareholders meeting, at which the board of directors is elected. If the CEO decides to treat it as a major event for communicating with investors, then the investor relations staff may be deeply involved in its planning. See the Annual Meeting Planning and Voting chapter for more information.
- *Analysts' day.* If a company has a particularly unique production facility or campus, it may be useful to schedule a day during which the company conducts tours for analysts and key investors, as well as hosting a variety of meetings about the company and its industry. See the Sell Side and Buy Side chapter for more information.
- *Earnings call.* Many public companies have a conference call with investors and analysts immediately following their release of quarterly earnings. See the Earnings Call chapter for more information.
- *Investor relations web site.* The investor relations section of the company web site is one of the first places that investors will access when they research a company. We have provided full coverage of this topic in the Investor Relations Website chapter.
- *Regulatory approval report.* If a company's products are subject to regulatory approval, as is the case in the pharmaceuticals industry, consider publishing a report that itemizes the current regulatory approval status of each product. This can be the most important investor relations document in those industries where regulatory approval has a major impact on company revenues.
- *Road show.* The investor relations officer and other members of the senior management team may go on road shows throughout the year to meet with investors and analysts. This topic is addressed in the Road Show chapter.
- *SEC filings.* The Securities and Exchange Commission (SEC) requires that a company issue a number of standard disclosures, such as the quarterly Form 10-Q, the annual Form 10-K, and the Form 8-K for significant changes impacting the company. Though these issuances are handled by a company's accounting department and legal staff, the investor relations officer may have input into the information presented in these filings. The contents and timing of these filings are described further in the SEC Filings chapter.

Of the additional forms of communication just noted, the investor relations staff tends to have the most control over the investor relations website and the analysts' day. The other forms of communication tend to be more regimented, or are controlled by other parties.

## The Communications Review Process

There should be a standard procedure for reviewing all types of written documentation that are to be released to the public. Consider following these review rules:

- All investor communications other than SEC filings are released by the investor relations department. They are responsible for sending press releases to a press release distribution service and the annual report to the printer, so this department is a natural chokepoint for controlling information releases. The investor relations officer should control *when* information is released, since many communications are prepared in advanced and held for release on specific dates.

- The company's legal staff reviews and formally approves every information release. This means that an approval form is attached to each document proposed for issuance, and that copies of both the document and the approval form are kept on file.
- If an information release contains financial information, it is reviewed and formally approved by a senior-level accounting person.

The use of these rules is particularly important in a larger company, where there is a potential for information to be released from multiple sources within the organization, and in a disjointed manner.

## The Communications Calendar

Given the considerable number of communications methods noted in this chapter, the investor relations officer should construct a communications calendar, on which are noted when the various methods are to be used. This is particularly useful for the following items:

Annual events:

- Annual meeting
- Annual report
- Analysts' day

Quarterly events:

- Earnings call
- Quarterly SEC filings

Other scheduled events:

- Road show
- Industry conferences

The investor relations officer can use this calendar to prepare for information releases on regularly scheduled dates, year after year.

## The Communications Mailing List

Much of the information released to the investment community is routed through either the SEC or a press release distribution service. However, both of these distribution channels represent a scattershot approach – the information is made available, but intended recipients may not see information intended for them. Consequently, the investor relations department should maintain a set of mailing lists that it can use to make it more likely that specific individuals will receive information about the company. There may be separate mailing lists for:

- Anyone signing up through the company's investor relations website
- Analysts following the company
- Key investors for which e-mail addresses are available
- All current investors for which e-mail addresses are available
- Local journalists
- Journalists who have issued stories about the company in the past
- Anyone within the company who is authorized to talk to the investment community
- All investor relations and public relations firms employed by the company

The use of communications mailing lists does *not* mean that a company is selectively issuing information (which may be a violation of Regulation FD). Instead, mailing lists are merely intended to ensure that a specific general-release item is received by a specific individual.

## Handling Negative News

The primary intent of every type of communication described in this chapter is to present the best possible image of a company to the outside world. However, there are times when there will be negative news. Examples of such events are:

- A lawsuit
- A product recall
- Failure of a drug application
- A labor strike
- The initiation of a hostile takeover attempt
- A supply chain failure
- An unexpected loss on the income statement

### The Negative News Response System

It is possible that investors will adjust their views of a company based on not just the bad news, but also how it *reacts* to the bad news. Thus, it is of some importance for the investor relations officer to have a firm grasp of how negative news is to be handled. The response to bad news can follow one of two paths, which are:

- *Prepackaged response*. If a problem has arisen in the past, or has already happened to a competitor, or is foreseen as being a likely event in the near future, prepackage a plan of action. This plan states who is to be contacted, which actions to take, and who is allowed to make statements to representatives of the media. There may also be a set of pre-written press releases and Form 8-K filings that only require minor updating to adjust for the actual event. For example, every competent airline has a plan in place for dealing with a plane crash.

- *Response procedure*. If a problem arises that is completely unique, there will probably not be a prepackaged response on hand. Instead, there should be a procedure in which a reaction team is contacted to handle the situation. For example, this group might include the company safety officer, chief financial officer, corporate counsel, and investor relations officer. Only one person is allowed to speak to representatives of the media, so that a single, coordinated statement is always made.

**Tip:** It is particularly important to have a list of backup personnel to contact if a negative event occurs, since someone on the primary contact list is bound to be out of touch at any given time.

Having either of these response paths in place reduces the time that a company needs to take whatever steps are needed to calm a potentially jittery investment community.

**The Negative News Early Warning System**

It is particularly important to maintain relations with the media even in the face of a negative news event. This is useful not only for having a ready pool of listeners when the company wants to give its own view of a situation, but also because members of the media may contact the company about negative events as they are unfolding. This early warning system gives management somewhat more time in which to formulate the most appropriate response.

Another source of early warning information is the industry analyst. This person wants to gain a reputation for making early calls on industry events, and so should have cultivated a large number of quality contacts throughout the industry who regularly forward information to him. An analyst is therefore likely to know about damaging events before most other people. If the investor relations officer has properly maintained relations with analysts, a possible benefit is being contacted by them concerning negative events.

**Tip:** If the company employs a lobbyist, have that person issue updates to the investor relations officer whenever it appears that pending legislation will impact the company.

In addition to these early warning channels from outside the company, it is also useful for the investor relations officer to maintain a strong communications network *within* the company, in order to be alerted at once of any internal issues that may eventually become public knowledge. For example, corporate counsel can advise the investor relations officer of any notifications of new lawsuits or insider stock sales, the engineering manager can warn of impending product recalls, and the controller can forward summaries of any problems expected to be reported in the next set of financial statements. The audit committee could also forward any correspondence received from the company's auditors, warning of control breaches found or other audit-related concerns.

## The Contagion Effect

The contagion effect arises when a competitor suffers from negative news that investors think might also apply to other companies within the same industry. A common result is that the stock prices of every company in the industry are driven down. The proper response by the investor relations department is to immediately issue a press release, stating that the company has not been impacted by the same issue. For example:

- If another company has lost money due to a lack of hedging, point out that the company has an active hedging program in place.
- If a competitor has had a supply chain disruption, note that the company has long-term supply agreements in place for all of its key raw materials.
- If the government has issued new regulations that require extensive capital expenditures within the industry, state that the company has already paid for the required upgrades.

By taking these steps, any initial decline in a company's stock price should hopefully be reversed within a relatively short time, as investors bid the stock price up to its previous level.

## The Nature of the Response

When dealing with negative news, the goal of the investor relations officer should be to put it behind the company as soon as possible. Otherwise, the business media will keep the story running in front of the investment community for a lengthy period of time. The best way to shorten the life span of any negative news event is to issue a comprehensive statement about the event, explaining the company's role in it and culpability (if any), and promising to investigate and remediate the situation as rapidly as possible. If a company were to take the reverse approach and attempt to obfuscate the facts or shift the blame elsewhere, the event may worsen over time, eventually resulting in a much worse impact on the reputation of the company than would otherwise have been the case.

If a company is the target of several negative news items at once or within a short period of time, it is especially important to put all of it behind the company in short order. This massive news hit will likely result in a significant one-time drop in the company's stock price. However, this is better than the alternative of a continuing stream of bad news that appears to drag on for months; in the latter case, expect investors to eventually abandon their stock holdings and move elsewhere, leaving behind a severely depressed stock price. Even worse from the perspective of management, a lengthy string of bad news events will result in less confidence in the management team, which may lead to their expulsion by the board of directors.

> **Tip:** Do not hide bad news in the disclosures that accompany the financial statements, since this makes it look as though the company is deliberately obfuscating information. Instead, deal with each significant bad news item in a separate press release, giving each one the attention it deserves.

There may be other cases in which it appears that negative news will fade away quickly and have no long-term impact on the company's stock price. For example, a brief interruption in a company's supply chain may be corrected so quickly that it is barely worth commenting on, and will not be remembered by investors after a few days. In these cases, the investor relations officer may choose to not deal with the issue at all. Conversely, a major event such as a product recall brings up multiple issues about the viability and safety of a company's products, and so requires an extensive response.

There may be situations where the remediation of a situation requires a number of months or years. If so, the investor relations officer should be very careful about how many public mentions are made of the issue during the remediation period. It is generally best to only make a public statement when there has been a material change in the situation, or when the entire issue has been settled.

Finally, there may be situations where the negative news is so bad that the investor relations officer will find it impossible to retain a large part of the investor base, and may also lose analyst coverage. If so, more drastic action may be required, such as:

- Selling off those subsidiaries that caused the trouble
- Purging the management team if they caused the trouble
- Selling the entire business to a competitor
- Entering entirely new lines of business

If the board of directors decides to continue the company as an independent business, it should consider taking the company private for a cooling off period and then taking it public again, possibly under a different name and perhaps repositioned into a different market category.

In short, when deciding upon the most appropriate response, the investor relations officer should advocate complete and immediate disclosure, with the intent of preserving the long-term valuation and reputation of the business.

## Risk Mitigation by the Investor Relations Officer

The investor relations officer could take the aggressive step of proactively advocating certain changes that may keep negative news from ever arising. For example:

- Recommend the creation of a succession plan for the CEO, to eliminate investor concerns about having a backup in place for the CEO position.
- Recommend that the company obtain business interruption insurance and relocate facilities if a key plant is situated in a flood plain.

- Recommend that the company institute a hedging program to offset the risk of increased raw material prices.

The investor relations officer is not responsible for any of the areas for which negative news typically arises, and so cannot force through any risk mitigation steps. Nonetheless, stating the case in favor of risk mitigation makes it more likely that the necessary steps will eventually be taken to reduce a company's risk profile.

**Summary**

The true quality of an investor relations officer is most readily apparent during a negative news event. An investor relations officer who prepares contingency plans and updates them regularly will appear vastly more prepared than someone who only reacts to these events as they occur. An especially canny investor relations officer will monitor how other companies deal with similar types of negative news, and will adopt those responses that appear to work best. And finally, a key element of negative news responses is to have an early warning system in place both within and outside of a company, and which is monitored constantly.

## Summary

This chapter has primarily dealt with different methods for communicating with investors. The investor relations officer will likely find that the press release is the most frequently-used tool. It is also worthwhile to have an up-to-date fact sheet on hand, since it can be a standard handout at investor meetings. The other communication methods noted in this chapter tend to be used with less frequency, but can still play a significant role in imparting information.

In the following Regulation FD chapter, we will cover the rules regarding the fair disclosure of information, and how to create a system for ensuring that information is released to the investment community as promptly as possible.

# Chapter 4
# Regulation FD

## Introduction

One of the more important investor relations functions is to ensure that information is properly disseminated to the investing public. An SEC rule that governs some aspects of this information dissemination is Regulation FD ("Fair Disclosure"). In this chapter, we discuss the reasons for and contents of Regulation FD, as well as how to create a reporting system that keeps a public company in compliance with its provisions.

## The Essentials of Regulation FD

Regulation FD was created in response to a number of situations in which companies were found to have given material non-public information, such as advance notice of earnings results, to a select few outsiders. The outsiders were able to use the information to make trades that placed them in an unfair competitive position in relation to other, less well-informed investors. Company managers were also allegedly able to manipulate analysts by giving advance information to those who portrayed the company favorably in their research reports.

To combat these issues, the SEC issued Regulation FD, which mandates that a company immediately release to the general public any material non-public information that it has disclosed to certain individuals outside of the company.

The following text from Regulation FD has been heavily edited to compress a large amount of legalese into a format that states the essence of the Regulation:

a. Whenever an issuer, or any person acting on its behalf, discloses any material nonpublic information regarding that issuer or its securities to [a broker, dealer, investment advisor, investment company, or holder of the issuer's securities], the issuer shall make public disclosure of that information:
   1. Simultaneously, in the case of an intentional disclosure; and
   2. Promptly, in the case of a non-intentional disclosure. Promptly means as soon as reasonably practical after a senior official of the issuer learns that there has been a non-intentional disclosure. In no event shall this public disclosure be later than the longer of 24 hours or the commencement of the next day's trading on the New York Stock Exchange.
b. Paragraph (a) of this section shall not apply to a disclosure made:
   1. To a person who owes a duty of trust or confidence to the issuer (such as an attorney, investment banker, or accountant);
   2. To a person who expressly agrees to maintain the disclosed information in confidence;
   3. In connection with a securities offering registered under the Securities Act, if the disclosure is by a registration statement, or an oral communi-

cation made in connection with the securities offering after filing the registration statement.

Note that the regulation is triggered by disclosures only to those individuals who are either investors or who work in the investment industry. There is no mention of disclosures to spouses or other family members, since such a requirement would call for a truly oppressive amount of information tracking by the investor relations staff.

Regulation FD states that "public disclosure" of material non-public information is considered to be a Form 8-K filing (see the SEC Filings chapter), or disseminating the information "through another method of disclosure that is reasonably designed to provide broad, non-exclusionary distribution of the information to the public." Most companies deal with the situation by issuing a Form 8-K. Note that this is one of the rare occasions when you are not allowed the standard four business days in which to issue an 8-K. Instead, the expectation is that the 8-K will be released within 24 hours of a disclosure event coming to the attention of a senior official of the company.

---

**Tip:** A possible alternative form of dissemination of material nonpublic information is a press release that is broadly distributed through a newswire service.

---

A small number of public companies update their company blogs with information that would normally be found in distributed press releases. We do not recommend the use of blogs for meeting the dictates of Regulation FD, since they might be construed as not providing sufficiently broad distribution to the public.

## Compliance with Regulation FD

There are a number of ways to mitigate the risk that there will be a material non-public disclosure of information. Most of the following possibilities require either the adoption of policies and procedures that govern the release of information, or the active participation of the investor relations staff. Compliance best practices include:

Policies and Procedures

- *Quiet period.* Mandate that there will be *no* communications with the investment community from the period when the company's results become reasonably apparent, until quarterly earnings are released in the Form 10-Q or the annual results in the Form 10-K. The quiet period could be quite long when annual results are being released, since the company must wait for the outside auditors to complete their audit of its financial records.
- *Post everything.* The company could make a standard practice of posting all of its presentations to the investor relations section of its website. At a minimum, this would mean posting the presentation PowerPoint slides and any written script that goes along with it. However, since a presenter could depart from the script, an even better approach is to make a video recording of every presentation and the following question-and-answer sessions, and

make these videos available on the website. This latter approach ensures that all presenter commentary is made available to the investment community.

- *Standard Q&A list*. Compile a list of standard questions that are being asked of the company, along with the standard answers to those questions. A problem with this approach is that the information in the list can become stale within a short period of time, so have a mechanism in place for refreshing the list with new information and distributing it on a regular basis.
- *Standard forbidden topics list*. If there are some aspects of the company that should only be discussed with outsiders by a few well-trained individuals, make sure that all other employees know they are prohibited from discussing those topics.
- *Impose employee non-disclosure agreements*. Wherever possible, have employees sign a non-disclosure agreement, in which are stated a number of topics which they are not allowed to discuss with outsiders. The agreement should state the penalties for revealing this information, such as immediate termination, so that employees will understand the seriousness of any violation.

Investor Relations Participation

- *Most meetings handled by investor relations officer*. Have the investor relations officer be solely responsible for the bulk of all presentations to the investor community. Centralizing communications with the one person most knowledgeable about current disclosures makes it less likely that non-public information will be released. This also means that most employees are specifically *not* cleared to speak with analysts and investors.
- *Discuss non-earnings information*. Steer the conversation away from earnings information, where most non-public disclosures tend to be, and focus instead on general strategy, industry trends, risks, and other information that is more likely to be publicly available.
- *Scripting*. Meet with every employee who is about to talk to an analyst or investor, and talk about what the person is allowed to say, based on the information the company has already released to the public. This can (and should) include assisting employees with the construction of their presentations by reviewing preliminary speech drafts and observing dress rehearsals of speeches.

---

**Tip:** Insist that all presentations to the investment community be heavily scripted, since this reduces the risk of making a stray comment that contains material non-public information.

---

- *Debriefing*. Once an employee has met with an analyst or investor, debrief him to see if there has been any unintentional disclosure of non-public information.

- *Investor relations attendance*. Have the investor relations officer or another investor relations employee attend meetings between company employees and outsiders. This person should be authorized to shut down a question if answering it would involve non-public information. At a minimum, the attendee can note any disclosures of non-public information, so that it can be released to the public immediately.

The preceding points all relate to the prevention of or prompt response to non-public disclosures. At a more subtle level, it is also possible that an employee reviewing a preliminary analyst report might inadvertently give away additional information by providing a correction to the report that implies the existence of certain non-public information. To avoid this problem, only provide feedback to analysts based on information that has already been fully disclosed.

> **Tip:** Formulate all of the preceding points into a disclosure policy statement, and have the CEO sign off on it. This document becomes the basis for how disclosures are handled.

In addition to the preceding points, it is also useful to keep a written record of situations in which material non-public information has been released, and how the company handled each situation. Doing so provides a paper trail if there are ever any accusations of having violated Regulation FD, and also serves as a trigger for filing a Form 8-K or making other arrangements to release information to the general public. A sample form to be completed for each material non-public disclosure follows.

> **Tip:** Whenever anyone submits a material non-public disclosure form, schedule them for a short discussion about the company's disclosure policy, since they have just admitted to a violation of the policy.

## Summary

Most of the disclosure problems discussed in this chapter can be resolved by tightly restricting the access of the investment community to employees, so that only a few trained employees are allowed to talk to them. Typically, this group is confined to the chief executive officer, chief financial officer, and investor relations officer.

Another way to minimize the impact of Regulation FD is to be proactive in issuing a constant stream of press releases and 8-K disclosures on every conceivable aspect of the company. By doing so, it will be extremely difficult for an employee to even find a topic on which there is a shred of information that can be considered both material and non-public.

**Sample Form for Material Non-Public Disclosures**

# Material Non-Public Disclosure Form

Complete this form when you have made a material non-public disclosure to an outside party.

If the recipient of material non-public information was one of the following, you *do not* have to submit this form.

- An attorney, investment banker, or accountant working for the company
- Someone who has signed a non-disclosure agreement
- Someone working with the company on a securities offering

If the recipient was anyone else, complete the next information block and forward this form to the investor relations officer.

| Name and occupation of other party | Date and time of disclosure |
|---|---|
| Information disclosed | |
| Employee signature | |

| 8-K issuance date and time | Corporate counsel signature |
|---|---|
| Press release issuance date and time | Investor relations officer signature |

Note: Attach 8-K and press release copies, and file

# Chapter 5
# The Earnings Call

## Introduction

Many public companies schedule periodic conference calls with the investment community, in which a presentation team discusses recent financial results, issues guidance regarding expected future performance, and responds to questions. The investor relations officer is deeply involved in the scheduling, preparation for, and operation of this conference call, which is known as an *earnings call*. In this chapter, we describe the participants in earnings calls, how these calls are scheduled and operated, their content, and what *not* to do during a call.

## Earnings Call Attendees

The primary participants in the earnings call are the CEO and CFO. They discuss all of the financial and operational results and projections (if any) of the business. The investor relations officer may be involved in the introduction to and conclusion of the earnings call, but otherwise operates in the background or as a discussion moderator. The investor relations officer may also record questions asked by callers, as well as coordinate the use of scripted answers to questions. Other employees may be added to the call from time to time to discuss areas of the company in which they are experts, but their participation should be considered the exception. They are most likely to be used when a question is anticipated that calls for an unusual level of expertise in one area of the company.

The investment community likes to hear the CEO on the earnings call, since it implies that this individual is actively involved in the financial management of the company. However, it may be acceptable for the CFO to lead the earnings call instead of the CEO, as long as the CFO has an excellent all-around knowledge of the company and is trusted by the investment community.

## Earnings Call Logistics

The earnings call is normally scheduled for a date immediately following the release of a company's quarterly Form 10-Q or annual Form 10-K filing (See the SEC filings chapter). It is customary to schedule earnings calls one week in advance. A shorter notice period may result in fewer attendees, since they may have already scheduled time during the earnings call for other activities.

The traditional opinion of when to hold an earnings call and issue an accompanying press release is after the financial markets have closed for the day. This scheduling means that investors and analysts have the time to analyze the contents of both the press release and the earnings call before making any injudicious trades that might increase the volatility of the stock price. However, participants in late-day earnings calls tend to be more tired and combative, which can lend a negative tone to the proceedings. Consequently, an early morning call, when participants have more energy, is recommended.

Notice of the call is made by press release to gain the widest distribution, but can also be by e-mail to ensure that analysts and key investors receive timely notice. The notification should include the following information:

- The date and time of the call
- The phone number to call
- The purpose of the call
- The names of those company managers who will participate in the call
- Whether there will be a question and answer session

It may also be useful to state in the notification whether the company plans to update its guidance during the call.

---

**Tip:** If the company plans to issue bad news during its earnings call, consider scheduling the call in front of those scheduled by competitors. Analysts may then ask these other companies about the same issue that the company reported.

---

Earnings calls are usually handled by third party conference calling services that set up phone lines and handle the queue of callers who have questions for the management team. They also typically provide a recording of the entire call; consider posting this recording in the investor relations section of the company website, so that those unable to attend the call can still listen to it at a later date.

## Structure of the Earnings Call

The earnings call is normally divided into two sections, with the first part being a prepared set of remarks about the company's results, while the second part is set aside for a question and answer session with whomever is listening to the call. The call begins with the investor relations officer introducing those employees who are participating in the meeting. The investor relations officer reads a boilerplate safe harbor statement (see the Forward-Looking Statement chapter) and then hands off the meeting to the CEO. The CEO will personally address most of the material to be presented, with the occasional participation of the CFO to discuss more detailed financial topics. If the company provides guidance regarding its expectations for future results (see the Guidance chapter), this information is added after the discussion of the company's historical results.

The first part of the call follows a baseline script that is used repeatedly for all of a company's earnings calls. It is more efficient to use the same detailed format for each call, since the investor relations officer can drop the latest updates on the company's earnings into the script. Using the same format also ensures that the company does not inadvertently miss mentioning information during a call, which listeners might otherwise consider to be an intentional avoidance of information.

The use of a script does not mean that the company's presentation team always states exactly the same types of information – it is only a baseline. The investor relations officer can add text in areas where the CEO or CFO wants to place special emphasis on certain aspects of the company's business. Also, the baseline script will change incrementally over time, as the operations of the business and the company's message to investors gradually evolve.

> **Tip:** If you anticipate a difficult question during a conference call, such as the departure of a key employee, always address it in the scripted part of the earnings call. By doing so, management can make a thorough answer, rather than the "off the cuff" response it might otherwise make if the issue comes up during the question and answer session.

The scripted part of the earnings call should not last longer than 30 minutes, with 20 minutes being sufficient for most companies to state their results and guidance. Since the entire earnings call is expected to last no more than one hour, having a longer presentation cuts into the limited amount of time set aside for the question and answer session. If the prepared statements run overly long, and especially if the management team has a history of continually running long, expect listeners to drop off the call or have subordinates take notes in their place.

## The Question and Answer Session

Following the prepared statements in the first section of the earnings call, the CEO returns control of the meeting to the investor relations officer, who acts as the moderator for the question and answer session. Participants in the call state their questions, and the investor relations officer directs the question to the most appropriate person.

The investor relations officer can achieve a considerable amount of scripting even in the question and answer session. This is done by anticipating which questions are most likely to be asked during the earnings call, and then constructing a list of talking points that the CEO and CFO can reference when they answer a question. This level of preparation is extremely useful, since it makes the management team appear to be well prepared.

Some of the questions asked are ones that the company encounters on an ongoing basis, such as asking for an update on the sales levels for stores that have been open for at least one year. The investor relations officer merely has to update the stock answers that were provided for these questions in the last earnings call. Other possible questions may be gleaned from the questions that were asked recently during road shows or during meetings with analysts. In addition, assume that questions will be asked about any variances from historical results that appeared in the most recent set of the company's financial statements.

> **Tip:** Consider scheduling the company's earnings call to be a few days later than the earnings calls of other companies in the same industry. You can then listen to their earnings calls to see which questions are being asked, and then prepare for the same questions in the company's earnings call.

It is better to list the scripted answers to anticipated questions on the walls of the room in which the earnings call is taking place. This allows the CEO and CFO to quickly focus on the set of points they want to make in response to a particular question. It also avoids the interminable delays associated with shuffling a set of question and answer cards. The investor relations officer should know exactly where each question-and-answer combination is located in the room, and point out its location to the person who is answering a caller's question.

> **Tip:** Have a staff person write down each question on a white board as it is asked, so that the CEO and CFO do not have to worry about providing an answer to a question that they did not hear correctly.

It is impossible to anticipate all questions that may be asked, though the CEO and CFO should still follow a set of rules for how they answer *all* questions. For example:

- If a question is a vague one, do not answer the question that you *think* was asked; continually ask for clarification until you are sure of the question. Otherwise, listeners may be quite startled by a seemingly odd answer.
- If a question is multi-part, answer only the first part. Doing so keeps one person from hogging the question and answer period. If a caller wants to continue asking questions, he can re-enter the queue of callers, and will have an opportunity to ask his next question in due time.
- If a question is speculative, such as "what would you do if an earthquake toppled your main production facility," refuse to speculate. Instead, answer with factual information only, such as "we carry earthquake insurance for all of our facilities."

If the earnings call is scheduled to last for one hour (as is common), the investor relations officer may elect to shut down the call after one hour has passed, even if there are additional callers waiting to ask a question. This makes sense when the management team or listeners have only set aside one hour for the earnings call in their schedules. If the management team wants to restructure the call to permit more questions to be asked, consider the following options:

- *Single question rule*. Allow each caller one question, after which they go to the back of the queue if they want to ask additional questions. This tends to limit the number of inconsequential questions.
- *Time monitoring*. If the CEO and CFO tend to run over their allotted time in the first part of the call, warn them when they exceed their scheduled time allotments.

- *Extend call.* Ask the CEO and CFO to block out additional time in their schedules for the period immediately following the earnings call, in case they want to extend the call to take extra questions.
- *Additional session.* Consider scheduling an additional conference call that is set aside entirely for questions and answers.

## Earnings Call Variations

There are times when it might be reasonable to modify the basic earnings call format. One option is to skip the question and answer session entirely. This approach is essentially a verbal press release, and is usually designed to address a specific topic, rather than the more broad-ranging format of a normal earnings call. It is best not to over-use this abbreviated method, since the investment community finds more value in the question and answer portion of an earnings call.

Another variation on the earnings call is to include an educational element, where an expert on one portion of the business, such as the engineering manager or sales manager, makes a short presentation regarding a specific topic, and is also available to answer questions. Examples of topics that may be discussed include the characteristics of a new product that is being released, the specifics of a drug that was just approved by the government, or the company's expansion into a new sales territory. While the extra information imparted may be useful, these presentations can greatly extend the duration of the earnings call. Given the pressure to keep presentations short, it may be better to schedule them for a separate call, where they can be addressed in more detail.

The key point with introducing variations to the earnings call format is to retain the focus on *earnings*. Listeners want management's view of how the company is doing financially and operationally. If the discussion departs from that basic goal, it is doing a disservice to the investment community.

## Earnings Call Bad Behavior

There are a few types of behavior that should be avoided during an earnings call. First, do not turn it into a marketing pitch, where the CEO and CFO are lauding the phenomenal performance of the company. The people listening in on the call are interested in management's commentary on the specific results of the business and guidance about future results – in short, this is a fact-oriented group, and you are wasting their time with overblown attempts to pump the company's stock price.

The earnings call is also a bad place in which to castigate an analyst for making a stock recommendation that the CEO does not agree with. Again, listeners are not participating in the call in order to hear a dressing down. Further, it is extremely rude to do so, since an essentially private concern is being raised in a public forum. Instead, the company should *never* make public statements about its issues with any analyst.

If a short seller is on the call and asks questions designed to needle the CEO or CFO, do not get into a war of words concerning their activities. The best approach with a short seller is to make a direct and factual response to any question asked, and move on to the next caller.

In general, emotions have no place in an earnings call. If a management participant in an earnings call cannot control his temper, he should not be allowed to participate in these calls in the future.

> **Tip:** If there were aspects of an earnings call that did not go well, consider extracting that section of the call from the recorded session and listening to it with the responsible person. Then follow up with a discussion of how the issue might have been handled differently.

## Summary

The investor relations officer has a relatively minor role in the speaking part of an earnings call, but has a much larger role in its organization. This person arranges the logistics for the call, coordinates with the CEO and CFO to create the prepared remarks for the first part of the call, anticipates the questions that will be asked during the question and answer session, and takes notes about the topics addressed during the call. Thus, the investor relations officer may not have the visibility of the CEO, but is the coordinator whose participation makes an earnings call a success.

It may be useful to occasionally call back some of the participants in an earnings call for their comments about how the call was managed and whether its contents should be altered in the future. If the participants have cogent comments, relay them back to the earnings call presenters to see if they want to alter the earnings call format in the future. If they do, summarize the change in a memo, and be sure to reiterate it to the presenters prior to the next earnings call.

# Chapter 6
# Guidance

## Introduction

There is always pressure from the investment community for more information about a business, and especially the results it expects to achieve in the near future. Should you formulate guidance on what to expect, or only comply with the basic filing requirements of the SEC? Your decision can have an impact on whether the company will receive coverage from analysts, the variability of the stock price, and even the company's ability to sell stock.

This chapter explains the reasoning in favor of providing guidance, notes the scenarios where guidance should *not* be issued, and presents guidelines for the timing, content, and consistency of guidance information, as well as related topics.

> **Related Podcast Episode:** Episode 63 of the Accounting Best Practices Podcast discusses guidance. You can listen to it at: **accountingtools.com/podcasts** or **iTunes**

## The Case for Guidance

It is worthwhile to consider the information environment from the perspective of the investor. This person receives information about a business a minimum of four times per year, when the quarterly and annual financial statements are released. These documents are almost entirely oriented toward the historical results of a business, so the investor has little information to use as the basis for future projections. Also, a business may release information at random intervals during the year in the Form 8-K about various material events, such as major agreements entered into or terminated, or the sale or purchase of a business. While this additional information makes note of specific events, it does little to inform the investor about changes in the basic income-generating capabilities of a business. In short, the standard reporting structure mandated by the SEC does little to keep investors apprised of the likely *future* results of a business.

If analysts are following a company, they will periodically issue estimates of future results. Each analyst has his or her following of investors, so there will be some aggregation of investors around the opinions of their favorite analysts. If there are no analysts following a company, then individual investors must arrive at their own estimates of company performance, which can be wildly divergent from each other. The result is a potentially broad range of estimates regarding what the correct share price should be. Also, as more time passes between the release of the last set of financial statements and the arrival of the next set, there is a greater divergence in views regarding the proper stock price.

The result is a fairly large amount of stock price volatility. This is caused by a continuing series of stock purchases and sales at different price points. Each price point is based on the diverging views of what buyers and sellers believe the stock is worth. Thus, it is reasonable to state that a lack of information about the future prospects of a business increases the volatility of its stock price.

What are the impacts of stock price volatility on a business? One or more of the following issues may arise:

- *Short sellers attracted.* A volatile share price may attract short sellers (see the Short Sellers chapter), because they are more likely to encounter a stock price decline from which they can profit.
- *Investors driven away.* Institutional investors prefer to invest in stocks that reliably move within a relatively narrow range, and so are less likely to buy volatile stocks. Since institutional investors buy in large quantities, their absence and related lack of demand tends to reduce the price of a stock.
- *Fund raising.* As just noted, the absence of institutional investors tends to lower the stock price, as does the increased probability of having short sellers. With a lower stock price, any business that wants to raise funds by issuing shares will have to issue more shares than would otherwise be the case in order to raise a given amount of cash.
- *Stock option valuation.* When a business grants stock options to its employees, it must recognize compensation expense related to the options. The calculation of the value of stock options is partially based on their volatility, where more volatile stocks are considered to be more valuable. Thus, a company with volatile share prices must charge a larger amount to expense for any issued stock options than a company with less volatile share prices.

Of the issues just noted, the one that impacts a business the most is fund raising. The other factors tend to either drive down the stock price or increase the reported cost of stock options, but they do not impact the cash flow of the business. The price at which a business can sell shares, however, can limit its ability to raise funds. Thus, a business in need of capital can suffer from high stock volatility.

> **Tip:** A case can be made that an analyst injects information into the marketplace from his or her own research into a company, which may reduce its stock price volatility. Thus, an alternative to issuing guidance is to attract a few analysts. Of course, analysts are more willing to generate research for those companies willing to issue supplemental information, which brings us back to the need for guidance (!).

## Guidance Guidelines

We have established that a lack of information about the prospects of a business can reduce its stock price and make the price more variable, which can have a negative impact on the reported results of the business and its ability to obtain funding. The solution is to provide a sufficient amount of guidance to narrow the range of expectations for a company's stock price. This guidance should incorporate the following factors:

- *Timing.* As just noted, the amount of variability in investor expectations regarding company prospects increases as time passes since the last release of financial information. Thus, a consideration is how frequently guidance should be issued.
- *Type of information.* What types of information does the investment community want to see? The bare minimum is likely to be earnings per share, but you can go further and reveal a broad range of additional financial and operational information.
- *Guidance range.* Stock price variability will be reduced if you issue guidance that stays within a narrow range of possible earnings. This range is driven by the accuracy of the company's forecasting systems.
- *Consistency.* Investors like to see considerable consistency in the structure and content of guidance over a long period of time.

We discuss these factors at greater length through the remainder of this section.

## Timing

Guidance should be issued on a consistent schedule. Many businesses prefer to do so once a quarter, usually immediately following the release of the quarterly financial statements, as part of the earnings call (see the Earnings Call chapter). This schedule helps analysts, who can then combine the company's future estimates with the "hard" numbers shown in the quarterly financial statements to arrive at their own estimates of the company's prospects. This also allows analysts to issue their own recommendations to their followers on a consistent schedule.

---

**Tip:** If you decide to issue guidance, the investment community will assume that the most recent guidance given is still relevant. Consequently, if the company's outlook changes to a sufficient extent to make the existing guidance incorrect, consider issuing new guidance. This should only be necessary if there is a substantial change from the existing guidance.

---

In addition to the normally scheduled release of guidance, consider issuing some unscheduled guidance. This may be necessary when some or all of the analysts following the stock are issuing projections that clearly diverge from the company's internal projections. In these cases, there will be an inevitable (and potentially large) correction when the company issues its regularly-scheduled quarterly guidance. If the divergence appears to be unusually large, the investor relations officer may elect to issue unscheduled guidance, thereby keeping the price of the stock from becoming too volatile.

A considerably different approach to timing is when a business elects to replace guidance with actual monthly results, on the grounds that investors can create their own extrapolations from this more current information. This concept is rarely followed, since it requires a company to be especially careful in constructing its monthly financial statements, and calls for the release of a large number of press releases.

> **Tip:** If you elect to issue monthly financial results, do so on the same day of each month, to introduce some consistency to the release of information. Also, build several buffer days into the schedule, so that you can still release information on time even when there is unexpected difficulty in creating financial statements.

Issuing guidance at intervals of longer than three months is generally not recommended, since the absence of information increases investor uncertainty about the company's prospects, and can lead to an increased amount of stock price volatility.

> **Tip:** There are rare cases where a business finds itself growing extremely quickly, such as when a new product line has proven to be unusually successful. This can result in a fast run-up in the stock price, but has the downside of a heightened level of stock price variability, due to investor uncertainty about the company's ability to sustain its new growth. This is a good time to issue more frequent guidance, which manages investor expectations.

### Type of Information

The minimum amount of information to include in guidance is the projected earnings per share. Investors may expect other information taken from the income statement, such as revenues and net income. The gross margin number is also sometimes included in guidance, as well as the order backlog. It is generally not advisable to issue a massive amount of information, for investors will come to expect it, and generating this material on an ongoing basis may prove to be time-consuming and expensive.

> **Tip:** There may be special situations where investors have expressed concern about the ability of a business to manage its risk. If so, consider issuing additional information on such topics as price swaps, price collars, and call options, which can mitigate outlier risks that might otherwise impact earnings during a guidance period.

Some organizations may be uncomfortable with the issuance of any financial information, for the reasons outlined later in the "When Not to Issue Guidance" section. If so, an alternative may be to occasionally issue information about the company's long-term strategy, or speak in general terms about the company's financial or operational situation. Investors can incorporate this information into their own knowledge of the company to derive a view of the value of its shares. Examples of this type of information are:

- "The company plans to open 10 new retail stores per year for the next five years." If investors can estimate the current sales volume per store, they can use this statement to estimate the company's likely sales volume for the next few years.

- "The company is installing a just-in-time manufacturing system." Investors can infer from this statement that there may be trouble with short-term deliveries while the company adjusts to the new system, followed by a reduction in working capital levels as inventory is reduced.
- "The company plans to expand its product offerings in the __ market." Investors can decide for themselves whether the company can compete effectively in the designated market, and what the amount of profitability and asset usage will likely be from this foray.

Handing out this type of information for general consumption is called the *mosaic theory*, because investors have to fit together the mishmash of data available about a company in order to create a composite view of its prospects. It requires a considerable amount of work by the investment community to derive actionable information from the mosaic theory, so do not be surprised if some analysts drop their coverage of the company, rather than spending time analyzing the information that the business chooses to disseminate.

While the information noted in the preceding example statements may be useful, it does not result in overly precise estimates of a company's earnings. Consequently, if you elect to release this type of information instead of more traditional forms of guidance, expect to see a wider range of analyst estimates concerning company earnings, along with an increase in the volatility of the stock price.

### Guidance Range

It is impossible to tell investors in advance what the exact performance of any business will be, so instead give them a range of likely outcomes. This range should be relatively narrow for guidance covering the next quarter, and widen for periods further in the future, to reflect the increased level of uncertainty that accompanies more distant projections. There is no standard guidance range, since the possible outcome will vary by industry, company, and forecasting system. For example, a government contractor with a portfolio of long-term contracts may be able to give guidance within a tight range of possible outcomes, since its revenue stream is highly predictable. Conversely, a developer of software apps for a smartphone may not know from day to day what its results will be, and so must report guidance within an extremely broad range.

---

**Tip:** Only issue guidance for the time period over which you are comfortable. Thus, if there is considerable uncertainty about results more than a few quarters in the future, do not issue guidance past that time period.

---

An example of guidance that uses an expanding range for more distant time periods is:

> We have reduced our guidance for the fiscal year ended September 30. We now expect the year's revenues to be in the range of $200 to $225 million, resulting in net profits of between $19 and $22 million, and diluted earnings per share of between $1.90 and $2.20. For the following year, we expect sales to be in the range of $210 to $250 million, resulting in net profits of between $21 and $27 million, and diluted earnings per share of between $2.10 and $2.70.

In the example, notice that the revenue range for the current fiscal year was $25 million, which expanded to cover a range of $40 million in the following year. Similarly, the net profit range expanded from $3 million in the first year to $6 million in the second year. This reflects the increased uncertainty of the guidance as a company projects further into the future.

A variation on the guidance format is to use percentages instead of numbers. Analysts can plug this information into their own models to derive estimates of how the company should perform. The following example illustrates the concept:

> We expect that the company will experience revenue growth next year in the range of four to seven percent. Also, we expect supply constrictions to increase our cost of goods during the same period by two percent, which should place our gross margins in the range of 43 to 47 percent. Because of the supply issue, we expect our net profit to be reduced by roughly one percent next year, net of tax effects, which places it in the range of four percent to eight percent.

---

**Tip:** If you issue guidance within an excessively narrow range, you will be more likely to keep issuing updated guidance whenever it appears that actual results will fall outside of the original range. If there are too many updates, you probably need to widen the guidance range.

---

### Consistency

Once you have decided upon the timing and content of guidance, review your own guidelines to see if the company can routinely adhere to them. The investment community expects consistency, so the company must be able to generate the same information, calculated in the same way, and released on the same schedule, for years to come.

---

**Tip:** If the guidance information includes ratios or other metrics, include the exact calculations in a guidance procedure, as well as documentation of where the information is derived from, so that they can be calculated in exactly the same way, every time.

---

If the company does not issue guidance in a consistent manner or begins to exclude information, it is quite possible that investors will react negatively, possibly because of a perception that the company is trying to hide negative information. To avoid this perception, always be very clear about the reasons why the information being supplied has changed, or why some information is being dropped from or added to guidance. For example:

- "We are no longer giving guidance on changes in sales levels for existing stores, because we have changed to the franchise model."
- "We have altered our calculation of revenues, because we now define the company's business model as being an agent for third parties, which allows us to only recognize our commission on sales as revenue, rather than the gross amount of revenue from goods sold."
- "We are no longer presenting the sales per person metric, since we have outsourced the bulk of our employees to a foreign production company that manufactures goods on our behalf."

**Tip:** If you change the calculation of a metric that is included in guidance, use the new calculation for any historical periods that may be presented, so that the basis of comparison from period to period is consistent.

## How Guidance is Communicated

Guidance is nearly always communicated as part of the quarterly earnings call. This is a conference call in which senior management discusses the results of the most recent reporting period. If guidance is to be given regarding expected future results, it is included at the end of the earnings call. For more information, see the Earnings Call chapter.

## The Preannouncement

If a company decides to engage in a consistent pattern of providing guidance, the investment community comes to expect guidance to be issued on a series of regularly-scheduled dates, usually as part of the quarterly earnings calls. Some organizations find it useful to provide even more information with a *preannouncement* that is made before the normal date on which guidance is issued. A preannouncement usually takes one of two forms, which are:

1. *Notification.* At the most minimal level, a preannouncement states the date on which new guidance will be issued. By pointing out that new guidance will be made available soon, analysts are more likely to delay the issuance of their own recommendations until they learn about the guidance. This tends to keep investor expectations more closely aligned with what management expects to report.
2. *New information.* A preannouncement can be used to issue new information. This can be useful when investor expectations are diverging from the guidance that management plans to issue at the next earnings call. The additional information helps to keep stock prices from becoming excessively variable.

**Tip:** The preannouncement is also heavily used to give early notice of the earnings that a company expects to report in its forthcoming quarterly or annual results.

Actual practice reveals that companies are more likely to use preannouncements to drop negative information into the marketplace. This could be due to concerns that litigation could be initiated against a company for having known about bad news, but not having released the information as promptly as possible.

An alternative reason for issuing a preannouncement is when management is beginning a road show (see the Road Show chapter) and is concerned that it might inadvertently mention non-public information when meeting with investors. To eliminate this potential debacle, a preannouncement is issued that contains the information that management is concerned about. Once the information is public knowledge, the management team is free to discuss it with investors.

A preannouncement can take a variety of forms, such as a press release, conference call, or webcast. If a preannouncement is issued in the form of a press release and it contains material information that may cause a significant adverse reaction in the marketplace, it may be useful to also schedule a conference call immediately following issuance of the press release. The management team can use the conference call to clarify the information contained in the press release, as well as answer any questions posed by attendees.

> **Tip:** If your company is being covered by analysts, you should be more willing to issue preannouncements, on the grounds that analysts are more likely to continue their coverage if they receive a continual flow of information.

## The Guidance Schedule

The investor relations officer is responsible for monitoring when guidance should be issued. The easiest way to do so is to include it in the normal schedule of activities for each quarterly earnings call. Even if there is no update to previously issued guidance, the management team can simply state this fact during the call. If the company is in the habit of preannouncing its forthcoming quarterly earnings, this too can be included in a regular schedule of activities. However, if preannouncements are only being made to adjust existing guidance, there is no way to schedule them, since their use is likely to be sporadic.

If a company does not have earnings calls but does issue guidance, the investor relations officer will need to maintain a separate schedule for when guidance will be released.

> **Tip:** It is more efficient to carry forward the same boilerplate text for each guidance announcement from the last announcement, and just update the guidance numbers within the template.

## Aggressive Guidance

An overly enthusiastic CEO might be tempted to issue aggressive guidance, where projected revenue and profit levels are higher than has historically been the case. The benefit of doing so is that the investment community will then assume that the company is more valuable than it had previously estimated, and bid up the stock price. However, aggressive guidance is not such a good idea when the CEO continues to use it over the long term, for the following reasons:

- *Inability to meet targets.* It is extremely difficult to report actual results that come anywhere near aggressive guidance over a long period of time. Eventually, actual results will lag, which creates a credibility problem for the CEO. If there are a series of missed projections, the investment community will eventually give little credence to any guidance given.
- *Price variability.* If a business is always struggling to meet the guidance targets that its CEO has issued, the result will likely be initial increases in the stock price when guidance is announced, followed by sharp price declines when the company cannot make its numbers, and so on. Thus, aggressive guidance tends to create more stock price volatility. Lots of stock price volatility tends to attract short sellers, who drive down the price of the stock.
- *Ethical breaches.* A more pernicious issue with aggressive guidance is that the management team will find itself under increasing pressure to deliver the results that the CEO has promised, which creates pressure to bend the accounting rules. If so, and those ethical lapses are reported to the public, the impact on the company's stock price may be catastrophic.

A vastly better alternative to aggressive guidance is to develop projections that are squarely within the comfort zone of the management team. The intent is not to issue projections that are too easy for the company to meet, since this does not create any pressure to improve the business. Instead, the CEO needs to follow a fine line of setting reasonable stretch goals for the business, without making managers so desperate to achieve their assigned goals that the only practical way to do so is through fraudulent financial reporting.

This comfortable level of guidance is appreciated by the investment community, since they will find that the company can nearly always deliver on its promises – and a business that reports reliable results is one for which more analysts are willing to provide coverage.

The reverse of aggressive guidance is excessively conservative guidance. It is not useful for a business to routinely report results that are far better than its guidance, for investors begin to build this performance variance into their expectations of future performance. Thus, if a business were to routinely exceed its guidance by a wide margin and then report results that only meet its guidance, investors may take this as a sign that the company is in trouble, and will bid down its stock price. Consequently, settle upon mid-range guidance figures that are neither too high nor too low.

In summary, aggressive guidance is a bad idea, since it is unsustainable, causes large stock price fluctuations, and can lead to fraud. Instead, base guidance on financial projections that the company has a strong likelihood of achieving.

## The Consensus Earnings Estimate

The consensus earnings estimate is the average estimated earnings for a business, as derived from a poll of a group of analysts. This number may vary, sometimes considerably, from the guidance issued by a company. There can be a number of reasons for the variance, such as a history of companies routinely reporting numbers better than their guidance (or the reverse). Or, some analysts may believe that outside factors, such as a recession, will have a greater impact on a company's future results than the management team believes will be the case.

The trouble with a consensus earnings estimate is that a business may meet or even exceed its official guidance, and yet report less than the consensus earnings amount – which triggers a decline in its stock price.

It is rarely a good idea for management to attempt to meet or exceed a consensus earnings estimate that is higher than its own published guidance. This estimate is derived by people who have less knowledge of a company's capabilities than its own management team. Also, why should a company be forced to follow the lead of outsiders? Instead, the company should work to meet the guidance that it has issued, and not worry about the consensus earnings estimate. If doing so results in a temporary decline in the stock price, then so be it.

## When Not to Issue Guidance

We have just built a case for why a public company should provide guidance to the investment community, and what the form and timing of that information may be. However, there are several situations in which guidance may not be appropriate, or where it may even be counterproductive. They are:

- *Inadequate forecasting.* If a company's forecasting systems are unable to generate reliable guidance that the company can meet, it is best not to issue any guidance until the systems are improved. Otherwise, continually issuing guidance that the company does not attain reflects poorly upon the management team. It is better to not even mention that the company is having trouble with its forecasting. Instead, simply state that the company continues to evaluate whether it should provide guidance, and does not choose to do so at this time.
- *New markets.* A company may have just entered new markets where it is uncertain of revenue and profit levels, or the ability of the business to grow. If so, any guidance issued has a high probability of being wrong, and so is worthless to investors. In this case, the management team can either issue guidance with very wide estimated ranges, or forego guidance until results become more predictable.
- *Many acquisitions.* The strategy of a company may be to grow through acquisitions. It is very difficult to provide guidance under this strategy, since the ability of a company to complete an acquisition has a binary outcome – either an acquisition is completed, or it is not. If guidance assumes the completion of an acquisition, and the deal falls through, then the guidance could

be wrong by a substantial amount. This is a particular problem when acquisitions are quite large, and so contribute to a large proportion of a company's projected financial results.

- *Development stage company.* A small number of companies go public when they are still quite small, and do not yet have a clear idea of the size of their markets, market share, profitability, and so forth. In these cases, it makes sense to resolve the informational uncertainties and *then* issue guidance.

With the exception of the inadequate forecasting situation, you should explain to investors the reasons for not issuing guidance, and promise to periodically re-examine the situation periodically to see if the company's results have become sufficiently predictable to use as the basis for guidance.

The situations noted here are in the clear minority for public companies. Usually, a company has been in business for a number of years and reached a certain critical mass before going public, so it should have adequate systems and a sufficient knowledge of its markets and financial results to be able to provide reasonably accurate guidance.

## Summary

In this chapter, we have shown considerable favoritism toward the concept of issuing guidance on a regular basis. It is useful for regulating the expectations of the investment community, and thereby reduces the risk of having wild swings in the stock price. However, the concept can be taken too far. It is not necessary to continually issue incremental updates to guidance. Instead, it is more efficient to issue guidance around a moderately wide range, so that the company has a solid chance of meeting its projections. By doing so, you only have to issue corrective guidance at long intervals, when outlier events threaten to impact the company's results.

# Chapter 7
# The Forward-Looking Statement

## Introduction

The legal situation in the United States used to make it extremely difficult for a publicly-held company to issue any statements about its forecasted results, since there was a significant risk of lawsuits. In this chapter, we explore the reasons for that risk, key aspects of the Private Securities Litigation Reform Act, the safe harbor concept, and how the use of a cautionary statement mitigates the legal risk associated with a forward-looking statement.

> **Related Podcast Episode:** Episode 58 of the Accounting Best Practices Podcast discusses forward-looking statements. You can listen to it at: **accounting-tools.com/podcasts** or **iTunes**

## The Legal Basis of the Forward-Looking Statement

For many years, it was very risky for a publicly-held company to make any type of statement about the financial results that it expected to see in the future. Whenever the price of a stock declined, shareholders could attempt to link the decline with anything said about future plans, and use that as the basis for a securities fraud lawsuit. The result was a multitude of lawsuits, which companies had the choice of either fighting (at a substantial legal cost) or of settling out of court (for an equally substantial sum). In short, the risk of monetary loss was too great for most companies to take the risk of publicizing a financial projection.

More specifically, shareholders were bringing suit under section 10b-5 of the Securities Exchange Act of 1934, which states:

> It shall be unlawful for any person, directly or indirectly, by the use of any means or instrumentality of interstate commerce, or of the mails or of any facility of any national securities exchange:
>
> a. To employ any device, scheme, or artifice to defraud,
> b. To make any **untrue statement of a material fact or to omit to state a material fact** necessary in order to make the statements made, in the light of the circumstances under which they were made, not misleading, or
> c. To engage in any act, practice, or course of business which operates or would operate as a fraud or deceit upon any person,
>
> in connection with the purchase or sale of any security.

[text highlighted in bold by the author]

In short, if a business made a projection that did not come to pass, an investor could use this section of the Act to bring a lawsuit, stating that the company made an untrue statement of a material fact or omitted to state a material fact.

If a company elected to fight such a lawsuit, it would file a motion to dismiss the allegations, on the grounds that the facts alleged by the plaintiff were insufficient to create a liability under the Act. If the judge hearing the case ruled in favor of the company, then the company would have incurred minimal legal costs. However, if the judge ruled that the case could proceed, then the plaintiff's attorney was entitled to badger the company with requests for a potentially massive amount of information (which is part of the *discovery* process). A canny attorney could issue requests for so much information that it would be less expensive for a company to settle the case than to provide the information. In addition, the plaintiff's attorney might even find something during the discovery process that would yield a more favorable outcome in court.

Alternatively, if the company elected to incur the expense associated with discovery and continue to trial, it would be faced with a major risk – that the plaintiff might seek a *class certification*, under which the case would be converted into a class action lawsuit. Obtaining a class certification is not a simple process, since it involves the following steps:

1. Suit is filed on behalf of a proposed class, which consists of those persons or entities that have suffered a common injury.
2. The plaintiff files a motion to have the class certified, which may require discovery to ascertain the size and composition of the class.
3. The plaintiff responds to a variety of objections made by the defendant, such as whether the plaintiff sufficiently represents the class.
4. The court determines the ability of the plaintiff's attorney to prosecute the claim.
5. Notification of the class action is sent to the members of the class.
6. If there is a settlement, notification must be sent to the members of the class.

The preceding list should make it clear that a class action is especially expensive for the plaintiff to initiate. However, if a certification is successful and the defending company loses the case, the company could be faced with paying out an astronomical sum.

---

**EXAMPLE**

In a class action lawsuit against the Hegemony Toy Company, it has been determined that the plaintiff class is comprised of 25,000 shareholders. A shareholder in this class owns an average of 1,500 shares. The lawsuit claims that the average shareholder sustained losses of $12 per share. Thus, the potential claim that might be awarded may be as large as:

$$25{,}000 \text{ Shareholders} \times 1{,}500 \text{ Shares} \times \$12/\text{Share} = \$450 \text{ million}$$

Given the potential size of the damages that might be awarded, Hegemony's management is strongly inclined to settle the case out of court.

---

In short, the legal process at the time was structured to make it easy to bring lawsuits against public companies whenever their stock prices declined. Given the potentially massive payouts if a court case were to go against them, most companies settled out of court, even if they were not even remotely responsible for any stock declines.

The legal situation made it quite difficult to operate in the investor relations profession, since any statements made had to be heavily watered-down, if they were made at all. Many companies simply avoided giving guidance or issued extremely conservative guidance.

## The Private Securities Litigation Reform Act

Congress alleviated the litigation situation by passing the Private Securities Litigation Reform Act (PSLRA) in 1995. In general, the Act was designed to reduce the number of frivolous securities lawsuits. The Act does so by increasing the amount of evidence that a plaintiff must have before filing a lawsuit. In particular, the following three concepts apply (with text taken from the Act):

> The complaint shall specify each statement alleged to have been misleading, the reason or reasons why the statement is misleading, and, if an allegation regarding the statement or omission is made on information and belief, the complaint shall state with particularity all facts on which that belief is formed.

> The complaint shall, with respect to each act or omission alleged to violate this chapter, state with particularity facts giving rise to a strong inference that the defendant acted with the required state of mind. (Author's note: This means the defendant knew a statement was false at the time it was made, or was reckless in not recognizing that it was false)

> The plaintiff shall have the burden of proving that the act or omission of the defendant alleged to violate this chapter (of the Act) caused the loss for which the plaintiff seeks to recover damages.

All of these concepts were designed to place a considerable burden of proof on the plaintiff, requiring the presentation of substantial evidence before a judge would accept a case.

The Act also contains the following provisions, which make it less likely that a lawsuit will be converted into a class action lawsuit:
- The judge determines who is the most adequate plaintiff for a class action, which may not be the plaintiff that originally filed suit
- Investors must receive full disclosure of the terms of proposed settlements
- Favored plaintiffs cannot receive bonus payments

In short, the Act makes it more difficult for a plaintiff to file suit, for it is necessary to have evidence of fraudulent behavior without the discovery process (which is only allowed *after* the plaintiff has presented proof of fraud).

## The Safe Harbor for Forward-Looking Statements

In addition to the provisions of the PSLRA that were noted in the last section, it also contained a safe harbor provision. This provision states that an entity issuing forward-looking statements is protected from liability as long as:

> The forward-looking statement is identified as a forward-looking statement, and is accompanied by meaningful cautionary statements identifying important factors that could cause actual results to differ materially from those in the forward-looking statement.

However, the safe harbor provision does not apply in certain circumstances, including:

- An offering of securities by a blank check company
- A penny stock issuance
- Rollup transactions
- Going private transactions

In the Act, a forward-looking statement is defined as:

A. A statement containing a projection of revenues, income (including income loss), earnings (including earnings loss) per share, capital expenditures, dividends, capital structure, or other financial items;

B. A statement of the plans and objectives of management for future operations, including plans or objectives relating to the products or services of the issuer;

C. A statement of future economic performance, including any such statement contained in a discussion and analysis of financial condition by the management or in the results of operations included pursuant to the rules and regulations of the Commission;

D. Any statement of the assumptions underlying or relating to any statement described in subparagraph (A), (B), or (C);

E. Any report issued by an outside reviewer retained by an issuer, to the extent that the report assesses a forward-looking statement made by the issuer; or

F. A statement containing a projection or estimate of such other items as may be specified by rule or regulation of the Commission.

---

**Tip:** The safe harbor provision applies to both written and oral statements.

---

The Act does not require a company to continue to update forward-looking statements, even if the information contained in the last such statement becomes obsolete. Specifically, the Act states:

> Nothing in this section shall impose upon any person a duty to update a forward-looking statement.

From an ongoing investor relations perspective, a company should update its forward-looking statements, but from a legal perspective, it is not required to do so.

We provide examples of cautionary statements in the next section.

## The Cautionary Statement

A cautionary statement is required by the PSLRA. It is made along with a forward-looking statement, and notes the factors (i.e., risks) that can cause actual results to differ from the forward-looking statement. The Act only notes that a cautionary statement must be made – companies must develop their own verbiage that matches the risks to which they are subjected. The following three examples show variations on what a cautionary statement can look like:

### Sample Cautionary Statement Relating to Financial Projections

This release contains forward-looking statements concerning Hegemony, its fourth quarter 20xx revenue, demand for its products, growth opportunities in emerging markets, and the timing of future product releases, which are made pursuant to the safe harbor provisions of the Private Securities Litigation Reform Act of 1995. Forward-looking statements are commonly identified by words such as "would," "may," "expects," "believes," "plans," "intends," "projects," and other terms with similar meaning. Investors are cautioned that the forward-looking statements in this release are based on current beliefs, assumptions and expectations, speak only as of the date of this release and involve risks and uncertainties that could cause actual results to differ materially from current expectations. Risks include the possibility that [competitor's] pricing, marketing and rebating programs, product bundling, standard setting, new product introductions or other activities targeting the company's business will prevent attainment of the company's current plans; the company will be unable to develop, launch and ramp new products and technologies in the volumes and mix required by the market on a timely basis; global business and economic conditions will not continue to improve or will worsen resulting in lower than currently expected demand; demand for the company's products will be lower than currently expected; the company will require additional funding and may not be able to raise funds on favorable terms or at all; there will be unexpected variations in market growth and demand for the company's products and technologies in light of the product mix that it may have available at any particular time or a decline in demand; and the company will be unable to maintain the level of investment in research and development that is required to remain competitive. Investors are urged to review in detail the risks and uncertainties in the company's Securities and Exchange Commission filings, including but not limited to the Quarterly Report on Form 10-Q for the quarter ended ___.

### Sample Cautionary Statement Relating to a Presentation

The information highlighted in this presentation includes selected financial information and should be read in conjunction with our consolidated financial statements and notes and the Cautionary Statements Regarding Forward-Looking Information included in our press release dated ___, which is posted on Hegemony's website at ___, as well as our financial statements and notes, the trends and risk factors affecting us and other information provided in our annual, quarterly and current reports, proxy statement, and other filings made with the Securities and Exchange Commission under Sections 13(a), 13(c), 14 or 15(d) of the Securities

Exchange Act of 1934. This presentation includes "forward-looking statements" within the meaning of securities laws. The statements in this presentation regarding the business outlook and expected performance as well as other statements that are not historical facts are forward-looking statements. The words "estimate," "project," "forecast," "intend," "expect," "believe," "target," "providing guidance" and similar expressions identify forward-looking statements, which are estimates and projections reflecting management's judgments based on currently available information and involve a number of risks and uncertainties that could cause actual results to differ materially from those suggested by the forward-looking statements. With respect to these forward-looking statements, Hegemony has made assumptions regarding, among other things, customer growth and retention, pricing, costs to acquire customers and to provide services, and the timing of various events and the economic environment.

### Sample Abbreviated Cautionary Statement

The material may contain certain forward-looking statements within the meaning of the United States Private Securities Litigation Reform Act of 1995 with respect to the financial condition, results of operations and businesses of Hegemony and certain of the plans and objectives of Hegemony with respect to these items. By their nature, forward-looking statements involve risks and uncertainties because they relate to events and depend on circumstances that will or may occur in the future. Actual results may differ materially from those expressed in such statements, depending on a variety of factors.

If the company maintains a lengthy list of identified risks that you do not want to include in a press release, consider referring to the location where you maintain the list. Here are two examples:

(1) Additional information concerning these and other risks is described under "Risk Factors" and "Management's Discussion and Analysis of Financial Condition and Results of Operations" in the Company's reports on Forms 10-K, 10-Q and 8-K that the Company files with the U.S. Securities and Exchange Commission.

(2) Please refer to the cautionary statement on page __ of the full Hegemony Annual Report for further information on forward-looking statements.

These examples should make it clear that cautionary statements can be massive, and may reach a point where they exceed all of the other text in a press release.

A key consideration when constructing a cautionary statement is that it should be tailored to the business, and not be just a boilerplate version copied from the Internet. This means that the statement should contain issues specific to the business, such as:

- Airline – "We may be unable to properly hedge against sudden spikes in the cost of jet fuel."
- Guitar manufacturer – "We may be unable to secure sufficient supplies of the exotic hardwoods needed to construct our products."

- Laptop manufacturer – "Increasing competition from tablet computers may reduce our unit sales volume."

---

**Tip:** The price charged by the companies that issue press releases is based on the total word count of each press release. Since cautionary statements should be included in press releases containing forward-looking statements, and the statements can be quite long, expect the cost of your press releases to increase by a substantial amount.

---

**Tip:** If you are planning to maintain an archive of press releases on the company's web site, be sure to route all visitors to the site through a page where a cautionary statement is listed, along with a button they must click on, stating that they have read the statement.

---

The risk profile of any business changes over time, so review the contents of any cautionary statements used on at least an annual basis, to ensure that major risks are properly identified.

In summary, cautionary statements are a necessary part of the legal landscape for any company that wants to make forward-looking statements. They will make press releases more expensive, but that is a minor cost when compared to the potential legal liability that is being averted.

---

**Tip:** As is the case with any type of information released to the investment community, be sure to have the company's attorneys review all forward-looking and cautionary statements.

---

## Summary

This discussion of forward-looking statements is a crucial one for the investor relations department, for a massive amount of its communication activities involve forward-looking statements. Thus, it is critical to know when to add cautionary statements to informational issuances, including press releases, speeches, and presentations. Even though the PSLRA has made it more difficult to initiate lawsuits against companies, it is still possible to do so, and the fallout from an adverse legal judgment can be massive. Hence, the need for a thorough knowledge of the concepts upon which forward-looking and cautionary statements are based.

# Chapter 8
# The Investor Relations Website

## Introduction

The use of the Internet has overwhelmed other, more traditional channels of communication that had been used by the investor community. While some investors may only conduct their research and information gathering at one of the large finance-oriented websites, many others will proceed directly to a company's own website to learn more about its operations, financial results, and investor relations activities. For this latter group, it is of considerable importance to ensure that there is an investor relations section within the company website that presents a massive amount of carefully targeted information about the company.

In this chapter, we describe the contents and functionality of an investor relations website, as well as special topics related to Regulation FD disclosures, hyperlinks, interactive features, and more.

## Contents of the Investor Relations Website

The amount of information available in the investor relations section of websites has continually risen, to the point where features considered advanced a few years ago are now commonplace. Thus, an investor may feel that a company is not serious about its investor relations function if he does not find advanced functionality within the company's website. This impression may even go a step further, where investors believe that a poor website implies that the management team has minimal technological savvy. The potential for this negative impression means that the investor relations website not only cannot be ignored, but must be attended to with considerable care.

The following table contains a list of the types of information that can be found in an investor relations website, and the menu categories within which they are typically found. The seven categories can be contained within a dropdown menu bar that spans the top of each web page. If you want to expand the number of menu choices, it may not be possible to list them all in a header bar; instead, more categories will probably mandate using a menu structure that is presented in the left sidebar of the page.

**Sample Page Structure within the Investor Relations Website**

| Menu Category | Content Page |
|---|---|
| **Overview** | *About us.* Brief description of what the company does and its strategy. *Company history.* Description of how the company has evolved. *Products and services.* Description of the types of products and services that the company provides. *Markets.* Description of the markets within which the company operates, as well as the dynamics impacting those industries and recent industry trends. Consider including contact information for industry trade groups (see the Hyperlinks to Third-Party Information section). *Fact sheet.* Key operational and financial metrics about the company, some of which may be listed on a trend line. *Notable investors.* If it is agreeable to the investors involved, list the better-known ones. Stating the identities of a few respected investors in the business may attract other investors. *Frequently asked questions.* Responses to the most commonly asked questions concerning investor relations topics, such as whether the company has a dividend reinvestment plan. *Terminology.* State any terms that are specific to the industry, and which neophyte investors might not know about. *Photographs.* A set of descriptive photographs about the company, its officers and managers, and its operations. These are used by the media for their stories about the company. *Contact us.* Note the contact information for the investor relations department. |
| **Governance** | *Board of directors.* The biographies of the board of directors. *Board committees.* Brief descriptions of each committee and its charter, as well as which directors serve on each one. *Management.* The positions and biographies of key members of the management team. *Governance.* Corporate governance guidelines, as well as the corporate code of business conduct and ethics. |
| **News and Events** | *Press releases.* Listings of all press releases issued by the company, possibly including an archive of earlier press releases. This should be designed as a one-line summary of each press release, with a link taking the reader to the full text of each press release. *Related regulations.* A summarization of the key regulations to which the company is subjected. *Rumors.* If the company is subjected to rumors on an ongoing basis, use this page to state and respond to each type of rumor. *Calendar of events.* List the dates and locations of all scheduled investor relations activities. |
| **Financial Results** | *Filings.* A complete listing of the company's filings with the SEC, sorted alternatively by date and by type of filing. *Annual reports.* A PDF download of the most recent annual report issued to shareholders. *Key results.* A summarization of the company's historical annual results, as well as its quarterly results within the current year. |

| Menu Category | Content Page |
|---|---|
| **Presentations** | *Annual meeting.* Videos or at least the transcripts of highlights from the latest annual shareholder meeting. *Management presentations.* Videos, transcripts, or PowerPoint copies of presentations made by management on various topics. *Earnings calls.* Audio recordings and/or transcripts of the most recent earnings calls. |
| **Share Information** | *Price chart.* A real-time or time-delayed presentation of the company's share price and historical results. *Tools.* An interactive tool for comparing the company's share price and publicly-available metrics with those of competitors. Another possible tool is to enter one's share total to determine the current total value of the stock holding. *Ticker symbol.* The company's ticker symbol and the stock exchange on which it is traded. *Dividends.* Information about the company's dividend policy and its history of dividend payments. *Insider stock trades.* Note the amounts and dates of purchases and sales of company stock by corporate insiders, or at least post SEC Forms 3, 4, and 5, which contain this information. Some investors model their own trades on this information, in the belief that insiders know best when to buy and sell. |
| **Analysts** | *Analyst contact information.* The name, position, and contact information for each analyst who follows the company (see the Hyperlinks to Third-Party Information section). |

> **Tip:** Whenever possible, do not post links on the investor relations website that will send prospective investors *away* from the website. Instead, it is better to store unique information on the website, which will bring viewers *to* the site.

It is of particular importance to maintain a high level of engagement with the investment community through the website, which can be achieved with the use of push technology. In essence, visitors to the site should be encouraged to sign up for e-mail alerts, which the company can use to issue notifications about press releases, SEC filings, upcoming earnings calls, and investor relations events.

Something of a rarity in investor relations websites is a proper discussion of the industry in which a company operates, and of the company's place within that industry. This provides investors with valuable context that would normally only be available through analyst reports. If a company is too small to attract any analysts, it is entirely possible that the industry context discussion is not available anywhere else, which makes it even more important to include this topic in the website. An industry discussion might include:

- Barriers to entry
- The larger competitors and how they compete
- The level of regulation
- The level of competition within and from outside of the industry

- Key historical trends

Also, consider that including industry information in the website is a good way to present the company's viewpoint on the situation. Otherwise, investors will obtain their information elsewhere, along with a viewpoint that is skewed in favor of whoever is providing that information.

The amount of content suggested for an investor relations website may appear overwhelming. However, it does not necessarily all have to be included in the site immediately. Instead, work on developing a core set of offerings, and then gradually expand into other areas over time.

## Functionality of the Investor Relations Website

An investor relations site that is loaded down with an overwhelming amount of information may not attract viewers if the functionality of the site is at a medieval level. Instead, it should be easy to navigate and search, so that users can quickly find the information they need, and are logically transitioned from one page or topic to another. The following are all features of a highly functional investor relations website:

- *Search.* Be able to search on key words for just the investor relations section of the site, rather than for the entire company website. Otherwise, users may find themselves wading through product user manuals and the like.
- *Simple site structure.* Aggregate information into a small number of menu categories (as noted in the preceding section), and prominently label how to move from one category to the next within the site.
- *Site map.* Maintain an updated site map from which users can navigate directly to specific areas of the site.
- *Print optimization.* Optimize all pages for printing. This is a particular problem when information is presented in certain multimedia formats that cannot be printed. In addition, post a widget on each page that site users can click on to print the page.
- *Consistent navigation.* Use exactly the same menu structure in all pages within the investor relations section of the site, which makes it easier for users to navigate the site.
- *RSS feed.* Enable an RSS news feed on the site, so that the latest site information can be "pushed" to participating users.
- *Newsletter and alerts signup.* Have a link on every page to an e-mail signup, in which anyone can select from a menu of what types of information they want to receive from the company by e-mail, such as newsletters or the times and locations of forthcoming investor relations events.
- *Page loading speed.* The site should not be run from an ancient server with bandwidth issues. On the contrary, pages should load very fast, to keep impatient users from leaving the site. In addition, streamline all files to be downloaded by users to make the downloads faster. For example, remove unnecessary pages and graphics from those files containing presentations.

- *Page sharing and approval.* Include widgets on the site that users can click on to send links to certain pages to specified recipients, or to "like" the pages on their preferred social media websites.
- *Translation feature.* There are several language translation widgets available that users can click on to convert the information in a website to a different language. With this feature, it is not necessary to build and maintain entire websites in different languages.
- *Custom summary page.* Give registered users the option to assemble a customized web page for their own use, in which are collected the specific information items that they want to see. This is a difficult feature to offer, but can noticeably increase visitor retention. An alternative to a custom summary page is to assemble the key information that investors are most likely to want to see on the home page of the investor relations site; investors can then bookmark the page for easy access.

In general, make sure that someone reviews the site on a regular basis to ensure that all features are operational, and that the presented information is current. These are particular concerns in the investor relations area, since the site may contain a number of data feeds and information updates that may fail or not be present, respectively.

> **Tip:** Occasionally survey site users for their opinions of the usability and content of the website. In particular, ask about any breakages or errors in the site that need to be fixed.

## Multimedia

A traditional investor relations website is probably populated entirely with text. An alternative that appeals to the more Internet-savvy investor is to include an extensive amount of multimedia. Examples of such inclusions are streaming video from the latest annual shareholder meeting, audio from the latest earnings call, and any number of presentations with voice overlays.

If the site is designed to allow users to download entire multi-media files, the massive size of these files could be a problem. If so, either split up the files into separate downloads, or arrange to have the information streamed to the user.

## Using the Website for Regulation FD Disclosure

The SEC's Regulation FD mandates that a company immediately release to the general public any material non-public information that it has disclosed to certain individuals outside of the company (see the Regulation FD chapter). The traditional method for disseminating this information is through a Form 8-K filing. Can a company instead use its website to disclose this information, thereby eliminating the cost of constructing and filing a Form 8-K? The SEC weighed in on this question at some length in its "Guidance on the Use of Company Web Sites," dated August 2008. The SEC states:

> In order to make information public, it must be disseminated in a manner calculated to reach the securities market place in general through recognized channels of distribution, and public investors must be afforded a reasonable waiting period to react to the information. Thus, in evaluating whether information is public for purposes of our guidance, companies must consider whether and when: (1) a company web site is a recognized channel of distribution, (2) posting of information on a company web site disseminates the information in a manner making it available to the securities marketplace in general, and (3) there has been a reasonable waiting period for investors and the market to react to the posted information.

The SEC then points out that whether a website is considered a channel of distribution of information depends on the steps taken by a company to alert the market to the presence of its website and its practices for disclosing information through that website.

Further, the SEC states that there are several factors to consider when determining whether a website makes information available to the securities marketplace. These include:

- Whether and how companies let investors and the markets know that the company has a web site and that they should look at the company's web site for information. For example, does the company include disclosure in its periodic reports (and in its press releases) of its web site address and that it routinely posts important information on its web site?
- Whether the company has made investors and the markets aware that it will post important information on its web site and whether it has a pattern or practice of posting such information on its web site;
- Whether the company's web site is designed to lead investors and the market efficiently to information about the company, including information specifically addressed to investors, whether the information is prominently disclosed on the web site in the location known and routinely used for such disclosures, and whether the information is presented in a format readily accessible to the general public;
- The extent to which information posted on the web site is regularly picked up by the market and readily available media, and reported in, such media or the extent to which the company has advised newswires or the media about such information and the size and market following of the company involved. For example, in evaluating accessibility to the posted information, companies that are well-followed by the market and the media may know that the market and the media will pick up and further distribute the disclosures they make on their web sites. On the other hand, companies with less of a market following, which may include many companies with smaller market capitalizations, may need to take more affirmative steps so that investors and others know that information is or has been posted on the company's web site and that they should look at the company web site for current information about the company;

- The steps the company has taken to make its web site and the information accessible, including the use of "push" technology, such as RSS feeds, or releases through other distribution channels either to widely distribute such information or advise the market of its availability. We do not believe, however, that it is necessary that push technology be used in order for the information to be disseminated, although that may be one factor to consider in evaluating the accessibility to the information;
- Whether the company keeps its web site current and accurate;
- Whether the company uses other methods in addition to its web site posting to disseminate the information and whether and to what extent those other methods are the predominant methods the company uses to disseminate information; and
- The nature of the information.

The third element to consider in the SEC's guidance was whether "there has been a reasonable waiting period for investors and the market to react to the posted information." The SEC considers the following factors when determining the duration of a reasonable waiting period:

- The size and market following of a company
- The extent to which investor information on the website is regularly accessed
- The steps taken by the company to make the investment community aware that it uses the website as a key source of important information about the company
- Whether the company has actively disseminated the availability of the information posted on the website
- The nature and complexity of the information

The SEC pointed out that the waiting period concept was a qualitative evaluation, as it notes in the following statement:

> What may be a reasonable waiting period after posting information on a company web site for a particular company and a particular type of information may not be one for other companies or other types of information. For example, a large company that frequently uses its web site as a key resource for providing information, has taken steps to make investors and the market aware of this, and reasonably believes that its web site is well followed by investors and other market participants, may get comfortable with a waiting period that is shorter than a waiting period for a company that is not in the same situation. If the information is important, companies should consider taking additional steps to alert investors and the market to the fact that important information will be posted – for example, prior to such posting, filing or furnishing such information to us or issuing a press release with the information. Adequate advance notice of the particular posting, including the date and time of the anticipated posting and the other steps the company intends to take to provide the information, will help make investors and the market aware of the future posting of information, and will thereby facilitate the broad dissemination of the information.

Here, the SEC appears to be backing away from any recommendation to solely rely on information distributed through a website, since it recommends a press release or SEC filing for the more important disclosures. However, the SEC then essentially reverses this qualification with the following statement:

> We now believe that technology has evolved and the use of the Internet has grown such that, for some companies in certain circumstances, posting of the information on the company's web site, in and of itself, may be a sufficient method of public disclosure under Regulation FD. Companies will need to consider whether and when postings on their web sites are "reasonably designed to provide broad, non-exclusionary distribution of the information to the public." ... Because the company has the responsibility for evaluating whether a method or combination of methods of disclosure would satisfy the alternative public disclosure provision of Regulation FD, it remains the company's responsibility to evaluate whether a posting on its web site would satisfy this requirement.

To summarize this verbose guidance from the SEC, we can reasonably conclude that a smaller public company whose website is less frequently accessed by the investment community should probably not rely solely on website postings for its Regulation FD disclosures. Conversely, a large public company with an extensive investor and analyst following, and which heavily markets its website, may be in a better position to rely solely upon its website postings for Regulation FD disclosures.

## Hyperlinks to Third-Party Information

Many companies include on their websites hyperlinks to other websites that are not related to their own businesses. The SEC weighed in on the use of hyperlinks in an August 2008 commentary. In general, the SEC pointed out that a company could be held liable for any hyperlinks it uses. In particular:

> A company can be held liable for third-party information to which it hyperlinks from its web site and which could be attributable to the company ... whether third-party information is attributable to a company depends upon whether the company has: (1) involved itself in the preparation of the information, or (2) explicitly or implicitly endorsed or approved the information. In the case of company liability for statements by third parties such as analysts, the courts and we have referred to the first line of inquiry as the "entanglement" theory and the second as the "adoption" theory.

The SEC then gave examples of situations in which a company could be considered to have "adopted" hyperlinked information. They are:

- Context of the hyperlink – what the company says about the hyperlink or what is implied by the context in which the company places the hyperlink;
- Risk of confusing the investors – the presence or absence of precautions against investor confusion about the source of the information; and

- Presentation of the hyperlinked information – how the hyperlink is presented graphically on the web site, including the layout of the screen containing the hyperlink.

The SEC believes that a company can be considered to have "adopted" the information to which it is hyperlinking when the business has "explicitly or implicitly approved or endorsed the statement of a third-party such that the company should be liable for that statement." The concept of implicit endorsement is a difficult one, which the SEC expands upon as follows:

> The key question in the hyperlinking context, therefore, is: Does the context of the hyperlink and the hyperlinked information together create a reasonable inference that the company has approved or endorsed the hyperlinked information? We believe that in evaluating whether a company has implicitly approved or endorsed information on a third-party web site to which it has established a hyperlink, one important factor is what the company says about the hyperlink, including what is implied by the context in which the company places the hyperlink.

> In considering the context of the hyperlink, we begin with the assumption that providing a hyperlink to a third-party web site indicates that the company believes the information on the third-party web site may be of interest to the users of its web site. Otherwise, it is unclear to us why the company would provide the link. To avoid potential confusion or misunderstanding about what the company's view or opinion is with respect to the information to which the company has provided a hyperlink, the company should consider explaining the context for the hyperlink – and thereby make explicit, rather than implicit, why the hyperlink is being provided. For example, a company might explicitly endorse the hyperlinked information or suggest that the hyperlinked information supports a particular assertion on the company's web site. Alternatively, a company might simply note that the third-party web site contains information that may be of interest or of use to the reader.

> The nature and content of the hyperlinked information also should be considered in deciding how to explain the context for the hyperlink. The degree to which a company is making a selective choice to hyperlink to a specific piece of third-party information likely will indicate the extent to which the company has a positive view or opinion about that information. For example, a company including a hyperlink to a news article that is highly laudatory of management should consider explanatory language about the source and why the company is providing the hyperlink in order to avoid the inference that the company is commenting on or even approving its accuracy, or was involved in its preparation. Conversely, the more general or broad-based the hyperlinked information is, the company may consider providing a more general explanation. For example, if a company has a media page and simply provides hyperlinks to recent news articles, both positive and negative, about the company, the risk that a company may have liability regarding a particular article or that it endorses or approves of each and every news article may be reduced. In this case, a title such as "Recent News Articles" may be all the explanation that a company may determine is needed to avoid being considered to have adopted the materials.

In short, it is apparent that hyperlinks cannot be sprayed throughout a website without first giving considerable thought to how to preface the link with additional information that probably has to be reviewed, if not written, by corporate counsel.

The SEC also pointed out the option of using exit notices for hyperlinks, while continuing to warn of a company's continuing liability if it uses them. The comment is:

> A company also may determine to use other methods, including "exit notices" or "intermediate screens," to denote that the hyperlink is to third-party information. While the use of "exit notices" or "intermediate screens" helps to avoid confusion as to the source of the third-party information, no one type of "exit notice" or "intermediate screen" will absolve companies from antifraud liability for third-party hyperlinked information.
>
> For example, if there is only one analyst report out of many that provides a positive outlook on the company's prospects, and the company provides a hyperlink to the one positive analyst report and to no other, and does not mention the fact that all the other analyst reports are negative on the company's prospects, then even the use of an "exit notice" or "intermediate screen" or explanatory language may not be sufficient to avoid the inference that the company has approved or endorsed the one positive analyst's report. With regard to the use of disclaimers generally, ... we do not view a disclaimer alone as sufficient to insulate a company from responsibility for information that it makes available to investors whether through a hyperlink or otherwise. Accordingly, a company would not be shielded from antifraud liability for hyperlinking to information it knows, or is reckless in not knowing, is materially false or misleading. This would be the case even where the company uses a disclaimer and/or other features designed to indicate that it has not adopted the false or misleading information to which it has provided the hyperlink. Our concern is that an alternative approach could result in unscrupulous companies using disclaimers as shields from liability for making false or misleading statements. We again remind companies that specific disclaimers of antifraud liability are contrary to the policies underpinning the federal securities laws.

The SEC has gone to some lengths in its guidance to point out the significant potential for liability if a company includes hyperlinks to third-party sites in its website. While the risk of liability can clearly be mitigated by carefully framing the context in which each hyperlink is provided, it is certainly easier to impose a blanket rule that no hyperlinks will be allowed on the website.

## Interactive Website Features

A company may elect to include blogs (such as CEO and investor relations blogs) or electronic shareholder forums on its website. These features are subject to the antifraud provisions of the federal securities laws, so it is helpful to understand the SEC's position about them, which it clarified in guidance issued in August 2008. The SEC points out the following:

Companies should consider taking steps to put into place controls and procedures to monitor statements made by or on behalf of the company on these types of electronic forums ... Accordingly, we are providing the following guidance for companies hosting or participating in blogs or electronic shareholder forums:

- The antifraud provisions of the federal securities laws apply to blogs and to electronic shareholder forums... Companies are responsible for statements made by the companies, or on their behalf, on their web sites or on third party web sites, and the antifraud provisions of the federal securities laws reach those statements. While blogs or forums can be informal and conversational in nature, statements made there by the company (or by a person acting on behalf of the company) will not be treated differently from other company statements when it comes to the antifraud provisions of the federal securities laws. Employees acting as representatives of the company should be aware of their responsibilities in these forums, which they cannot avoid by purporting to speak in their "individual" capacities.
- Companies cannot require investors to waive protections under the federal securities laws as a condition to entering or participating in a blog or forum. Any term or condition of a blog or shareholder forum requiring users to agree not to make investment decisions based on the blog's or forum's content or disclaiming liability for damages of any kind arising from the use or inability to use the blog or forum is inconsistent with the federal securities laws and, we believe, violates the anti-waiver provisions of the federal securities laws.

A company is not responsible for the statements that third parties post on a web site the company sponsors, nor is a company obligated to respond to or correct misstatements made by third parties.

Given the existence of a liability under the securities laws, a company considering the use of interactive website features should first have a monitoring system in place for statements made, as well as a system of policies and training that all employees must be aware of before they are allowed to use the interactive features. If a company does not have these protective systems in place, it should not install interactive features on its website.

## Website Information Removal

Though the investor relations site will certainly contain a massive amount of information, there is no need to clutter up the message being sent to investors by including older information or statements that have been superseded and so are no longer accurate. For example, consider removing the following from the site:

- Video recordings or transcripts from older shareholder meetings
- Video recordings, transcripts, or PowerPoint presentations associated with earlier investor presentations, product launches, or other public announcements
- Audio recordings of more dated earnings calls

The SEC has stated in its interpretive guidance on websites that a company should clarify which information is *not* current, so that investors are not confused by it. The SEC points out the following:

> In circumstances where it is not apparent to the reasonable person that the posted materials or statements speak as of a certain date or earlier period, then to assure that investors understand that the posted materials or statements speak as of a date or period earlier than when the investor may be accessing the posted materials or statements, we believe that previously posted materials or statements that have been put on a company's web site should be:
> - Separately identified as historical or previously posted materials or statements, including, for example, by dating the posted materials or statements; and
> - Located in a separate section of the company's web site containing previously posted materials or statements.

Thus, you could shift older information into an archive section of the site, where it is still available for those investors who want to delve into the company's history in greater detail.

---

**Tip:** Monitor the download volume for the older files and consider deleting them from the site if they are no longer being accessed.

---

## The Website and the IPO

A company that is about to go public through an initial public offering (IPO) has an enormous amount of work to do to prepare for its IPO, and may not want to divert any effort into the enhancement of its website. This is an incorrect mindset, since the period surrounding the IPO is when investors are most curious about the company, and go straight to its website to learn more about it. The volume of visitors to the site will spike massively during this IPO period and then fall off shortly thereafter. Thus, a company has a one-time opportunity to impress the investment community.

When prospective investors arrive at the company website, they will be most impressed by a stylish, well-constructed site that thoroughly describes the company's operations. There may not yet be an investor relations component of the site before the IPO event, but the company should launch one as soon as the company's stock begins trading on an exchange.

In short, consider the company website to be a key element of the IPO, not only from an investor relations perspective, but also from a public relations viewpoint, in order to take advantage of the massive surge in public interest that accompanies any IPO. If the company simply does not have the manpower to update its website, then hand off this task to a firm that specializes in building websites, and do so sufficiently far in advance for the site to be completed and tested before the IPO event occurs.

## Third Party Providers

The nature of some of the information needed for an investor relations website makes it particularly difficult to construct in-house. A number of third-party services can create and maintain entire investor relations websites for a company. These websites incorporate instant posting of company press releases, interactive stock quotes and charts, investment calculators, all SEC filings, investor relations event calendars, and webcasting. The sites can also be configured for viewing on a mobile device. Thus, a company can pay a monthly fee to have someone else manage their site.

If a company wants to maintain some of the information on its investor relations site, while accessing custom data feeds of market information, there are several firms, such as Quote Media, that will provide the requisite information for a monthly fee. These data feeds can be configured to match the color and font scheme of the website, so they give the appearance of being highly integrated website components.

It may also be useful to hire a search engine optimization (SEO) firm to work with the company to improve the ranking of its investor relations pages in the major search engines. They can assist with rewriting pages to emphasize key words, and introducing more easily searchable sub-headings and bullet points.

In short, third parties will likely be needed for some component of an investor relations site. The component most commonly outsourced is the data feeds, which a company cannot readily create by itself.

## Summary

Every publicly held company should have a well-populated investor relations section within its website. This website should be feature-rich even for a smaller public company, since it is likely to be the first place that a prospective investor will visit when researching a business.

The minimum amount of information considered necessary for an investor relations website is continuing to increase. To see if your company's offering is at least adequate, conduct a periodic survey of the investor relations sites of competing public companies, or of "best in class" organizations to see what types of information or features might be useful additions to your company's website.

# Chapter 9
## The Sell Side and the Buy Side

## Introduction

In this chapter, we describe the many players in the investment community, and how to deal with them. They are generally classified into two groups, the *sell side* and the *buy side*. The sell side assists investors in making investment decisions. The buy side is comprised of the money management entities that buy large numbers of securities for money management purposes. The investor relations department uses both the sell side and the buy side to reach out to the investment community, both to tell the company's story and to raise funds.

> **Related Podcast Episode:** Episode 79 of the Accounting Best Practices Podcast discusses dealing with an analyst. You can listen to it at: **accounting-tools.com/podcasts** or **iTunes**

## The Sell Side

The sell side is comprised of those firms that assist the investing public in making investment decisions. Of this group, the investor relations officer is most concerned with analysts, who generate the advice relied on by investors. There are likely to be only a few analysts covering a company, but their presumably large number of followers makes them quite important to the investor relations department. Next in importance is the stockbroker community. Stockbrokers manage their own networks of investors, so it is certainly useful to curry favor with this group. However, there are many more stockbrokers than analysts, so it is a much greater chore to maintain relations with them. In addition, we make note of investment bankers, who assist the company with fund raising activities. They locate buyers for the company's securities, and can assist with shifting the ownership of large blocks of stock from one shareholder to another. In this section, we describe all of these members of the sell side.

### The Analyst

An analyst investigates a public company, and creates an analysis of where he thinks the company's stock price will go. Based on this recommendation, stockbrokers may suggest to their clients that they alter their positions in a company's stock. Given the multiplier effect of an analyst's opinion, it is important to understand what analysts do and how to deal with them.

We begin with the analyst report. It is updated several times per year, and typically includes the following information:

- *Overview*. Describes the company and what it does.
- *Competitors*. Describes key competitors of the company and their relative positioning in the industry.
- *Analysis*. States the analyst's opinion of how well the company is performing. This may include an analysis of how larger industry trends may impact the company.
- *Financial results and forecast*. States recent historical results and the analyst's projections for future results.
- *Valuation*. Uses one or more methods to arrive at an estimated valuation for the company. Usual valuation tools are discounted cash flow analysis and a comparison of the company to the market valuations of its peer group.
- *Recommendation*. Recommends that investors either buy, sell, or hold shares.
- *Research notes*. Includes source information that more sophisticated investors can research to arrive at their own conclusions.

If an analyst distributes reports on a subscription basis, she sends the report directly to clients. The clients are paying for this advice, so they want to see good insights into each company being reviewed. If there isn't, then they stop paying the analyst.

If an analyst works for a brokerage, she presents her "buy" recommendations to the assembled sales staff before the markets open each morning, which is known as the *morning call* (the brokerage's buy side customers may also access the call). The sales staff will be looking for a sales pitch to use for each stock, and so it is useful for the analyst to provide key points about a recommended company that will be memorable for clients. If clients buy a recommended company's stock, the brokerage earns a commission, which in turn secures the employment of the analyst. Conversely, if an analyst only has a "hold" recommendation on a stock, it is not recommended to the sales staff, which therefore generates no commissions. Thus, analysts working for brokerages are always looking for stocks for which they can reasonably issue a "buy" recommendation, and thereby earn a profit for their employers.

---

**Tip:** The investor relations staff can generate a list of selling points that the sales staff of a brokerage can use, and pass them along to those analysts covering the company. It can also include these points in its presentations to stockbrokers during any non-deal road shows.

---

The better analysts have four skills that make them more likely to make projections that are justified by actual results. Those skills are:

- *Industry specialization*. An analyst should have a detailed knowledge of an industry, including the competitive postures of the various participants, key factors that impact the entire industry, its cost structure, the financial condition of the major players, and so forth.

- *Contacts*. An analyst should have a working relationship with most of the key players in the industry. This should include someone in the senior management of most major companies in the industry, as well as industry pundits and consultants. These contacts provide up-to-date information about changing trends within the industry.
- *Analysis skills*. An analyst needs to know how to interpret all of the preceding information to arrive at reasonable estimates of future conditions, not only for the industry as a whole, but also for individual companies within the industry.
- *Communication skills*. Even if an analyst understands the direction of an industry, she is not truly successful without being able to communicate this information effectively. This means having excellent report writing skills, as well as the ability to speak comfortably at industry conferences and in a television studio.

Some of the better analysts have used their analysis and communication skills to attract a following of wealthy investors and institutional investors, who are more likely to make investments based on their recommendations. To attract these investors, analysts strive to attain high rankings in various analyst rankings that are conducted by third parties.

Why does a public company need this specialized individual? There are several reasons for attracting the attention of not just one analyst, but a number of them, including:

- *More investors*. If a well-known analyst decides to follow a company and issue recommendations about its stock, that is an indicator to some investors that the company has the seal of approval of that analyst – which can lead to a larger number of investors.
- *Contacts*. A good analyst has a large number of contacts, which he or she can share with the company if there is ever a need to raise funds or place large blocks of stock.
- *Bandwagon effect*. Once a few analysts start following a company, other analysts are more likely to jump on the bandwagon and also begin following it. This means that a secondary group of investors who follow the recommendations of these other analysts will be more likely to invest in the company.

We have built a case in favor of attracting analysts. However, doing so is not easy, for several reasons. First, the population of analysts has declined along with the profits of the brokerage houses. Whenever profits decline in the financial services industry, the brokerages that employ the bulk of all analysts are more likely to lay off a fair number of them. Second, independent analysts who issue paid newsletters have fewer subscribers when there is an industry downturn, and especially when there is so much free "analysis" available on the Internet. The result is a decline in the number of independent analysts.

The impact of this downturn in the analyst population has been especially severe on micro cap and nano cap companies. The reason for the lack of analyst coverage for this group is the manner in which an analyst generates revenue for a brokerage. When an analyst makes a "buy" recommendation on a stock, that recommendation needs to generate a sufficiently large commission to create a large profit for the brokerage, net of the cost of the analyst and related overhead. Thus, if an analyst spends a large amount of time researching a nano cap company, the potential amount of trading volume that will be generated will be too small to manufacture a sufficiently large profit for the brokerage – there is simply not enough stock available to support the required volume of stock sales.

---

**Tip:** An analyst may be willing to provide to the investor relations officer information about the minimum market capitalization, daily trading volume, and overall liquidity that a company must have before consenting to provide coverage.

---

If a micro cap or nano cap firm wants to obtain analyst coverage despite this structural difficulty, it will need to find alternative ways to do so. One possibility is for the investor relations staff to search for smaller boutique brokerages that specialize in the company's industry. These analysts are most easily found by researching who provides coverage for competing firms. These analysts have already done the research needed for the industry as a whole, and so may be inclined to provide coverage for the company, if only because not much additional work would be required to do so. They will be especially interested in providing coverage if the company is uniquely positioned, or if it appears to be unreasonably undervalued.

---

**Tip:** Competing firms may list the analysts who cover them in the investor relations sections of their websites. These analysts are among the more likely ones to extend their coverage to the company, since they are already involved in the industry.

---

It may also be possible to hire an investor relations consultant who has an in-depth knowledge of the analysts who cover other businesses in the same market space as the company. This consultant may be able to provide an introduction to the most likely analyst prospects.

In those rare cases where a large number of analysts are willing to provide coverage, you may need to decide which ones to most vigorously support. To do so, obtain copies of the research reports issued by them. When compared, it will be readily apparent which of the analysts conduct the most in-depth research and have the most complete understanding of how the industry operates. Also, look at which analysts are asked to give presentations (especially keynote addresses) at industry conferences; this is a strong sign that the conference organizers have a high opinion of those analysts. Other selection methods are to pick analysts with the most industry experience, or those having earned the chartered financial analyst credential.

Another option is to obtain the services of an analyst that works for a sell side firm with which the company does business related to the sale of stock or acquisitions work. This coverage will be free, but the coverage may not necessarily be favorable. There is supposed to be a fire wall between the analysis portion of a sell side firm and the rest of the business, where there is no pressure on analysts to provide favorable coverage. Indeed, Section 501 of the Sarbanes-Oxley Act even mandates that a sell side firm cannot retaliate against its own analysts that provide negative recommendations for the stock of a client company.

Though the option of obtaining free analyst coverage may seem reasonable, please note that there is *always* a cost – if the company does not continue to do business with the investment bank, then the analyst coverage will probably not last long.

---

**Tip:** If a company is being pursued by several investment bankers, consider apportioning some of the company's business to all of them, so that the company obtains coverage from the analysts that work for all of the bankers.

---

Another possibility is to pay an analyst to provide a report about the company. This is expensive, and may not generate a large amount of investor activity. Also, the analyst is supposed to state on the report that he or she is being paid by the company, which may weaken the impact of the report.

If a company has attracted the attention of analysts, how do you deal with them? It is illegal to pass confidential information to analysts, as per Regulation FD, but there are some options available for making them feel more welcome, including:

- *Provide guidance.* If the company is not already providing guidance, start doing so (see the Guidance chapter). Issuing estimates of future earnings reduces the work load of analysts, since they do not have to rely so much on their own models to derive earnings estimates. Also, if there is a sudden change in the company's prospects, issue updated guidance soon thereafter, so that analysts can react to it and modify their own projections concerning the company.

- *Keep guidance reasonable.* The CEO should not make outlandish claims for stratospheric earnings, since this will engender an ongoing series of stock price increases, followed by steep declines when the company cannot meet its own earnings targets. Analysts do not like hefty stock price volatility, since there may be a sharp price decline right after an analyst has issued a "buy" recommendation. If an analyst is embarrassed too many times by aggressive guidance, he or she may decamp in search of companies that issue more conservative guidance.

- *Schedule earnings calls.* Give analysts the opportunity to ask questions of management by scheduling earnings calls following the release of quarterly and annual results.

- *Allow direct meetings.* If an analyst wants to meet with senior management or obtain a tour of the company facilities, by all means do so. These meetings give analysts excellent background information about the company, which they can use in their analyses. For example, they can estimate how many people work for the company by counting the cars in the parking lot, or back into its working capital requirements by estimating the amount of inventory in the warehouse. Management can also discuss their views of the industry as a whole, or of competitors, which gives analysts additional information about the competitive environment, as well as how the senior management team thinks.

- *Send filings and press releases.* Whenever the company issues a filing to the SEC, or issues a press release or fact sheet, send a copy to the analyst. There should be a mailing list for all analysts covering the company, to track who should receive these materials.
- *Schedule analysts' day.* If a number of analysts follow the company, schedule an annual analysts' day. This is an on-site series of presentations that can include speeches by people analysts do not normally meet, such as the technical staff, customers, and industry experts. There may also be a plant tour and product demonstrations. Alternatively, the senior management team could set up shop for a day in New York City, where many analysts are based; a New York analysts' day may also attract analysts from Europe, since flights into New York are quite convenient, with the least time zone differential from Europe. It may take several years to build up attendance at an analysts' day, so be prepared to schedule it every year for the foreseeable future.

---

**Tip:** Consider scheduling an analysts' day to immediately precede or follow the annual shareholder meeting, so that shareholders can attend both events.

---

**Tip:** There is a significant chance that an employee being interviewed by an analyst will impart information that has not been disclosed to the public, which is a violation of Regulation FD. To monitor these instances, have an investor relations person sit in on all interviews, and note any such items that should be included in a Form 8-K for immediate release.

---

If the company elects to allow meetings between analysts and employees, exercise considerable care in determining which employees should meet with the analysts. The selected individuals should be briefed in advance on standard questions and answers, when to pass queries along to someone more qualified to answer them, and which types of information have not yet been released to the public, and therefore should not be discussed. Generally, it is easiest to restrict meetings with analysts to just a few people who are routinely briefed on company activities, and who know how to deal with analysts. This means the CEO and CFO should be prepared to talk to analysts on a regular basis.

> **Tip:** Listen in on the earnings calls of competing firms to determine the types of questions that analysts are asking, and prepare answers to the same questions.

> **Tip:** Analysts want to talk to management, not listen to a presentation. At most, have background materials available that an analyst can read, but leave the meeting time completely open for a free-ranging discussion.

A better analyst will want to verify the information provided by the company, and does this by talking to competitors, suppliers, and customers – essentially everyone in the industry who can give them confirming information. Accordingly, be prepared to give contact information to any analyst who asks for the information, and to make introductions where necessary.

When an analyst writes a research report about a company, he may send a copy to the investor relations officer or CEO, asking for comments. If so, it is acceptable to fact-check the document and give feedback on any items that are demonstrably incorrect. However, do not re-write the report, since a litigation-minded investor could use a marked-up report version as evidence that the company is unduly influencing those analysts providing coverage. Further, do not question or otherwise comment upon the conclusions reached by an analyst, since doing so implies that the company is bringing pressure to bear upon the analyst to change his opinion.

> **Tip:** If the company gives feedback on preliminary versions of analyst reports, it should retain a copy of the original and marked-up versions, to provide evidence in case a plaintiff ever questions the probity of the company.

When an analyst issues a report about the company or its industry, pay close attention to it. Many analysts have exceptionally broad knowledge of an industry and excellent insights into its workings, so their opinions are worth discussing. In particular, the management team should make note of the following three issues:

- *Strategic flaws.* Has the analyst legitimately spotted a flaw in the company's strategic direction that requires correction?
- *Analyst assumptions.* If the analyst has provided backup information about how he derived certain numbers in the report, make note of those assumptions; they could be used as indicators of how the analyst will react to changes in the company's performance in the future.
- *Stock price impacts.* If the analyst has noted an issue that impacts his perception of the company's value, assume that the rest of the investment community sees the same problem. The issue may require correction if the management team wants the company to achieve the highest possible stock price.

When dealing with analysts, the CEO must understand that there will be times during the life cycle of a business when the stock price will be undervalued, and there will be times when it is overvalued. The first case will result in "buy" recommendations from analysts, and the latter situations will necessitate "sell" recommendations – this is simply part of the ongoing ebb and flow of stock prices. Even if a company is doing well, an analyst may downgrade the stock of every company in an industry if there is a perception that outside forces are about to put the industry into a tailspin. Thus, the CEO should not post favorable analyst reports on the company web site, and then yank them off when a subsequent report inevitably turns less favorable. This type of subjective behavior smacks of favoritism, where the company is only publishing good news. It also appears to give the company's endorsement to a favorable report.

> **Tip:** Only post analyst contact information in the investor relations section of the company's website. Investors can use this information to contact analysts directly for research reports. By doing so, the company gives the appearance of being impartial in its dealings with analysts.

A better approach to both positive and negative analyst reports is to not publicly acknowledge them at all. The only action that a company should ever take, and only on rare occasions, is to contact an analyst or that person's supervisor regarding a factual error in a published or forthcoming report. In nearly all situations, it is better to simply flood the market with information about the company, and let analysts create reports based on this complete set of information.

Conversely, do not publicly castigate an analyst who has issued an unflattering report, or reduce the flow of information to that person. Doing so does not give the investment community a flattering view of the management team. Also, giving less information to an analyst who has issued an "outlier" analysis makes it more likely that the analyst will continue to issue reports that differ from the consensus opinion, simply because he now has less input for his analysis model.

Many analysts prefer to avoid placing an outright "sell" recommendation on a stock, since this is most likely to annoy a company's CEO, who might seek retribution by excluding them from meetings with management. Instead, there are a number of terms that indicate to investors that a stock might be overvalued, such as "underperform," "moderate buy," "accumulate," or "long-term buy". An approximate replacement for the damaging "hold" recommendation is "moderate buy," which at least gives the appearance that an investor should buy a few shares. A knowledgeable investor knows what an analyst is trying to say, and will likely reduce his ownership of the shares on which such designations have been placed. These terms reflect the politics that an analyst must deal with in order to be truthful with investors, while still maintaining access to company management.

We have given some insights into the difficult environment in which an analyst operates. To make their job easier, and hopefully to attract more analysts, make sure that they receive all information that has been issued to the public, offer solidly achievable guidance, and give them ongoing access to the senior management team. By doing so, they will have a thorough understanding of the company's operational and financial structure, and so should be able to arrive at their own estimates of company results that roughly coincide with what the company eventually reports.

**The Stockbroker**

A stockbroker is a person or business that executes the buy and sell orders of an investor in exchange for a commission. Stockbrokers are important, because they can influence the purchasing decisions of their client investors. Thus, there is a multiplier effect when dealing with them. Unfortunately, it is quite a task to keep all stockbrokers informed about the company. According to the Financial Industry Regulatory Authority (FINRA), there are more than 630,000 stockbrokers registered with it. It is difficult for even a large investor relations department to keep in touch with a fraction of this massive group.

There are two keys to success when dealing with stockbrokers. First, make bulk presentations to large groups of stockbrokers during non-deal road shows (see the Road Show chapter). This allows the presentation team to engage with many stockbrokers at one time using a standard presentation format, which is highly efficient. The second key to success is to give stockbrokers a short set of memorable talking points about the business. They use this information to convince their clients to buy the company's stock. The intent is to essentially prepackage their sales pitch; this makes it not only more likely that they will represent the company to their clients, but also gives the company some control over what is said.

> **Tip:** Talk to stockbrokers about the sales points they need when they discuss the company with their clients, and write several variations on the sales pitch for them. Also, send to interested stockbrokers copies of any articles written about the company, which they can forward to their clients.

The presentation to a group of stockbrokers should *briefly* discuss what the company does and its future prospects, while leaning heavily on selling points. A sample presentation outline appears in the following exhibit, where the emphasis is on a small number of PowerPoint slides, with selling points appearing at the beginning and end of the presentation. Note the brevity of the entire presentation.

**Sample Structure of a Stockbroker Presentation**

| Duration | Topic |
| --- | --- |
| 1 minute | **Company overview**. Should nearly duplicate the final slide, and provides key talking points for stockbrokers. Should state what the company does, its prospects, and why it is a good investment. |
| 3 minutes | **Company fundamentals**. State the positioning of the company in the market, key products, and competitive strengths. |
| 2 minutes | **Company results**. Show the financial results of the company, especially its profits and cash flow on a trend line. Point out key items in the financials as necessary. |
| 2 minutes | **Growth opportunity**. Show how the company plans to grow. Place an emphasis on the company's internal organic growth rate wherever possible, since it is more controllable than growth by acquisition. |

| Duration | Topic |
|---|---|
| 1 minute | **Valuation impact.** Show the current and projected valuation of the company, based on the growth opportunity just stated. Also, translate the valuation into earnings per share, and compare it to the company's current earnings per share. |
| 1 minute | **Summary.** Should nearly duplicate the first slide. List key talking points about what the company does, its prospects, and why it is a good investment. |
| **10 minutes** | **Total duration of presentation** |

**Tip:** Always have copies of the presentation available for stockbrokers, since they can use the talking points listed on the presentation document when describing the opportunity to their clients.

A key point when making stockbroker presentations is that the explanation of what the company does should be extremely simple. If the company is involved in many disparate activities, it will be difficult to explain to stockbrokers – and if they do not understand it, they probably will not bother to present it to their clients. Thus, it may make sense to focus the company on a specific and tightly-defined business area before attempting to present it to stockbrokers.

A micro cap or nano cap company may have a considerable amount of trouble attracting stockbrokers who are able to recommend its stock to their clients. The trouble is that stockbrokers working for larger firms will be told which stocks to pitch to their clients, and those larger firms are only interested in selling stocks for which there is considerable liquidity. It may be possible to attract the attention of stockbrokers who have more seniority, since this group is sometimes allowed more leeway in recommending stocks to their clients. Another option is to retain the services of an investor relations consultant who knows stockbrokers who are willing to deal with micro cap and nano cap stocks – these stockbrokers usually work for small boutique brokerages that specialize in the stocks of smaller public companies.

**Tip:** If you are in direct communication with the company's investors, ask them who recommended the stock to them. If this was a stockbroker, attempt to create a long-term relationship with that broker, who may then be more inclined to steer other investors toward the company's stock.

### The Investment Banker

An investment banker raises equity or debt funding on behalf of its clients. When a company engages the services of an investment banker, the primary point of contact is the CFO, not the investor relations officer. The CFO works with the investment banker to create a multi-year forecast of the company's estimated profits and cash flows. The investment banker then sends this forecast, along with supporting information about the business, to a list of institutional investors and/or individual investors. The banker aggregates the list of interested clients by city, and arranges a road show for the CEO and CFO, who will travel to each city in turn, presenting the company's request for funding to all interested parties (see the Road Show chapter).

95

The banker then contacts the people who met the presentation team during the road show to see who is interested in funding the business, and on what terms. The banker settles the terms of the deal, arranges for payment, and takes a percentage of the final funding amount as a transaction fee.

Subsequent to the deal being closed, the investor relations officer may be involved in sending copies of the company's public filings and other press releases to the new investors, if the investors have requested this information. It may also be prudent to do so in order to maintain good relations with these investors, in case they might be interested in additional rounds of funding at a later date.

**Summary**

The bulk of this section has been concerned with the analyst, since the opinions of that person are listened to throughout the investment community. The basic points when dealing with analysts are to provide them with a broad range of information from which they can derive their own projections, while managing the business in such a predictable manner that it is relatively easy for them to forecast the company's future performance.

The situation is quite different with stockbrokers. In this case, the investor relations team needs to impart a streamlined view of the business on a highly repetitive basis to many people. There should be an emphasis on imparting a clear and easily understandable vision of what the company does and why its stock is valuable. The information imparted is probably going to be repeated to many clients, so it has to be so simplified that it can be easily repeated.

## The Buy Side

The buy side refers to institutional investors, such as pension funds, mutual funds, and insurance companies. These entities have enormous cash reserves available for investment, and so can be considered *the* heavyweight investors in the investment community. The investor relations department may or may not want to pursue investments by this group, since their buying and selling activities are so large that they can roil stock prices, and also effectively reduce the amount of tradable stock. Conversely, individual investors are generally welcomed, since they usually hold stock positions longer than other types of investors, and may remain loyal to a company long after other, more quantitatively-driven investors have departed the scene. Thus, we include both institutional and individual investors in the following discussion of the buy side.

### The Institutional Investor

Institutional investors are always looking for profitable new investments in which they can generate a return on their cash, and so are continually being pursued by public companies. However, their sheer heft makes them unlikely investors in micro cap and smaller businesses, since there are not enough available shares for them to move easily in and out of ownership positions. If they were to do so, their initial purchases would drive up the stock price, while any subsequent stock sales would depress the stock price. In addition, most institutional investors have adopted internal investment rules that constrain them from buying the stocks of smaller companies. Thus, this type of investor is not available to smaller public companies.

In cases where an institutional investor *has* elected to purchase a company's stock, the extent of its investment may soak up the majority of available shares, which restricts the ability of other investors to buy the stock. Most investor relations officers are willing to put up with this inconvenience, for two reasons:

- *Stock placements*. Institutional investors are usually quite willing to buy stock when a business has an initial public offering or secondary offering, if the initial purchase price is low enough to increase the odds that the investor can eventually sell the shares for a profit.
- *Stock transfers*. If an investor wants to sell a large block of shares, the investor relations officer may be able to convince a single institutional investor to acquire the entire block.

There are also several risks associated with institutional investors, which are:

- *Stock price*. When an institutional investor eventually sells its shares, the volume of shares being sold can trigger a significant decline in the stock price. Some investors attempt to mitigate this effect by liquidating their positions over a relatively long period of time.
- *Votes*. An institutional investor may own so many shares that it can influence the voting for directors at the annual meeting, as well as votes on other issues.

It is difficult to determine whether institutional investors as a group tend to be longer-term or shorter-term investors. It is obviously preferable from a public company's perspective for an institutional investor to retain its stock position for as long as possible, if only to avoid any downward pressure on the stock price. However, institutional investors (like any investors) must continually review the fundamentals of the companies and industries in which they invest, and liquidate positions where the long-term outlook is not good. Some investors are quicker to move their holdings than others; one company may experience considerable annual churn in its institutional shareholders, while another sees little change from year to year.

The investor relations officer may decide to pursue institutional investors, with the objective of increasing the proportion of shares held by this type of investor. If so, be aware that the investment strategies of only a small number of these investors may even allow them to invest in the company. For example, they may only invest in certain countries, industries, or companies having a certain market capitalization. Others may only invest in companies having a certain growth profile, or perhaps only those that pay dividends, or only those listed in certain stock indices. There may also be rules about never investing below a certain stock price, or where the result will be an excessive amount of ownership in a business. A few even base their decisions on the ethical or social responsibility profile of a company. Further, their rules may not allow them to invest more than a certain percentage of total funds in any one industry. In short, the investment rules of an institutional investor can constrain it from making an investment.

> **Note:** Being moved from one stock index to another can impact a company's stock price. For example, a company grows enough to be shifted from the Russell Microcap Index into the Russell 3000 Index. The proportion of investors buying all of the stocks in the Microcap Index may be less than the proportion buying stocks in the 3000 Index, resulting in a sudden run-up in the company's stock price as demand increases for the company's stock.

Investment decisions within institutional investment firms are usually made by a small number of fund managers. These managers typically rely upon the advice of their own in-house analysts, or the reports of one or more outside analysts to make investment decisions. The investor relations officer can draw the attention of these managers to the company by requesting a meeting between the fund manager, the in-house analyst, and the company's CEO or CFO. If the fund manager is interested, this may lead to a series of additional meetings. The fund manager and analyst will be particularly interested in the dynamics of the business and the industry in which it operates, as well as barriers to entry, competitors, and expected future growth rates. They will also want to learn about the backgrounds and accomplishments of the senior management team. The analyst will be particularly interested in drilling down into the operational results and cash flows of the business, to ascertain whether the company's products and services can continue to grow in a profitable manner. For more information about meeting with institutional investors, see the Road Show chapter.

An investment by a high-quality institutional investor may result in a flurry of additional investments from other investors who follow the holdings of that institutional investor. Thus, it may be particularly worthwhile for the investor relations officer to maintain relations with a select group of fund managers on an ongoing basis.

> **Tip:** Before approaching an institutional investor about buying the company's shares, research whether the investor has a history of quickly flipping its shares, or of being an activist investor. If either is the case, it may be best to contact other investors instead.

### The Buy Side Analyst

The buy side analyst is employed by fund managers to conduct research into specific investment opportunities. The reports created by a buy side analyst are only used by the employing fund manager in making investment decisions. By restricting access to this information, buy side analysts hope to achieve a research edge over other investors.

We only mention the buy side analyst here to point out their different orientation from the sell side analyst who was described in the preceding section.

**The Hedge Fund**

A hedge fund is essentially a mutual fund for wealthy investors. Investors must be accredited (see the Accredited Investor section in the Sale of Restricted Stock chapter), and the fund usually requires a minimum investment period of one year. Hedge funds are aggressively managed, and use a variety of strategies to maximize returns for investors. A hedge fund manager can follow almost any investment strategy, which allows them to invest anywhere, and in unusually large concentrations in certain industries. They may also employ leverage (debt) to maximize returns. A hedge fund may be an acceptable investor if it has a history of making longer-term investments.

**Sovereign Wealth Funds**

A sovereign wealth fund manages large amounts of cash from national governments. These funds are used to manage the reserves generated by trade surpluses. They are mostly owned by the oil producing countries in the Middle East, as well as China and Singapore. Examples of sovereign wealth funds are:
- Abu Dhabi Investment Authority
- China Investment Corporation
- Kuwait Investment Authority
- Qatar Investment Authority
- Temasek Holdings (Singapore)

If the country behind such a fund requires ready access to its invested cash, then the fund will probably only invest in very liquid public debt instruments.

If a sovereign wealth fund has a longer-term investment strategy, it may invest in the stock of public companies. However, the massive amounts of funds involved usually mandate that investments be restricted to larger companies. As is the case with other institutional investors, a sovereign wealth fund has difficulty trading large blocks of stock in smaller companies without causing adverse stock price effects.

**The Individual Investor**

When looking at the stock register of any public company, there will be a great many individual investors listed, though their stock holdings may be dwarfed by those of a vastly smaller number of institutional investors. These investors may buy shares directly, or through a stockbroker (in which case the shares may be held in the name of the stockbroker).

The objectives of this large group of investors can be difficult to ascertain (see the Investing Strategies chapter), so you will find that a small number of individual investors move in and out of the stock with great rapidity, while a larger number tend to hold onto their shares for long periods of time.

> **Tip:** If the investor relations officer is looking for unusually loyal investors, a good source may be near the company's facilities. Local investors may have a personal relationship with the company, and so are more inclined to hold the stock, even when its price declines. They may also be more inclined to support management if there is a proxy battle.

The investor relations staff should always be on the hunt for high net worth individuals, since they may buy large blocks of stock and then hold the shares for long periods of time. It may be possible to locate these investors through an investor relations consultant, or by asking current shareholders for the names of their advisors, and then educating the advisors about the company; this may indirectly lead to referrals. If high net worth individuals contact the company about investing, the investor relations staff should be prepared to give them a considerable amount of individual attention.

> **Tip:** If the company sells outstanding products, consider adding a notice to the product packaging that the company is publicly held, and state its ticker symbol. This may result in a few customers becoming investors.

A micro cap and nano cap firm will have an especially difficult time attracting individual investors. The trouble is that there may be very few shares available for sale, so that a buy order may take several days to fill – and the price may change substantially during that time. The same problem arises with selling shares, since the price may drop dramatically before a sufficient number of buyers can be found. Thus, only high net worth investors who are willing to accept these risks in exchange for the possibility of outsized gains will be interested in smaller companies.

It can be difficult to cost-effectively find individual investors who are willing to invest in a business, especially when some of their stock purchases may turn out to be in quite small quantities. Thus, it may make sense to try several approaches to attracting these investors and compare the costs of doing so to the number of shares purchased, to determine which method is the most cost-effective.

Once a company has obtained a significant base of individual investors, it should have a long-term plan for retaining them. One option is to put a particularly large amount of work into the annual report, so that it contains much more than just the annual financial statements. Another possibility is to go to some lengths to notify investors of the annual shareholders meeting, and provide enough unique content for investors to be interested in attending. Yet another option is to schedule periodic shareholder conference calls, where investors can question senior management about the business. The amount of effort expended on these activities will probably increase if the company has a large proportion of individual investors.

## The Foreign Investor

There is a strong tendency for companies to only sell to investors located in their headquarters country, which artificially narrows the field of potential investors. Consider expanding the company's investor relations activities to other countries if there have been a number of inquiries from those areas for information, or if the company already appears to have achieved thorough coverage of its home country's investors.

Here are several options for making it more likely that foreign investors will invest in the company:

- *Multi-language version of website.* Give website users the option to switch to a different language version of the site. This option is available through several services, where site users click on a popup button that allows them to switch to over a dozen alternative languages.
- *Investor days at subsidiaries.* It is generally easier to attract investors in countries where the company already has a subsidiary, so consider organizing an investor day at one of these facilities. This will probably only attract investors within a short distance of the facility, but may be an indicator of the overall level of interest to be expected in a country.
- *International road show.* A good starting point for an international road show is Europe, where there is an excellent infrastructure in place for organizing road shows. By far the best location to start is London. Other excellent choices that are homes to large concentrations of institutional investors are Amsterdam, Edinburgh, Frankfurt, Geneva, Paris, and Zurich. There tends to be less interest in United States companies in the Far East investment centers, though possible road show choices are Tokyo, Hong Kong, and Singapore.

---

**Tip:** It is nearly mandatory to engage the services of one or more local investment banks to arrange international road shows, since the company will likely have no contacts in these locations. Also, consult with them to learn about local financial terminology. For example, when a British investor asks about your company's turnover, he is referring to sales, not inventory.

---

European investors tend to be less interested in smaller cap stocks. Also, given the higher logistical cost of foreign road shows, it is usually not cost-effective for smaller firms to engage in them. Thus, the road show option is effectively restricted to mid cap and large cap companies.

If you are planning a road show that will involve visits to multiple countries, be especially careful to make arrangements around local holidays and vacation seasons. For example, it can be quite difficult to find anyone to talk to in Europe during August, which is their traditional vacation month. Also, have your investment banker investigate the timing of road shows by other companies, so that your road show does not conflict with their meeting dates. This can be a particular problem when there are major sporting events, such as the British Open and Wimbledon, since presentation teams are in the habit of combining their road shows with attendance at these events.

> **Tip:** If you are going to pursue foreign investors over the long term, you should schedule at least one road show per year to the areas where current international investors are concentrated. Where possible, this should include one or more members of the senior management team.

### Investment Clubs

An investment club is a group of individual investors that votes to buy or sell investments with their pooled funds. There is a multiplier effect when making a presentation to an investment club, since their pooled investments can represent a moderately significant purchase. Investment clubs tend to retain securities that they have acquired for a longer period of time than most other investors, so convincing them to invest can have a particularly long-term payoff. Thus, it can be worthwhile to occasionally make a presentation directly to an investment club.

You can purchase the mailing list of the National Association of Investors Corporation to obtain access to its member investment clubs, or sponsor its events, or advertise in its *Better Investing* magazine. Unfortunately, the number of investment clubs has been declining for a number of years, as on-line investing systems have attracted a larger proportion of individual investors.

### Summary

The investor relations department will find that it must deal with a broad array of investors, each with its own risk tolerances and investment styles. Indeed, the investment preferences of one investor may lead it to sell a company's stock, while the preferences of another investor will lead it to buy shares. The investor relations staff must be available to provide information to both incoming and outgoing investors, so that they all have sufficient information to make informed decisions about their holdings in the company's securities. We delve into the reasons why investors buy and sell shares in the Investing Strategies chapter.

## Summary

We have noted in this chapter a large number of players in the investment community. Of this group, an effective investor relations officer of a larger public company will want to maintain particularly good relations with outside analysts and any institutional investors – in the first case, because their opinions impact many other investors, and in the second case, because they may own a large chunk of the company.

The investor relations officer of a smaller public company may not be able to attract any outside analysts or institutional investors, in which case the focus of attention shifts to other players. Under these circumstances, the most effective use of investor relations time is to communicate with a large number of stockbrokers through an ongoing series of non-deal road shows (see the Road Show chapter), since these people influence the buying decisions of their clients.

It is useful for the investor relations staff to collect information from all of the players noted in this chapter about their perceptions of how the company is operating, and how this impacts their views of what the stock price should be. The investor relations officer should summarize these comments and forward them to the CEO and CFO; the result may be changes to the company's strategy and/or tactics to maximize its value in the eyes of the investment community.

# Chapter 10
# Investing Strategies

## Introduction

There are a number of strategies that investors follow when making decisions to invest in or sell the securities of a business. Some of these strategies are based on the operations, finances and industry sector of a business, while others are related to technical issues that cause stock trading to occur even in the absence of any triggering company event. In this chapter, we cover the basic types of strategies that investors follow, and how those strategies impact the investor relations function.

## Investing Strategies

The traditional investing strategies have been the growth, value, and income approaches, which are described first in the following bullet points. We follow those strategies with a number of more specialized techniques, such as ones relating to expected or rumored merger activity. Also, high frequency trading comprises a large part of all trades in a company's securities, though it is not based on a long-term investment strategy. The most common approaches to investing are:

- *Growth strategy*. Some investors buy shares of companies in their early stages of development, on the assumption that these businesses will ramp up quickly and experience high rates of revenue growth. They then sell their shares once a company's fundamentals appear to be maturing, with lower growth rates and a steady proportion of market share. These investors are particularly focused on the rate of growth of a company's revenues and earnings per share, as well as the speed with which they are growing in comparison to the rest of the industry. Once a business reports a slower rate of growth, expect these types of investors to sell out, which may put downward pressure on the stock price.

- *Value strategy*. Some investors will only buy stock when it is trading at multiples notably lower than those of the industry at large. They will hold the shares until such time as they believe the shares have returned to the industry average, and then sell the shares. These investors are most interested in the ratio of a company's share price to its book value, which they will compare to the same ratio for other companies in the same industry. In addition, they delve into the basic earnings fundamentals of a business, to ensure that the current low valuation is not caused by financial issues that could derail their investment. Also, they are more likely to buy a company's shares shortly after it declares a profit warning, since the warning probably triggers a price decline. An interesting side effect of having value investors is that their purchasing activities tend to keep a share price from dropping too low, while their planned selling tends to keep share prices from rising too high. Thus, value investors tend to have a moderating influence on stock price volatility.

- *Income strategy.* Some investors are only concerned with the dividend payments they receive from their investments. The issuance of a continuing series of dividends will attract this group of investors, and they will leave immediately if a company reduces, delays, or eliminates its dividend. These investors are most interested in an uninterrupted history of dividends, a continuing increase in the dividend amount paid per share, and enough information about the fundamentals of the business to gain assurance that the dividend will not be reduced.

- *Growth at a reasonable price.* Some investors are positioned midway between the growth and value strategies. They buy shares when the current market valuation of a business appears inordinately low, but only in conjunction with a reasonable prospect for future growth. They will still sell their shares when a company's valuation has reached a certain point in relation to the industry average, but may also retain their holdings somewhat longer if the prospect of additional revenue growth appears to warrant the risk of retention.

- *High frequency trading.* The majority of all securities trades are now initiated by entities that engage in high frequency trading. These firms are essentially market makers, since they buy shares from sellers at the bid price, and then sell the shares to other investors at the offer price a few moments later, earning a fraction of a cent per share. This can be called an investing strategy, since the traders are buying and selling – they are just not holding shares for very long. Clearly, these investors have no interest in the financial condition of a company whose shares they are trading.

- *Technical analysis strategy.* Some investors are extremely active with their investments, closely tracking the historical behavior of stock prices and using this information to estimate where stock prices will be in the very near future. One of the more popular versions of technical analysis is *momentum investing*, which is the theory that securities that have done well in the recent past will continue to do so in the near future. These investors have only a moderate interest in a company's fundamentals, since they are moving in and out of investment positions on a continual basis.

- *Merger arbitrage strategy.* Investors buy the shares of companies that they believe will be acquired, and profit from the eventual (and presumably higher) price at which acquisitions are completed. This strategy can result in massive surges and declines in stock volume as acquisition rumors ebb and flow.

- *Roll up strategy.* There are rare cases where a company is unusually good at acquiring and wringing excellent results out of other businesses. Investors look for a continuing history of acquisitions that routinely result in accretive increases in earnings. They buy shares in acquiring businesses that show accretive earnings, in hopes that the gradual accumulation of purchasing power and other advantages by the acquirer will yield outsized earnings, and therefore sharp increases in the stock price.

- *Theme investment strategy.* Some investors prefer to obtain deep knowledge about a particular industry or commodity, and only invest in those areas. For example, an investor may choose to either invest in the automobile manufacturing market or sell it short. As another example, an investor may be an expert on the impact of changes in the price of copper on many industries, and chooses investments based on those impacts. This type of investor is less concerned with the fundamental profitability of a specific business; instead, he tends to buy or sell the shares of clusters of similar companies.

Note the different types of information that growth and value investors use. Growth investors are most concerned with the information appearing on a company's income statement, while value investors are more concerned with the book value information appearing on the balance sheet. A technical investor or a theme investor has less interest in either information source. The investor relations staff should be aware of these differences in orientation when dealing with the various types of investors.

The following bullet points do not describe additional investment strategies; instead, they address the circumstances under which a person comes into the ownership of company shares. These sometimes inadvertent investors may have no real strategy for what to do with the stock. Where possible, we have noted their possible reactions to stock ownership. The "strategies" are:

- *Company employees.* Some people own shares in a business simply because they happen to be employees of the company. The company may have issued shares to them as part of an initial public offering, or for other reasons. These shares are likely to be initially restricted, with a waiting period and other requirements being imposed before they can be sold. Not all employees are financially sophisticated, and their shareholdings may also be extremely small. For both reasons, there tends to not be much activity in these shares. If anything, company employees tend to forget that they even *own* the shares. If employees do remember their shareholdings, they are more likely to retain them out of loyalty to the company.

- *Inheritance.* An individual may inherit shares. If so, there are two possible outcomes. One is that the recipient is barely aware of the shares (usually when the shareholding is quite minor), in which case the shares are unlikely to be traded. The other outcome is that the recipient is financially sophisticated, and will immediately roll the shares into his or her portfolio; if the shares do not match the person's investment strategy, they will be sold. Also, there may be inheritance tax issues that require the recipient to sell the shares in order to pay the taxes. In general, the death of a shareholder is more likely than not to trigger the sale of the deceased person's shares in the near future.

- *Stock options.* Members of the management team, and sometimes other employees that a business wants to retain will be issued stock options, under which they have the option to purchase company shares at a certain price within a specific date range. Any shares purchased under a stock option plan are likely to be restricted, and so will not be traded for some time. However, the recipients of shares purchased under stock option plans will face a tax burden from their earnings, and so will likely sell at least some of these shares as soon as possible in order to generate enough cash to pay their tax obligations. Thus, an exercised stock option will likely lead to the sale of a portion of the related shares as soon as they become unrestricted.

- *Stock purchase plans.* Some companies offer stock purchase plans to their employees, under which the employees can buy shares through ongoing payroll deductions, and usually at a discount to the market price. Participants in stock purchase plans tend to be somewhat more financially sophisticated, and so will be more likely to sell their shares at the right price.

This last group of points indicates that the circumstances under which shareholders come by their shares can have an impact on their propensity to hold or sell the shares.

## Implications for Investor Relations

As the profile of a business changes over time, the different types of investors and investment strategies noted in this chapter will come and go. The ownership of a company will never be purely of any one type of investor, but the mix of investors will certainly change. For example, the declaration of a company's first dividend will almost certainly trigger a reduction in the number of investors following a growth strategy, to be replaced by a new set of investors who follow the income strategy.

The investor relations officer may choose to present exactly the same information to the investment community, irrespective of what types of investors own its shares. However, if the company wants to attract and retain a certain type of investor, it is acceptable to slant the presented information to emphasize the requirements of a certain type of investor. For example, if senior management finds that income investors tend to be long-term investors (which it presumably wants), it might make sense to begin emphasizing the size, frequency, and trend of dividend payments. If senior management elects to make such an emphasis, it should discuss its plans with the board of directors, since the result may be a substantial change in the ownership of the company.

> **Tip:** If senior management decides to alter the company's message to attract a certain type of investor, coordinate the change with the public relations and marketing departments, since the message should be consistent across all of the company's modes of communication with the public.

## Summary

If the nature of a business changes over time, it is reasonable to assume that some portion of its investors will also change. Departing investors will have valued the company for its prior operational profile, while the investment views of incoming investors will drive them to buy shares in the company. There will also be a group of investors who never change their holdings, possibly because of indifference.

The investor relations staff will see these changes in the investor profile over time. The presence of any particular type of investor should not be of great concern to the investor relations officer. However, it may be worth pointing out to senior management and the board of directors what the impact on the company's ownership will be if the company adopts certain actions, such as changing the level of investment in research and development activities, paying dividends, or expanding into a new industry.

# Chapter 11
# Short Sellers

## Introduction

Short selling is investment activity that assumes the price of a company's stock will decline, rather than increase. Company managers and mainstream investors consider short selling activities to be counter-productive, since the result is a decline in the price of the company's stock. As we will see in this chapter, some short sellers engage in marginally ethical activities to force down stock prices. However, others do an excellent job of poring through the financial and operational information of businesses to detect potential indicators of downturns, and use this knowledge to drive stock prices more quickly to where they should be. Thus, short selling (when done correctly) serves as an early warning indicator of financial difficulties.

This chapter describes the short selling strategy, the ideal target for a short seller, the short interest measurement, and how to deal with short sellers.

> **Related Podcast Episode:** Episode 74 of the Accounting Best Practices Podcast discusses short sellers. You can listen to it at: **accountingtools.com/podcasts** or **iTunes**

## The Short Selling Strategy

A short seller is someone who expects a company's stock price to decline in the near term; he sells borrowed stock with the expectation of earning a profit later, when he buys back the stock at a lower price. The basic short selling process involves these steps:

1. Set up a margin account at a brokerage firm, where the investor uses the value of his investments placed with the brokerage firm to borrow money.
2. Place a short sale transaction with the brokerage firm. The short seller is borrowing the target company's stock from the broker. The broker, in turn, is borrowing the shares either from its own inventory, or another brokerage firm, or the account of another client.
3. Wait for the stock price to decline, and then authorize the broker to sell the shares on the open market. The broker also buys shares on the open market to close out the transaction.

Short selling is a very risky activity. For example, if a company's stock sells for $5 and its price drops all the way to zero, then a short seller can earn a maximum of $5. However, if the price increases to $100, then the short seller has just lost $95. Thus, there is a limited upside potential and a massive downside potential for a short seller.

---

**EXAMPLE**

An investor believes that the market for games is decreasing, and so decides to sell short a total of 10,000 shares of Hegemony Toy Company. The investor borrows the shares from his broker and sells them for $10 each. After two weeks, the market price of Hegemony stock has dropped to $8, so he buys 10,000 shares and returns them to the broker. His net earnings from the short selling transaction were:

$100,000 Initial sale price - $80,000 Price at which bought shares = $20,000 Profit

A few months later, the investor believes that an additional stock price drop is about to occur. Accordingly, he decides to sell short another 10,000 shares of Hegemony stock. The investor borrows the shares from his broker and sells them for $8 each. However, Hegemony releases unexpectedly robust earnings information, and the stock price zooms to $14. The investor is now forced to buy 10,000 shares at $14 each and return them to the broker. His net loss from the transaction is:

$80,000 Initial sale price - $140,000 Price at which bought shares = $60,000 Loss

---

To increase the risk to a short seller even more, the entity that loans the shares to the short seller can demand that the short position be closed at any time, which means that the short seller must buy shares at whatever the current market price may be, and return the shares. The lender (usually a broker) requires the return of its shares when it has concerns about the creditworthiness of the short seller.

Even if a short seller uncovers critical information about a business that absolutely, positively appears to presage a drop in its stock price, it is very difficult to determine *when* the price change will occur. This increases the risk for a short seller, who may be tempted to keep a short position open for a long time, waiting for the anticipated drop to occur. During that time, the stock price may very well increase instead, which may result in the brokerage imposing a margin call, where the investor must put more funds into his account with the brokerage. Consequently, short sellers also have a timing risk.

In summary, the investments of short sellers can be wiped out from the unlimited nature of short selling losses, by being forced to close out their positions with whichever entity loaned them shares, and because of fluctuations in stock prices while they are waiting for the price of the target stock to decline.

Short sellers rely upon a number of techniques to decide when to sell short, as well as when to accelerate matters with their own actions. These techniques include:

## Ethical Techniques

- *Financial statement examination.* Short sellers review the financial statements and other information released by a company, and may conduct their own investigations as well, looking for evidence of an impending downturn in the company's financial results.

- *Restricted stock monitoring.* The SEC's Rule 144 mandates a certain waiting period before the holders of restricted stock can have the restriction removed and can sell their shares. Short sellers can track the earliest dates by which these restrictions can be lifted, which is an indicator of when company insiders are likely to sell their stock and thereby drive down prices. Short sellers can sell shares in advance of the anticipated sell-off dates, when prices are higher, and buy them back after the sell-off dates, when prices should be lower.
- *Momentum monitoring.* Short sellers monitor the short interest ratio (see the Short Interest section), and sell short if they see an upward trend in the ratio. In essence, they are waiting to see if other investors are betting against the company, and then follow the crowd.
- *Road shows.* When a company issues more stock, this dilutes the earnings per share of existing stock, which can lead to a reduction in the price of the stock. Thus, short sellers watch for evidence of an impending stock sale, such as a road show by company management, and sell shares in advance of the offering.

Less Ethical Techniques

- *Messages on bulletin boards.* Short sellers can create multiple aliases on investment bulletin boards, and then create what appears to be a groundswell of support for selling the stock of a specific business. This activity can include the creation of false rumors about a target company.
- *Investor conference calls.* Short sellers may enter an investor conference call and pose questions that make the company look bad. Their intent is to plant the idea with other investors that management does not know what it is doing, which can cause investors to sell their shares, triggering a price drop. This works especially well if the management group answering questions on the call does not give the appearance of being prepared.
- *Naked short selling.* Short sellers can take advantage of trading loopholes to sell shares that they cannot actually borrow, resulting in a failed delivery to the buyer within the standard three-day settlement period. When used in large volume, naked short selling can place an undue amount of downward pressure on share prices. This practice is illegal. The SEC's Regulation SHO is designed to reduce the volume of naked short selling.

Given the high risk level associated with short selling, it should be no surprise that short sellers can push ethical boundaries to increase the odds that the price of a stock will decline. We can speculate that a sudden stock price increase might even trigger ethical breaches, since short sellers are then facing potentially massive losses.

## The Short Seller Target

What type of company is an ideal target for a short seller? Any company can be targeted, but here are some characteristics for companies that are more likely to be impacted:

- *Smaller float*. If a company has a small number of shares outstanding, it is easier for a relatively small number of trades to create large changes in the price of the stock.
- *Available shares*. If investors have placed large amounts of the company's stock in their margin accounts, these shares are probably available to be loaned to short sellers by the brokerages managing those accounts.
- *Earnings variability*. If a business has a recent history of large fluctuations in its reported earnings, its stock price has also probably bounced around in conjunction with the earnings. High stock price variability attracts short sellers, who are more likely to experience price drops that they can take advantage of.
- *Aggressive guidance*. If the CEO has a habit of stretching the credulity of the investment community with aggressive guidance, it is more likely that there will be an earnings shortfall at some point, which will yield a drop in the stock price.

Conversely, there are some situations that are *less* likely to attract short sellers. A company that has a well-defended market position and which faces minimal competitive pressure can be reasonably assured of consistent profitability. A high level of earnings consistency (especially if buttressed by a reliable and long-term dividend payout) will keep the stock price from fluctuating very much, which in turn tends to deflect the attention of short sellers.

## Short Interest

Short interest is the number of shares in a company that investors have sold short and not yet closed out. *Closing out* means that an investor has finalized a short sale by purchasing stock on the open market and returning it to the lending entity.

Short interest as a gross number is a reasonable indicator of the view of the investment community regarding the direction that a company's stock price is likely to take. This is particularly effective when tracked on a trend line, so that unusual changes in short interest become more readily apparent. However, tracking short interest as a simple gross number is of less use when a company is either buying back or selling stock, since the grand total number of shares is changing. Under these circumstances, consider using the *short interest ratio* instead.

The short interest ratio is the number of shares being sold short, divided by the average daily volume of shares traded. The ratio states short interest as a proportion of trading volume, and so is a better measure than short interest as a gross number. Track the ratio on a trend line, to spot changes in sentiment regarding the future direction of the stock price.

**EXAMPLE**

The short interest in the stock of Hegemony Toy Company is 1,000,000 shares, and the average daily trading volume is 3,000,000 shares. Thus, the short interest ratio for Hegemony stock is calculated as:

1,000,000 Shares sold short ÷ 3,000,000 average daily trading volume
= 33% Short interest ratio

The ratio also shows the number of days of average trading that it takes before short sellers can cover their positions. As the ratio goes up, it becomes more difficult for short sellers to cover their positions, which means that they'll have to scale back on their short positions or else run the risk of having stock prices climb to levels that would wipe out their investments. A high ratio may even prevent prospective short sellers from taking short positions in a stock.

**EXAMPLE**

Hegemony Toy Company reports poor quarterly earnings, and short sellers attack the stock. The short interest increases to 9,000,000 shares. Since the average daily trading volume of Hegemony shares is 3,000,000 shares, this means that it will take three business days for short sellers to cover their positions.

A *short squeeze* can occur when short sellers find that the price of a stock is increasing, rather than declining, so there is a scramble to close out positions by purchasing shares. When a large number of short positions must be closed out within a short period of time, this places upward pressure on the stock price, which can create substantial losses for short sellers. A short squeeze is more likely to occur when trading in small cap stocks, since the relatively small supply of shares makes it easier for a sudden demand spike to run up the price.

## Dealing with Short Sellers

What can a company do about short sellers? The CEO may be tempted to force them out by issuing guidance for better-than-expected earnings results. This kind of publicity may initially increase the stock price, which creates an untenable situation for short sellers. In the short term, such guidance may quite possibly drive them away.

**Tip:** You can monitor short selling on a web site called shortsqueeze.com, which provides varying levels of short selling information, depending on your membership level.

The problem is that the more aggressive guidance will make it very hard to meet investor expectations. If the CEO keeps issuing higher and higher guidance numbers, all the short sellers have to do is wait quietly until the stock price is clearly much too high, and then sell short in even greater quantities and turn a massive profit when the stock price inevitably craters. In short, the CEO's own actions have manufactured profits for short sellers.

So obviously, increasing guidance is a bad idea. There are several other actions to consider that are more workable. They are:

- *Never issue aggressive guidance.* Increasing the expected results of the business only raises the stock price to an unsustainable level. Instead, issue conservative guidance which the company can comfortably meet on a long-term basis. This approach reduces stock price volatility; with minimal stock volatility, short sellers will see little point in targeting the company.
- *Issue press releases.* Monitor the larger investor message boards to see if there are sudden increases in negative discussions about the company. Those increases may coincide with short selling. If there appears to be a smear campaign going on, consider issuing a press release that addresses the substance of the allegations.

**Tip:** Never mention short sellers in a press release, since this gives the appearance of opening a dialog with them. Instead, focus squarely on providing factual information that happens to offset their allegations.

- *Rumors web page.* Consider creating a web page on the company website, on which the company responds to any rumors being spread about it. This page will probably not be accessed a great deal, and so is unlikely to have much of an impact on the actions of the investment community.
- *Issue all bad news at once.* Issue every scrap of bad news to the investing public at one time. For example, if you report a bad quarter, short sellers may start monitoring the company, and possibly selling short, because they expect that the business will issue a string of more bad news that will drive the stock price down even further. Thus, when you know there is bad news, dump *all* of it on the market at once, so there will be no additional bad news for short sellers to feed on. The result should be a one-time drop in the stock price – and no further.

**Tip:** When the preliminary financial statements clearly indicate poor quarterly results, see if there are any additional expenses that can be legitimately recorded within the quarter, thereby leaving a clean slate for the next reporting period.

- *Preparation.* Prepare for every reasonably foreseeable emergency. You can create boilerplate press releases for such issues as product recalls, litigation, or the departure of a manager. Having these canned responses ready gives the appearance of a management team that reacts promptly to a crisis. If management appears competent, there tends to be less stock volatility, and that repels short sellers.

- *Abbreviated responses.* Short sellers may pose difficult questions during investor conference calls. If so, the worst action you can take is to get into an argument, or to give a long-winded and rambling answer. Instead, make a short and well-reasoned reply, and immediately move on to the next caller.
- *Limit road shows.* Limit the number of people who are aware of any plans to sell more company stock. Since a stock issuance can drive down earnings per share, and therefore the stock price, short sellers are more likely to sell short if they know stock is about to be issued.
- *Shift company stock out of margin accounts.* Company insiders may keep their stock in margin accounts. If so, they have probably signed a hypothe-cation agreement with their broker, under which the broker can extend a margin loan in exchange for lending out any security in the account as collateral to raise the capital needed to fund the loan. This means that shares in the company held by company insiders may be used for a short seller attack on the company. To avoid this situation, have all insiders move their company shares to a cash account with their brokerages.

---

**Tip:** If outside investors complain that short sellers are driving down the value of their investments, have the investors move their holdings in the company's stock to a cash account with their brokers. Doing so reduces the number of shares available to short sellers.

---

## The Passive Approach

One option is to not react at all to the activities of short sellers. By doing nothing, the investor relations staff is not wasting time reacting to the activities of investors who are beyond its control. Instead, the focus should be on issuing a consistent message to the investment community, which is updated regularly to reflect changes in the company's business.

While attractive, this view is not entirely tenable. The trouble is that the investor relations staff has probably gone to a good deal of trouble to attract a core group of long-term investors, and the activities of short sellers are most definitely impacting the value of their investments. Thus, if the company takes a completely hands-off approach to short sellers, it may find that some key investors will be driven away.

Retaining key investors does not necessarily mean that the company should go through a wild series of gyrations to counteract every depredation made by short sellers. If some investors continually complain that their investments are being shredded by nefarious short sellers, the company probably does not need those investors.

There is a middle ground between utter passivity and aggressive responses. A reasonable approach is to track the amount of short selling (as noted in the Short Interest section), as well as making a moderate number of inquiries into the nature of the latest short selling attack. By doing so, the investor relations staff at least presents the appearance of being knowledgeable about the extent and nature of any short selling, and may even uncover an issue that it can counteract with a judiciously-constructed press release.

In short, there is a strong argument in favor of reacting to short sellers in a low-key manner, if only to give the impression to existing shareholders that the company is aware of short selling activity and may take action to mitigate the more egregious situations.

## Summary

The investor relations staff probably considers short sellers to be an annoyance. However, short sellers serve a purpose in the marketplace, and so will always be a part of the environment for any public company. The real question is not whether investors should be allowed to sell short, but rather how to deal with them.

The overriding goal in dealing with short sellers is to temper your response. Never increase earnings guidance or alter company operations in order to drive away short sellers. Instead, keep guidance conservative, and react to rumors with well thought-out press releases. A strong case can even be made for only monitoring short selling activity, without taking any offsetting actions at all.

A low-key approach essentially accepts short selling activity and the related downward pressure on company stock, but keeps the investor relations staff focused on the larger goal of presenting the company and its results to the investment community.

# Chapter 12
# Stock Exchanges

## Introduction

Any publicly held company should strive to have its shares listed on a stock exchange, since doing so makes it much more likely that there will be regular trading in its stock. The investor relations officer is not usually responsible for establishing or maintaining this listing, which is more likely to be administered by the company's attorneys or CFO. Nonetheless, it is useful for the investor relations officer to be aware of the reasons why stock exchanges can be so useful, as well as the listing requirements of the primary stock exchanges. This chapter addresses both topics.

## Stock Exchange Overview

A stock exchange is a physical location or an electronic system, on which investors buy and sell securities. A stock exchange creates an orderly market, which makes it easier for transactions to be completed. They also impose listing requirements that keep the securities of less financially stable companies from being listed. Thus, investors use stock exchanges for their transactional efficiency and the supposition that the securities being traded come from issuing companies that have passed minimum financial benchmarks.

From the perspective of a publicly held company, why bother with a stock exchange listing? There are numerous reasons for doing so, including:

- *Trading volume*. Many investors only trade securities that are listed on an exchange, so moving onto a stock exchange makes it much more likely that daily trading volumes will increase.
- *Price volatility*. When there are only occasional trades, share prices are usually quite volatile. With the increased trading volume associated with a stock exchange, it is much more likely that prices will stabilize.
- *Acquisition currency*. The increased trading volume of a stock exchange makes it easier to convince the owners of an acquisition target to accept stock in exchange for their company, since they can sell the shares with relative ease.
- *Prestige*. There is a distinct difference in the prestige level of public companies that are listed on a national exchange, and those that are not. This can have an impact on the decisions of lenders, customers, and suppliers to do business with a company.
- *Reduced bid-ask price spread*. When there are a larger number of buyers and sellers, the difference between the bid price and ask price for a stock are reduced. This means that the transaction cost associated with buying or sell-

ing shares on an exchange is reduced. The investor relations officer can use this argument to attract new investors.

If a company wants to be traded on a stock exchange, it must first qualify under the standards set by the exchange. Generally speaking, the qualification standards are easiest for the American Stock Exchange and the most difficult for the New York Stock Exchange. These standards focus on a variety of factors, such as net income, cash flow, market capitalization, shareholders' equity, and total assets. All of the stock exchanges offer multiple alternative sets of criteria under which a company can qualify for listing. For example, a company with strong cash flow but little net income can qualify under one set of criteria, while another business with less income or cash flow can still qualify if it has a large market capitalization. The different sets of criteria are designed to allow the securities of a variety of types of businesses to be listed.

If a company's owners decide to list its securities on a stock exchange, they must apply to the exchange. The steps for doing so vary somewhat by exchange, but generally follow these steps:

1.  *Alter bylaws*. The company alters its bylaws to comply with the governance requirements of the stock exchange. This usually requires that the board establish audit, nominating, and compensation committees.
2.  *File application*. The company completes the exchange's listing application and submits it, along with a filing fee.
3.  *Investigation*. The stock exchange assigns an analyst to the company, who investigates the application and asks additional questions on a variety of topics. This may result in a comment letter that points out changes the company must make before its application will be approved.
4.  *Reserve ticker symbol*. The stock exchange reserves a ticker symbol for the company, in anticipation of the successful completion of the application process.
5.  *Set trading date*. If the listing application is approved, the parties agree on a date when trading in the company's stock on the exchange will begin.
6.  *Begin trading*. Depending on the exchange, the CEO of the company may be asked to appear at the stock exchange at the beginning of the first day of trading in the company's stock.

> **Tip:** Though it should not be a primary consideration in selecting a stock exchange, there are differences in the fees charged by the various exchanges, with higher fees being charged by those exchanges having more rigorous listing requirements.

A publicly held company is not necessarily listed on a stock exchange. If a company is still submitting timely filings to the SEC, but either does not qualify to be listed on a stock exchange or does not choose to do so, then it is listed on the over the counter market. A trading symbol for a company that trades on the over the counter market is OTB:[ABCD]. See the Over the Counter Bulletin Board section for more information.

At the most minimal level, a company can stop its periodic reporting to the SEC, in which case it cannot be listed on a stock exchange or the over the counter market. Instead, the most recent trades are listed on the Pink Sheets. A trading symbol for a company that trades on the Pink Sheets is PINK:[ABCD]. See the Pink Sheets section for more information.

In the next few sections, we cover the initial listing requirements imposed by several of the larger stock exchanges, so you can see how different exchanges are oriented toward different types and sizes of companies.

## The New York Stock Exchange

The stock exchange that has the most prestige and sets the most difficult listing standards is the New York Stock Exchange (NYSE). The standards are set high in order to limit the exchange to a smaller group of securities whose issuers are the most qualified by being financial stable. It is less common for a company to initially list its shares on the NYSE, because it takes time to build sufficient mass to justify being on this exchange.

Some institutional investors are only allowed by their internal investment rules to invest in the shares of companies listed on the NYSE, which is why growing companies tend to start with other stock exchanges, and later switch to the NYSE when they are large enough to qualify for it.

The listing standards of the NYSE involve meeting minimum standards in multiple areas, which are noted in the following table.

**NYSE Initial Listing Financial Criteria**

| | Alternative 1 Earnings Test | Alternate 2a Cash Flow Valuation | Alternate 2b Revenue Valuation | Alternate 3 Affiliated Company* | Alternative 4 Assets and Equity |
|---|---|---|---|---|---|
| Market capitalization | | $500 million | $750 million | $500 million | $150 million |
| Market value of public shares | $40 million | $40 million | $40 million | $40 million | $40 million |
| Revenues | | $100 million | $75 million | | |
| Operating history | | | | 12 months | |
| Aggregate 3-year income** | $10 million | | | | |
| Aggregate 3-year cash flow | | $25 million | | | |
| Total assets | | | | | $75 million |
| Stockholders' equity | | | | | $50 million |
| Round lot shareholders | 400 | 400 | 400 | 400 | 400 |
| Publicly held shares | 1,100,000 | 1,100,000 | 1,100,000 | 1,100,000 | 1,100,000 |
| Minimum price | $4 | $4 | $4 | $4 | $4 |

\* For new entities with a parent or affiliated company listed on the NYSE

\** With a minimum of $2 million in each of the last two years; third year must be positive; or, aggregate 3-year income of $12 million, with at least $5 million in the most recent year and $2 million in the next most recent year.

# The NYSE Amex

The New York Stock Exchange purchased the American Stock Exchange, and now calls this exchange the NYSE Amex. This exchange is designed for much smaller companies than those found on the NYSE. The listing standards of the NYSE Amex are noted in the following table.

**NYSE Amex Initial Listing Standards**

| Criteria | Standard 1 | Standard 2 | Standard 3 | Standard 4 |
|---|---|---|---|---|
| Pre-tax income | $750,000 | N/A | N/A | N/A |
| Market capitalization | N/A | N/A | $50 million | $75 million or At least $75 million total assets and $75 million revenues |
| Market value of public float | $3 million | $15 million | $15 million | $20 million |
| Minimum price | $3 | $3 | $2 | $3 |
| Operating history | N/A | 2 years | N/A | N/A |
| Shareholders' equity | $4 million | $4 million | $4 million | N/A |
| Public shareholders / Public float (shares) | Option 1: 800 / 500,000 Option 2: 400 / 1,000,000 Option 3: 400 / 500,000 | | | |

Note how the initial listing standards are designed to accept many types of smaller businesses. A company can qualify by having a moderate amount of pre-tax income, or with a moderate amount of shareholders' equity, or if it has one of several measures of business mass, such as assets or market capitalization. None of the requirements are especially difficult to meet, which means that many smaller firms find the NYSE Amex to be a reasonable starting place in which to list their shares. Later, as a company presumably grows, it may want to move to an exchange with higher minimum standards, in order to obtain access to a larger group of investors.

# The NASDAQ

The NASDAQ is a computerized system that provides price quotations and facilitates the purchase and sale of securities. The NASDAQ operates several exchanges, each with different listing standards that are designed to attract different types and sizes of companies. The listing standards of three of these exchanges are described in the remainder of this section.

### The NASDAQ Global Select Market

The Global Select Market has the most rigorous standards, because it is designed to compete with the NYSE. Its listing standards are noted in the following table.

**NASDAQ Global Select Market Initial Listing Standards**

| Criteria | Standard 1 | Standard 2 | Standard 3 | Standard 4 |
|---|---|---|---|---|
| Pre-tax earnings | ≥ Aggregate $11 million in prior three fiscal years* | | | |
| Cash flows | N/A | ≥ Aggregate $27.5 million in prior three fiscal years** | N/A | N/A |
| Market capitalization | N/A | ≥ $550 million 12-month average | ≥ $850 million 12-month average | $160 million |
| Revenue | N/A | ≥ $110 million | ≥ $90 million | N/A |
| Total assets | N/A | N/A | N/A | $80 million |
| Stockholders' equity | N/A | N/A | N/A | $55 million |
| Bid price | $4 | $4 | $4 | $4 |
| Market makers | 3 or 4 | 3 or 4 | 3 or 4 | 3 or 4 |
| Round lot / total shareholders | 450 / 2,200 | 450 / 2,200 | 450 / 2,200 | 450 / 2,200 |
| Publicly held shares | 1,250,000 | 1,250,000 | 1,250,000 | 1,250,000 |
| Market value of publicly-held shares*** | $45 million | $45 million | $45 million | $45 million |

\*    And with pre-tax profits of ≥ $2.2 in each of the two most recent fiscal years, with no losses in any of the three years

\*\*   With no losses in any of those three years

\*\*\*  The stated market value is for initial public offerings. The figure is $110 million for seasoned companies.

## The NASDAQ Global Market

The NASDAQ Global Market has listing standards that sandwich it between the NASDAQ Global Select Market and the NASDAQ Capital Market. Its listing standards are noted in the following table.

**NASDAQ Global Market Initial Listing Standards**

| Criteria | Income Standard | Equity Standard | Market Value Standard | Total Assets / Total Revenue Standard |
|---|---|---|---|---|
| Income from continuing operations* | $1 million | N/A | N/A | N/A |
| Stockholders' equity | $15 million | $30 million | N/A | N/A |
| Market value of listed securities | N/A | N/A | $75 million | N/A |
| Total assets and total revenue | N/A | N/A | N/A | $75 million and $75 million |
| Publicly held shares | 1.1 million | 1.1 million | 1.1 million | 1.1 million |
| Market value of publicly held shares | $8 million | $18 million | $20 million | $20 million |
| Bid price | $4 | $4 | $4 | $4 |
| Round lot shareholders | 400 | 400 | 400 | 400 |
| Market makers | 3 | 3 | 4 | 4 |
| Operating history | N/A | 2 years | N/A | N/A |

\* In the latest fiscal year or in two of the last three fiscal years

## The NASDAQ Capital Market

The NASDAQ Capital Market imposes the easiest listing standards, which makes it a direct competitor to the NYSE Amex. Its listing standards are noted in the following table.

**NASDAQ Capital Market Initial Listing Standards**

| Criteria | Equity Standard | Market Value Standard | Net Income Standard |
|---|---|---|---|
| Stockholders' equity | $5 million | $4 million | $4 million |
| Market value of publicly held shares | $15 million | $15 million | $5 million |
| Operating history | 2 years | N/A | N/A |
| Market value of listed securities | N/A | $50 million | N/A |
| Net income from continuing operations* | N/A | N/A | $750,000 |
| Bid price | $4 | $4 | $4 |
| Publicly held shares | 1 million | 1 million | 1 million |
| Round lot shareholders | 300 | 300 | 300 |
| Market makers | 3 | 3 | 3 |

* In latest fiscal year or in two of the last three fiscal years

# The Toronto Stock Exchange

The major stock exchanges described in the preceding sections are by no means the only ones on which a company can list its shares. In this section, we note the listing standards of one of the more active smaller exchanges, the Toronto Stock Exchange. The following table shows that this exchange has found a number of alternative ways to allow a company to list its securities, with different categories for businesses engaged in technology, research and development (R&D), and industrial activities. There is even a category for businesses that are not yet profitable, but forecast that they will be in the near future. Its listing standards are noted in the following table.

The Toronto Stock Exchange, and other exchanges like it, have designed their listing requirements to make it relatively easy for a smaller company to be listed. This type of exchange can be a good starting point for a company, after which it can graduate to an exchange with tougher listing requirements (which has a larger pool of investors).

There are dozens of stock exchanges on which a company could list its shares. Many exchanges are designed for the listings of businesses located in the same country as the exchange, but the following exchanges tend to attract a broader clientele:

- Australian Securities Exchange
- Deutsche Bourse
- Hong Kong Stock Exchange
- London Stock Exchange

- Shanghai Stock Exchange
- Tokyo Stock Exchange

**Toronto Stock Exchange Listing Standards**

| Criteria | Technology Issuer | R&D Issuer | Forecasting Profitability Issuer | Profitable Issuer | Industrial Issuer |
|---|---|---|---|---|---|
| Earnings or revenue | N/A | N/A | Evidence of pre-tax earnings for current or next year of at least $200,000 | Pre-tax earnings from operations of at least $200,000 in the last year | Pre-tax earnings from operations of at least $300,000 in the last year |
| Cash flow | | | Evidence of pre-tax cash flow for current or next year of at least $500,000 | Pre-tax cash flow of $500,000 in the last year | Pre-tax cash flow of $700,000 in the last year, and an average of $500,000 for the past two years |
| Net tangible assets | | | $7,500,000 | $2,000,000 | $7,500,000 |
| Working capital and capital structure | Funds to cover all planned development, capital, and administrative expenditures for one year | Funds to cover all planned R&D, capital, and administrative expenditures for 2 years | Sufficient working capital to carry on the business, plus an appropriate capital structure | Sufficient working capital to carry on the business, plus an appropriate capital structure | Sufficient working capital to carry on the business, plus an appropriate capital structure |
| Cash on hand | At least $10 million cash on hand, with the majority raised through a prospectus offering | At least $12 million cash on hand, with the majority raised through a prospectus offering | | | |
| Products and services | Evidence of advanced stage of development for products, or management has expertise to develop the business | 2+ year operating history with R&D activities; evidence of technical expertise to advance the R&D program | | | |
| Public distribution | 1 million shares and 300 round lot shareholders | 1 million shares and 300 round lot shareholders | 1 million shares and 300 round lot shareholders | 1 million shares and 300 round lot shareholders | 1 million shares and 300 round lot shareholders |
| Market capitalization | $10 million market capitalization, $50 million total capitalization | $4 million market capitalization | $4 million market capitalization | $4 million market capitalization | $4 million market capitalization |

## Delisting from an Exchange

Thus far, we have noted the initial listing requirements that stock exchanges impose. There are also *ongoing* listing standards that companies must meet in order to continue to be listed. These ongoing standards vary by stock exchange, but are always less than the initial listing requirements. Ongoing standards may include the maintenance of minimum amounts for a combination of:

- The number of publicly traded shares
- Total market value
- Stock price
- The number of shareholders

If a company does not meet an ongoing listing standard, the exchange on which its securities are listed will contact it regarding the issue, and will give the company a certain amount of time in which to rectify the matter. If the company does not resolve the issue, then the stock exchange will delist the applicable securities.

When a company is delisted, it may also lose its market makers. A *market maker* is a broker-dealer that facilitates trading in a security by displaying buy and sell quotations for the issuing company's shares, for which it may sell from its own inventory. Once a company is delisted, its stock trading volumes will likely decline precipitously, while the variability of its stock price will increase. Market makers will then be at risk of incurring losses on their holdings of a company's stock, and so will terminate their roles as market makers.

## The Over the Counter Bulletin Board

The over the counter market is known as the Over the Counter Bulletin Board, or OTCBB. It is a stock listing service that shows real-time quotes, last-sale price, and volume information for all securities listed on the OTCBB.

This is not a formal stock exchange, but rather the default designation given to a company that is not listed on a stock exchange but which is current in its filings with the SEC. There are no other requirements for being listed on the OTCBB. If a company is not current with its filings, it is instead classified as being listed on the Pink Sheets (see the next section).

Companies that are current with their SEC filings but not listed on an exchange are likely to have small amounts of revenue and/or assets, and may have irregular earnings. As such, investments in OTCBB companies are considered to be risky. Also, because there is not much trading activity in these stocks, there tends to be a large spread between bid and ask prices, which makes investments in these stocks especially risky for investors.

It is very difficult for an investor relations officer to interest investors in acquiring company stock if the company is languishing on the OTCBB. Rather than wasting time trying to attract investors, it is more productive to convince management to apply to and be listed on *any* stock exchange. Once such a listing has been obtained, it is much easier to find an interested audience.

## The Pink Sheets

If a company is remiss in its SEC filings or has gone private, its shares will be listed on the Pink Sheets. This is essentially the default listing for the securities of a company that does not expend any effort to make its financial results known to the public. The Pink Sheets are administered by OTC Markets Group, Inc. Share prices will be listed on the Pink Sheets even if a company no longer has *any* interest in the trading of its shares. If a business finds that its stock has fallen into the Pink Sheets category, OTC Markets Group will likely contact the company to see if it is interested in moving the stock listing into a different listing category that contains recent financial information about the company – which requires an ongoing fee.

A company that has dropped into the Pink Sheets classification clearly has little interest in maintaining an investor relations function, since the business is only in this category if it has stopped filing the mandatory reports with the SEC that investors rely upon to make share purchase and sale decisions.

## Summary

If a company is publicly held, then it should be listed on a stock exchange. Doing so confers the benefits of a higher volume of stock trading, though this comes at the cost of annual listing fees and some changes to the governance structure of a business. Once a company is listed on an exchange, the investor relations officer should have an ongoing interest in advancing the business to an exchange that is used by a larger number of investors, thereby increasing the volume of trading in company stock. The increased level of demand for the stock may increase its price, as well as reduce its price volatility.

A large part of this chapter contained summaries of the listing standards required by the various stock exchanges. Please note that these were only *summaries* – the more critical requirements were listed, but a large number of variations and qualifications were excluded. Also, we did not include governance requirements, which usually call for modifications to a company's bylaws, and perhaps to the committees reporting to the board of directors. In short, refer to the official listing requirements of an exchange to obtain a comprehensive view of *all* requirements.

# Chapter 13
# Share Management

## Introduction

One of the primary goals that an investor relations officer pursues is to attract liquidity; liquidity entails a high volume of trading in a company's stock. The liquidity goal is much easier to achieve if there are a large number of registered shares available for trading, which is known as *float*. The investor relations officer can influence the management of a company's shares to improve the probability that liquidity will be achieved.

In this chapter, we describe many of the considerations involved in managing a company's shares to increase its float. We also address several techniques for selling small amounts of additional shares, discuss the advantages and disadvantages of dividends and stock buyback plans, and other similar issues.

## Float Management

A key consideration for the investor relations department is the number of shares available for trading. A large float creates a significant level of liquidity, which means that investors can easily buy and sell shares without any undue delays to find counter parties. Also, a large float means that investors can buy and sell large blocks of stock without having their actions impact the stock price, which is of particular importance to institutional investors, which routinely invest large amounts in a company's securities.

The investor relations staff can have an impact on a company's float by paying attention to the following float management activities.

### Activities to Increase the Float

- *Issue more shares.* When a company has the option of raising funds through a debt or equity issuance, the finance staff usually favors obtaining a loan, since it is (usually) quicker and less expensive to obtain than funds raised through a stock offering. However, if the company has an unusually small float, it could make quite a difference from a stock liquidity perspective to obtain funds through selling stock, and then registering those shares as soon as possible. Going to the trouble of issuing new shares may be less worthwhile if the company already has a sufficient float.

- *Register stock (company initiative).* If a company has a large amount of unregistered stock, consider having the company's securities attorneys file with the SEC for a stock registration. This will take a number of months to accomplish, as well as a significant amount of legal fees, but can be worthwhile if the result is a large amount of registered shares. Indeed, some shareholders may have *required* the company to register their shares as part of a private placement of the company's stock. Since these investors are likely to sell their shares immediately following registration, it increases the amount of readily available stock.

- *Register stock (employee initiative)*. If employees hold unregistered stock and the company has no plans to register the shares for them, inform the employees of their right under the SEC's Rule 144 to have their shares automatically registered after a six month holding period. This can include the recommendation of brokerages to employees who can sell the shares for the employees once the holding period has been completed.
- *Only issue common stock*. When a company issues a wide range of securities, only some may be registered for trading. Alternatively, each type may be registered, but the volume of securities of each class represents too small a float to create an active market. Accordingly, consider simplifying the capital structure of the business, so that it is only comprised of a large pool of common stock. At a minimum, keep an offer open to the holders of all other types of securities to swap them for whatever number of common shares appears appropriate, so that the common stock float gradually increases over time.
- *Minimize stock repurchases*. When a company has an excess amount of cash, a common use is to repurchase some of the outstanding stock. Doing so tends to prop up the stock price, and also increases the earnings per share for the remaining shares. However, a stock repurchasing initiative also reduces the float. This is a minor issue when a company already has a large float. Nonetheless, if the amount of the repurchase is expected to be large, or if the existing float is small, it may not be a good idea to repurchase shares.
- *Break up stock blocks*. A company may have a large number of registered shares outstanding and yet have a relatively small float, if some investors have accumulated large positions in the company's stock. These large holdings have effectively withdrawn stock from circulation, leaving a vastly smaller effective float. It may be worthwhile to contact these investors about selling off at least a portion of their holdings, which may represent a substantial increase in the size of the available float.
- *Conduct road shows*. The company should regularly engage in non-deal road shows (see the Road Show chapter) to create interest among investors to own the company's stock. From a float perspective, road shows are particularly effective if the presentation team visits entirely new geographic regions on regular basis, thereby accessing new pools of potential investors.

### Activities to Delay Stock Sales

If a company has issued large amounts of shares as payment for acquisitions, it may be faced with potentially massive stock sales when the holders of those shares want to convert their holdings to cash. This intense selling pressure can seriously depress the stock price, especially when shareholders want to sell so many shares that it may take days or weeks of selling to liquidate their positions. This aggravation can be ameliorated to some extent by imposing *lock-up agreements* on the new recipients of company stock. Under a lock-up agreement, shareholders are constrained from selling their shares for a certain period of time, such as six months. Alternatively, the agreement may state that a shareholder can only sell in certain volumes per time period, such as 10,000 shares per month. Thus, the lock-up agreement spreads the downward price pressure over a longer period of time; during that time, a company can work on increasing its float, which thereby shrinks the proportional impact of the shares being sold.

In short, the investor relations staff should pay continual attention to the size of the float, and take steps to keep it as large as possible. This is especially important in a smaller firm, where there is a tendency for the float to shrink over time, reducing the ability of investors to easily move in and out of ownership positions.

## The Direct Stock Purchase Plan

A company may set up a direct stock purchase plan (DSPP), under which shareholders can buy shares directly from the company's stock transfer agent without going through a stockbroker. This approach avoids paying a stockbroker commission. To encourage buying through a DSPP, a company may offer a discount to the current market price of the stock.

There is usually a maximum purchase amount built into a DSPP in order to control the amount of shares purchased through the plan. However, if a company wants to raise a significant amount of new capital, it can waive the maximum purchase limitation to bring in more cash. Conversely, if the market price of the stock drops too low, the company can freeze the DSPP and not allow any additional purchases until such time as the stock price increases again.

A DSPP is attractive to the investor relations department, because it tends to attract long-term investors who are interested in buying the shares of the company over the long term. Other investors move in and out of stock positions more quickly, and so would have little interest in a DSPP that may require a long period of time to acquire a significant number of shares.

## The Employee Stock Purchase Plan

A public company can create an employee stock purchase plan (ESPP), under which employees make regular payments (usually through payroll deductions) to purchase shares of the company's stock at regular intervals. The shares do not involve a stockbroker commission, and may be offered at a modest discount to the current market price.

A company can file a Form S-8 with the SEC to register the shares issued to employees under an ESPP; this is an inexpensive and quick registration method, and allows employees to sell their shares relatively quickly.

An ESPP does not usually generate a great deal of cash for a company, and requires a modest amount of administrative overhead. However, it *does* improve the level of employee engagement with the business, and can be considered part of the employee benefits package.

## Dividend Reinvestment Plans

Dividends are a distribution of a company's earnings, and are paid from its retained earnings. A company can set up a dividend reinvestment plan (DRIP), under which shareholders can elect to reinvest their dividends in the purchase of additional company shares. The company can purchase shares through the plan on the open market, which has the advantage of ensuring that the stock is already registered. Alternatively, the company can issue new shares and have them registered, thereby increasing the float.

From the perspective of an investor, a DRIP reduces the cost of acquiring shares, since no stockbroker is involved, and therefore no stockbroker commission. Also, since cash from dividends is being reinvested, a DRIP is essentially a long-term savings plan.

From the perspective of the company, dividends are being retained within the business, which increases the amount of cash available for a variety of other purposes.

An anomaly with a DRIP is that it contravenes the objectives of an *income investor* (see the Investing Strategies chapter), which should be the primary type of investor who is interested in a company that issues dividends. An income investor is most interested in receiving income from dividends, rather than increased share holdings. Thus, it is less likely that an income investor would enroll in a DRIP.

## Stock Splits

If a company enjoys a continuing run-up in the price of its stock, the price may eventually be so high that it prevents individual investors from buying large blocks of stock. The resulting reduction in demand is not large, and is unlikely to have a significant impact on the price of the stock. Nonetheless, companies occasionally choose to split their stock, so that one share is converted into two or more shares. The result is a reduction in the stock price to a level that is presumably more affordable for investors.

---

**EXAMPLE**

An investor holds 100 shares of stock that are currently trading at $100 each. The market value of these shares is $10,000 (calculated as 100 shares × $100 each). The issuing company decides to initiate a 1-for-5 stock split. This means that the investor swaps out his old certificate for 100 shares for a new one for 500 shares. The market price should drop to $20 to reflect the increased number of shares, which means that the investor still has holdings worth $10,000 (calculated as 500 shares × $20 each).

---

The board of directors should be cautious about authorizing excessively large stock splits, since the result drops the stock price substantially lower; any additional decline in the price of the stock could classify it as a penny stock, at which point institutional investors may be required by their investment rules to sell the stock.

If a lower share price will increase trading volume, the investor relations officer should certainly be in favor of a stock split. However, if the price drops so low that some investors are selling off their positions, the investor relations officer might instead recommend a *reverse stock split*, where the company exchanges a larger number of shares for a smaller number of shares. Doing so increases the stock price to the point where investors will feel more comfortable investing in the stock.

**EXAMPLE**

An investor holds 100 shares of stock that are currently trading at $2 each. The market value of these shares is $200 (calculated as 100 shares × $2 each). The issuing company decides to initiate a 10-for-1 reverse stock split. This means that the investor swaps out his old certificate for 100 shares for a new one for 10 shares. The market price increases to $20 to reflect the reduced number of shares, which means that the investor still has holdings worth $200 (calculated as 10 shares × $20 each).

In general, there is no real advantage to a stock split from the perspective of benefits experienced by the investor. However, there is a definite cost associated with a stock split from the perspective of the company, since there are a number of legal, accounting, and stock recordkeeping issues that must be addressed whenever a split is authorized.

## Dividend Payments

The decision to issue dividends to shareholders is made by the board of directors. If a company is planning to issue a dividend for the first time, it is worthwhile for the investor relations officer to discuss the issue with the board before they approve the transaction. When a company has followed a consistent revenue and earnings growth path, a reasonable proportion of its investors are probably investing in the company to take advantage of the increases in its stock price that are caused by company growth. A rapidly growing company is presumed to need all of its cash to fund growth, so no dividend is expected. Once the company issues a dividend, these growth-oriented investors will assume that the company is not planning to grow as fast, and so will sell the stock. They will be replaced by a different group of investors who are more interested in earning dividend income.

The change in the type of investor is neither good nor bad, but it does mean that there will be an increased amount of turnover among shareholders for a period of time. During this transition period, it is possible that the share price will be somewhat more volatile than usual.

If the board wants to find a use for the company's excess cash, but does not want to turn away its growth-oriented investors, then alternative uses for the cash are making acquisitions or paying off liabilities.

If the board of directors elects to go forward with an initial dividend payment, it is of considerable importance to signal to the marketplace that the company intends to continue to issue dividends at regular intervals. Otherwise, a one-time distribution to shareholders via a dividend will merely send the growth investors to the exits without creating an incentive for income investors to take their place, thereby creating downward pressure on the stock price.

> **Tip:** When initially announcing a dividend, point out the timing and expected size of future dividends, so that the investment community can properly value the shares on which dividends are being paid.

When embarking on a strategy of issuing ongoing dividends, begin with a small dividend that the company can easily support from its current resources and expected cash flows. By doing so, the board can comfortably establish a gradual increase in the size of the dividend that the investment community can rely upon, which should result in a slow increase in the price of the company's stock. Conversely, the worst type of dividend is one that is so large that the company has a difficult time scraping together the cash needed to pay it, which can endanger the ability of the company to operate on an ongoing basis.

It is also useful for the board of directors to consider the negative implications of not having sufficient cash to continue paying a dividend. If this were to happen, the income-oriented investors who are holding the stock precisely because of those dividends will sell their shares; this will trigger a supply and demand imbalance that will lower the price of the stock. Eventually, value-oriented investors will buy the stock when it has dropped by a sufficient amount, in hopes of a recovery in the stock price. Nonetheless, a dividend cancellation almost always triggers a steep stock price decline.

In summary, the board of directors should think long and hard about the decision to begin issuing dividends. Dividends work best when followed consistently over a long period of time, but doing so requires rock-solid cash flows. Any inability to meet a dividend obligation will trigger a rapid stock price decline. Thus, always consider a vote to issue dividends as a long-term strategic issue, not just a short-term payout.

**Note on dividend dates:** The *declaration date* is the date on which the board of directors sets the amount and payment date of a dividend. The *record date* is the date on which the company compiles the list of investors who will be paid a dividend. The *ex-dividend* date is the first date immediately following the declaration of a dividend, when the purchaser of a company's stock is *not* entitled to receive the next dividend payment; this is normally two business days prior to the record date. The *payment date* is the date on which the company pays the dividend to its investors.

## The Stock Buyback Option

Companies sometimes engage in stock buybacks, where the board of directors authorizes that a certain amount of cash be set aside for a repurchase program. There are three reasons why a company may engage in a buyback:

- To reduce the number of shares outstanding, which should increase the amount of earnings per share, and therefore provide pressure to increase the share price.
- Because management believes that the share price is currently too low, and does not adequately reflect the true market value of the business. Thus, if a buyback plan is announced that the company will buy back shares whenever the share price falls below a certain price point, there will be a tendency for the stock price to stay above that trigger point.
- To mop up excess shares that have been created through the issuance of stock options and warrants.

---

**EXAMPLE**

The Hegemony Toy Company has 5,000,000 shares of its common stock outstanding. These shares currently trade at $20. In the fiscal year just ended, Hegemony reported net profits of $2,000,000, which results in reported earnings per share of $0.40 (calculated as $2,000,000 profits ÷ 5,000,000 shares).

Hegemony's board of directors approves a $10,000,000 stock buyback. At the current $20 market price, this means the company can acquire 500,000 shares. By doing so, there will now be 4,500,000 shares outstanding. The altered share total changes the earnings per share figure to $0.444.

---

There are multiple problems with a stock buyback. One is certainly float management, since there will be fewer shares in circulation after the buyback has been completed, which reduces the liquidity of the stock. If a company already suffers from an excessively small float, this is a valid objection to a buyback.

Another problem is that companies have a strong tendency to acquire shares when they are flush with cash, which is usually at a point in their life cycles when they have a very high stock price. Thus, they are converting a relatively small number of shares to treasury stock in exchange for a large amount of cash, which does little to boost the earnings per share for the remaining shares outstanding. This is the reverse of what would be considered prudent behavior for an investor, who attempts to buy low and sell high. If a company were as prudent as an investor, it would only buy back shares when its stock price was very low.

Yet another issue is that a buyback signals to the investment community that a company has more cash than it needs for its operations, so growth-oriented investors suspect that the company will not grow as fast in the future as it has in the past. This signal may cause growth investors to sell the stock. Conversely, the company has not used its cash to issue dividends, so it has *not* sent a signal that will attract income-oriented investors (see the Investor Strategies chapter). Thus, a buyback tends to create selling pressure among one group if investors, while not attracting any new investors.

When a company has excess cash, it should consider a stock buyback to be one of the last potential uses for that cash. Instead, the sequence of possible uses should roughly follow this series of decision options:

1. *Invest in company operations.* This is assumed to be the best profit generator.
2. *Acquire related companies.* This approach is riskier than internal growth, but still focuses the company on its primary markets.
3. *Pay down debt.* This reduces the risk of not paying back loans. The approach can be extended to paying off leases and even reducing the amount of accounts payable.
4. *Build a reserve.* There is nothing wrong with building a large cash reserve to guard against a downturn in the company's fortunes.
5. *Buy back stock.* If all of the preceding steps have been taken, only then is a buyback warranted, and only if the stock is trading at a reasonably low price.

If, despite all of the preceding warnings, a company still decides to engage in a stock buyback program, it at least affords the investor relations officer an excellent opportunity to issue a series of announcements that the company has bought yet another block of its own stock.

---

**Tip:** In any press release mentioning a stock buyback, be sure to mention how long the company has been buying back shares and the amount of cash still reserved for more repurchases, so that investors get the impression that the company has a long-term commitment to supporting its stock price.

---

## The Stock Repurchase Safe Harbor Provision

Under the Securities Exchange Act, a company is not allowed to enter into any transactions related to its securities that will affect their prices or trading volumes. A stock buyback program is very likely to breach this provision, so the SEC promulgated Rule 10b-18 to create a safe harbor provision for companies engaged in stock buybacks.

To qualify for the safe harbor provision, a company must ensure that its stock buyback program complies with the following four conditions on a daily basis:

- *Purchase centralization.* Buyback purchases made on behalf of the company must be made by a single broker/dealer on any given day.
- *Time of purchases.* A buyback purchase must not be the opening purchase of the day or within the last 30 minutes before the close of trading. However, a company with a public float of at least $150 million and an average daily trading volume of at least $1 million can purchase shares until 10 minutes before the close of trading.
- *Price of purchases.* Buyback purchases must be at prices that do not exceed the higher of the highest independent bid or the last independent transaction price. If the shares are not quoted on an organized exchange, then the price cannot be higher than the highest bid obtained from three independent dealers.
- *Volume of purchases.* The total volume of buyback purchases in a single day cannot exceed 25% of the average daily trading volume for that security. The SEC does allow one block trade per week that is not subject to this 25% limitation, but only on the condition that the company makes no other buyback trades that day.

---

**Tip:** The Rule 10b-18 safe harbor provision only applies to buybacks of common stock. It does not apply to any other types of securities.

---

In short, the SEC's trading rules for a buyback program are designed to dampen the impact of buyback trades on the price of a company's stock, using a combination of controls over the centralization, timing, price points, and volume of purchases made.

## Odd Lot Shareholders

The investor relations officer normally has an intense interest in increasing the number of shares in circulation, as well as the number of shareholders. However, it is not cost-effective to maintain a large number of odd lot shareholders. An odd lot shareholder is an investor who holds less than 100 shares of a company's stock. The annual cost of issuing proxy statements and annual reports to odd lot shareholders is not cost-effective, so many investor relations officers take the position that these investors should either be eliminated or encouraged to increase their share holdings.

An additional factor favoring the elimination of odd lot shareholders arises when a public company wants to go private. Doing so requires a steep reduction in the number of shareholders, and one of the least expensive ways to achieve this reduction is the elimination of odd lot shareholders, since the company must buy back so few shares from them.

Odd lot shareholdings tend to form an unusually large proportion of the shareholder base in a public shell company (see the Initial Public Offering chapter). If a company goes public through the purchase of a shell entity, it may find that it is saddled with a large number of odd lot shareholders who are completely inactive.

There are three ways to mitigate the odd lot shareholder conundrum, which are as follows:

- *Buy back shares.* The company could contact odd lot shareholders and offer to buy back their shares. This requires a certain amount of labor, so a case can be made that it is even less cost-effective to buy back these shares than it is to leave them alone. Also, buying back shares can run afoul of the SEC's rules regarding tender offers, the avoidance of which requires widely-spaced transactions with individual shareholders.
- *Offer direct stock purchase plan.* The company can go out of its way to contact odd lot shareholders to make them aware of the company's direct stock purchase plan (see the Direct Stock Purchase Plan section). A few of the shareholders may take advantage of it to increase their shareholdings, thereby boosting them out of the odd lot classification.
- *Reverse stock split.* A company can conduct a reverse stock split, where a large number of shares are exchanged for a smaller number of shares. For example, a 100-to-1 reverse split would reduce the holdings of a shareholder who owns 99 shares to a fraction of one share, which allows the company to cash him out. Once the smaller shareholders have been cashed out in this manner, the company can conduct a forward stock split (such as a 1-to-100 split) to return the remaining shareholders to their pre-existing shareholding levels. The disadvantage of this approach is that it requires shareholder approval, some administrative effort, and the cash needed to pay off the fractional share holdings.

The odd lot shareholding issue never really goes away, because there are always methods by which someone might come into ownership of just a few shares. For example, the estate of a large shareholder may distribute his holdings among many relatives upon his death, or a reverse stock split may convert a large share holding into a small one, or employees may be issued small stock grants. Thus, the investor relations officer should periodically review the number of odd lot shareholdings and decide whether steps should be taken to reduce their number.

## Treatment of Abandoned Property

The state governments have all enacted unclaimed property laws, under which organizations are required to forward to the government any abandoned property, such as an abandoned bank account. In some states, these laws also apply to stockholder shares. When dealing with shareholders, their property is considered to be lost based on different laws, depending on the state. Typically, the issuer or its stock transfer agent is required to make note of any shareholder communications that are returned as being undeliverable, and then conduct a shareholder database search to attempt to locate the missing parties. If a shareholder cannot be found, the organization files an unclaimed property report with the applicable government, at which point the government is considered to be the owner of the missing shareholder's shares. If missing shareholders later appear, they must file with the government to reclaim their shares.

The Securities and Exchange Commission has issued Rule 17Ad-17, *Lost Securityholders and Unresponsive Payees*, to deal with this situation. The essential points of this rule are as follows:

- A lost securityholder is a holder of securities from whom an item of correspondence was returned as undeliverable, and for which there is no new address information.
- Transfer agents must exercise reasonable care to ascertain the addresses of lost securityholders, which requires that at least two database searches be conducted using at least one information database service.
- The first search must be conducted between three and 12 months of a securityholder being designated as lost, and again between six and 12 months after the first search.
- These searches are not needed if the aggregate value of security holder assets is less than $25 or the holder is not a natural person.

The abandoned property concept does not alter the number of shares outstanding, since share ownership simply shifts to the government. However, the investor relations function should keep copies of the unclaimed property reports, in case missing shareholders re-appear years later and want to reclaim their shares.

---

**Tip:** Do not ignore the need to remit abandoned property to the government, since governments routinely conduct abandoned property audits, and could fine a business that did not remit unclaimed property in a timely manner.

---

## Summary

Whenever a public company makes a decision that will impact its float, the investor relations officer should make those recommendations needed to ensure that a sufficient number of registered shares are available for trading. Otherwise, institutional investors will be less likely to take stock positions in the company, and the firm may struggle to attract interest from other investors who may also be concerned about holding a potentially illiquid stock.

When a company makes a change to any part of its stock management program, the investor relations officer should reconsider the entire marketing message being sent out to the investment community, to ensure that the message continues to reflect the actions of the company. For example, issuing a dividend may bring investors to question whether a company is still in growth mode, or if it has now become a mature business. Similarly, a stock buyback implies that a company can no longer find an in-house use for its available cash, which also implies a lack of growth prospects.

# Chapter 14
# SEC Filings

## Introduction

The investor relations officer must continually interact with investors, analysts, and other members of the investment community. The language spoken by these people is financial, so the investor relations officer must also have considerable facility with the financial information produced by a company. This chapter describes each component of the financial statements, as well as the contents of the three primary SEC filings most commonly perused by the investment community, and finishes with a discussion of the disclosure of non-GAAP information.

## The Income Statement

The income statement is an integral part of a company's financial statements, and contains the results of its operations during an accounting period, showing revenues and expenses, and the resulting profit or loss.

There are two ways to present the income statement. One method is to present all items of revenue and expense for the reporting period in a statement of comprehensive income. Alternatively, you can split this information into an income statement and a statement of comprehensive income.

There are no specific requirements for the line items to include in the income statement, but the following line items are typically used, based on general practice:

- Revenue
- Tax expense
- Post-tax profit or loss for discontinued operations and their disposal
- Profit or loss
- Extraordinary gains or losses
- Other comprehensive income, subdivided into each component thereof
- Total comprehensive income

A key additional item is to present an analysis of the expenses in profit or loss, using a classification based on their nature or functional area; the goal is to maximize the relevance and reliability of the presented information. If you elect to present expenses by their nature, the format looks similar to the following:

**Sample Presentation by Nature of Items**

| Revenue | | $xxx |
|---|---|---|
| | | |
| Expenses | | |
| Direct materials | $xxx | |
| Direct labor | xxx | |
| Salaries expense | xxx | |
| Payroll taxes | xxx | |
| Employee benefits | xxx | |
| Depreciation expense | xxx | |
| Telephone expense | xxx | |
| Other expenses | xxx | |
| Total expenses | | $xxx |
| | | |
| Profit before tax | | $xxx |

Alternatively, if you present expenses by their functional area, the format looks similar to the following, where most expenses are aggregated at the department level:

**Sample Presentation by Function of Items**

| Revenue | $xxx |
|---|---|
| Cost of goods sold | xxx |
| Gross profit | xxx |
| | |
| Administrative expenses | $xxx |
| Distribution expenses | xxx |
| Research and development expenses | xxx |
| Sales and marketing expenses | xxx |
| Other expenses | xxx |
| Total expenses | $xxx |
| | |
| Profit before tax | $xxx |

Of the two methods, presenting expenses by their nature is easier, since it requires no allocation of expenses between functional areas. Conversely, the functional area presentation may be more relevant to users of the information, who can more easily see where resources are being consumed.

Additional headings, subtotals, and line items are added to the items noted above if doing so increases the user's understanding of the entity's financial performance.

An example follows of an income statement that presents expenses by their nature, rather than by their function.

**EXAMPLE**

Hegemony Toy Company presents its results in two separate statements by their nature, resulting in the following format, beginning with the income statement:

Hegemony Toy Company
Income Statement
For the years ended December 31

| (000s) | 20x2 | 20x1 |
|---|---|---|
| Revenue | $900,000 | $850,000 |
| | | |
| Expenses | | |
| Direct materials | $270,000 | $255,000 |
| Direct labor | 90,000 | 85,000 |
| Salaries | 300,000 | 275,000 |
| Payroll taxes | 27,000 | 25,000 |
| Depreciation expense | 45,000 | 41,000 |
| Telephone expense | 30,000 | 20,000 |
| Other expenses | 23,000 | 22,000 |
| Finance costs | 29,000 | 23,000 |
| Other income | -25,000 | -20,000 |
| Profit before tax | $111,000 | $124,000 |
| Income tax expense | 38,000 | 43,000 |
| Profit from continuing operations | $73,000 | $81,000 |
| Loss from discontinued operations | 42,000 | 0 |
| Profit | $31,000 | $81,000 |

Hegemony then continues with the following statement of comprehensive income:

Hegemony Toy Company
Statement of Comprehensive Income
For the years ended December 31

| (000s) | 20x2 | 20x1 |
|---|---|---|
| Profit | $31,000 | $81,000 |
| | | |
| Other comprehensive income | | |
| Exchange differences on translating foreign operations | $5,000 | $9,000 |
| Available-for-sale financial assets | 10,000 | -2,000 |
| Actuarial losses on defined benefit pension plan | -2,000 | -12,000 |
| Other comprehensive income, net of tax | $13,000 | -$5,000 |
| | | |
| Total comprehensive income | $18,000 | $76,000 |

The investor relations officer should be familiar with the reasons for unusual revenue or expenditure levels in the income statement, as well as which expenses are aggregated into the various line items in the statement.

# The Balance Sheet

In most organizations, the balance sheet is considered the second most important of the financial statements, after the income statement. A balance sheet presents information about an entity's assets, liabilities, and shareholders' equity, where the compiled result must match this formula:

Total assets = Total liabilities + Equity

The balance sheet reports the aggregate effect of transactions as of a specific date. It is used to assess an entity's liquidity and ability to pay its debts.

There is no specific requirement for the line items to be included in the balance sheet. The following line items, at a minimum, are normally included:

Current Assets:

- Cash and cash equivalents
- Trade and other receivables
- Investments
- Inventories
- Assets held for sale

Non-Current Assets:

- Property, plant, and equipment
- Intangible assets
- Goodwill

Current Liabilities:

- Trade and other payables
- Accrued expenses
- Current tax liabilities
- Current portion of loans payable
- Other financial liabilities
- Liabilities held for sale

Non-Current Liabilities:

- Loans payable
- Deferred tax liabilities
- Other non-current liabilities

Equity:

- Capital stock
- Additional paid-in capital
- Retained earnings

Here is an example of a balance sheet which presents information as of the end of two fiscal years:

Hegemony Toy Company
Balance Sheet
As of December 31, 20X2 and 20X1

| (000s) | 12/31/20X2 | 12/31/20x1 |
|---|---|---|
| **ASSETS** | | |
| **Current assets** | | |
| Cash and cash equivalents | $270,000 | $215,000 |
| Trade receivables | 147,000 | 139,000 |
| Inventories | 139,000 | 128,000 |
| Other current assets | 15,000 | 27,000 |
| **Total current assets** | $571,000 | $509,000 |
| | | |
| **Non-current assets** | | |
| Property, plant, and equipment | 551,000 | 529,000 |
| Goodwill | 82,000 | 82,000 |
| Other intangible assets | 143,000 | 143,000 |
| **Total non-current assets** | $776,000 | $754,000 |
| | | |
| **Total assets** | $1,347,000 | $1,263,000 |
| | | |
| **LIABILITIES AND EQUITY** | | |
| **Current liabilities** | | |
| Trade and other payables | $217,000 | $198,000 |
| Short-term borrowings | 133,000 | 202,000 |
| Current portion of long-term borrowings | 5,000 | 5,000 |
| Current tax payable | 26,000 | 23,000 |
| Accrued expenses | 9,000 | 13,000 |
| **Total current liabilities** | $390,000 | $441,000 |
| | | |
| **Non-current liabilities** | | |
| Long-term debt | 85,000 | 65,000 |
| Deferred taxes | 19,000 | 17,000 |
| **Total non-current liabilities** | $104,000 | $82,000 |
| | | |
| **Total liabilities** | $494,000 | $523,000 |
| | | |
| **Shareholders' equity** | | |
| Capital | 100,000 | 100,000 |
| Additional paid-in capital | 15,000 | 15,000 |
| Retained earnings | 738,000 | 625,000 |
| **Total equity** | $853,000 | $740,000 |
| | | |
| **Total liabilities and equity** | $1,347,000 | $1,263,000 |

An asset on the balance sheet is classified as current when a company expects to sell or consume it during its normal operating cycle or within 12 months after the reporting period. If the operating cycle is longer than 12 months, use the longer period to judge whether an asset can be classified as current. All other assets are classified as non-current. The following are classified as current assets:

- *Cash.* This is cash available for current operations, as well as any short-term, highly liquid investments that are readily convertible to known amounts of cash and which are so near their maturities that they present an insignificant risk of value changes. Do not include cash whose withdrawal is restricted, to be used for other than current operations, or segregated for the liquidation of long-term debts; such items should be classified as longer-term.
- *Accounts receivable.* This includes trade accounts, notes, and acceptances that are receivable. Also, include receivables from officers, employees, affiliates, and others if they are collectible within a year. Do not include any receivable that you do not expect to collect within 12 months; such items should be classified as longer-term.
- *Marketable securities.* This includes those securities representing the investment of cash available for current operations, including trading securities.
- *Inventory.* This includes merchandise, raw materials, work-in-process, finished goods, operating supplies, and maintenance parts.
- *Prepaid expenses.* This includes prepayments for insurance, interest, rent, taxes, unused royalties, advertising services, and operating supplies.

A liability is classified as current when a company expects to settle it during its normal operating cycle or within 12 months after the reporting period, or if it is scheduled for settlement within 12 months. All other liabilities are classified as non-current. The following are classified as current liabilities:

- *Payables.* This is all accounts payable incurred in the acquisition of materials and supplies that are used to produce goods or services.
- *Prepayments.* This is amounts collected in advance of the delivery of goods or services by the entity to the customer. Do not include a long-term prepayment in this category.
- *Accruals.* This is accrued expenses for items directly related to the operating cycle, such as accruals for compensation, rentals, royalties, and various taxes.
- *Short-term debts.* This is debts maturing within the next 12 months.

Current liabilities include accruals for amounts that can only be determined approximately, such as bonuses, and where the payee to whom payment will be made cannot initially be designated, such as a warranty accrual.

A comparative balance sheet presents side-by-side information about an entity's assets, liabilities, and shareholders' equity as of multiple points in time. For example, a comparative balance sheet could present the balance sheet as of the end of each year for the past three years. The intent is to provide the reader with a series of snapshots of a company's financial condition over a period of time, which is useful for developing trend line analyses.

The comparative balance sheet is required by the SEC in numerous circumstances for the reports issued by public companies, particularly the annual Form 10-K and the quarterly Form 10-Q. The usual SEC requirement is to report a comparative balance sheet for the past two years, with additional requirements for quarterly reporting.

The following is a sample of a comparative balance sheet that contains the balance sheet as of the end of a company's fiscal year for each of the past three years:

**Sample Comparative Balance Sheet**

|  | as of 12/31/20X3 | as of 12/31/20X2 | as of 12/31/20X1 |
|---|---|---|---|
| **Current assets** | | | |
| Cash | $1,200,000 | $900,000 | $750,000 |
| Accounts receivable | 4,800,000 | 3,600,000 | 3,000,000 |
| Inventory | 3,600,000 | 2,700,000 | 2,300,000 |
| **Total current assets** | $9,600,000 | $7,200,000 | $6,050,000 |
| | | | |
| Total fixed assets | 6,200,000 | 5,500,000 | 5,000,000 |
| **Total assets** | $15,800,000 | $12,700,000 | $11,050,000 |
| | | | |
| **Current liabilities** | | | |
| Accounts payable | $2,400,000 | $1,800,000 | $1,500,000 |
| Accrued expenses | 480,000 | 360,000 | 300,000 |
| Short-term debt | 800,000 | 600,000 | 400,000 |
| **Total current liabilities** | $3,680,000 | $2,760,000 | $2,200,000 |
| | | | |
| Long-term debt | 9,020,000 | 7,740,000 | 7,350,000 |
| **Total liabilities** | $12,700,000 | $10,500,000 | $9,550,000 |
| | | | |
| Shareholders' equity | 3,100,000 | 2,200,000 | 1,500,000 |
| **Total liabilities and equity** | $15,800,000 | $12,700,000 | $11,050,000 |

The sample comparative balance sheet reveals that the company has increased the size of its current assets over the past few years, but has also recently invested in a large amount of additional fixed assets that have likely been the cause of a significant boost in its long-term debt.

As was the case with the income statement, the investor relations officer should be familiar with the reasons for unusual changes in the balance sheet, as well as which accounts are aggregated into the various line items in the balance sheet.

# The Statement of Cash Flows

The statement of cash flows contains information about the flows of cash into and out of a company; in particular, it shows the extent of those company activities that generate and use cash. The primary activities are:

- *Operating activities*. These are an entity's primary revenue-producing activities. Examples of operating activities are cash receipts from the sale of goods, as well as from royalties and commissions, amounts received or paid to settle lawsuits, fines, payments to employees and suppliers, cash payments to lenders for interest, contributions to charity, and the settlement of asset retirement obligations.
- *Investing activities*. These involve the acquisition and disposal of long-term assets. Examples of investing activities are cash receipts from the sale of property, the sale of the debt or equity instruments of other entities, the repayment of loans made to other entities, and proceeds from insurance settlements related to damaged fixed assets. Examples of cash payments that are investment activities include the acquisition of fixed assets, as well as the purchase of the debt or equity of other entities.
- *Financing activities*. These are the activities resulting in alterations to the amount of contributed equity and the entity's borrowings. Examples of financing activities include cash receipts from the sale of the entity's own equity instruments or from issuing debt, proceeds from derivative instruments, and cash payments to buy back shares, pay dividends, and pay off outstanding debt.

The *direct method* or the *indirect method* can be used to present the statement of cash flows. These methods are described below.

## The Direct Method

The direct method of presenting the statement of cash flows presents the specific cash flows associated with items that affect cash flow. Items that typically do so include:

- Cash collected from customers
- Interest and dividends received
- Cash paid to employees
- Cash paid to suppliers
- Interest paid
- Income taxes paid

The format of the direct method appears in the following example.

**EXAMPLE**

Hegemony Toy Company constructs the following statement of cash flows using the direct method:

Hegemony Toy Company
Statement of Cash Flows
For the year ended 12/31/20X1

| Cash flows from operating activities | | |
|---|---|---|
| Cash receipts from customers | $45,800,000 | |
| Cash paid to suppliers | -29,800,000 | |
| Cash paid to employees | -11,200,000 | |
| Cash generated from operations | 4,800,000 | |
| | | |
| Interest paid | -310,000 | |
| Income taxes paid | -1,700,000 | |
| Net cash from operating activities | | $2,790,000 |
| | | |
| **Cash flows from investing activities** | | |
| Purchase of fixed assets | -580,000 | |
| Proceeds from sale of equipment | 110,000 | |
| Net cash used in investing activities | | -470,000 |
| | | |
| **Cash flows from financing activities** | | |
| Proceeds from issuance of common stock | 1,000,000 | |
| Proceeds from issuance of long-term debt | 500,000 | |
| Principal payments under capital lease obligation | -10,000 | |
| Dividends paid | -450,000 | |
| Net cash used in financing activities | | 1,040,000 |
| | | |
| Net increase in cash and cash equivalents | | 3,360,000 |
| Cash and cash equivalents at beginning of period | | 1,640,000 |
| Cash and cash equivalents at end of period | | $5,000,000 |

**Reconciliation of net income to net cash provided by operating activities:**

| | | |
|---|---|---|
| Net income | | $2,665,000 |
| Adjustments to reconcile net income to net cash provided by operating activities: | | |
| Depreciation and amortization | $125,000 | |
| Provision for losses on accounts receivable | 15,000 | |
| Gain on sale of equipment | -155,000 | |
| Increase in interest and income taxes payable | 32,000 | |
| Increase in deferred taxes | 90,000 | |
| Increase in other liabilities | 18,000 | |
| Total adjustments | | 125,000 |
| Net cash provided by operating activities | | $2,790,000 |

The standard-setting bodies encourage the use of the direct method, but it is rarely used, for the excellent reason that the information required for this presentation is difficult to assemble; companies simply do not collect and store information in the manner required for this format. Instead, they use the indirect method, which is described next.

## The Indirect Method

Under the indirect method of presenting the statement of cash flows, the presentation begins with net income or loss, with subsequent additions to or deductions from that amount for non-cash revenue and expense items, resulting in net income provided by operating activities. The format of the indirect method appears in the following example.

---

**EXAMPLE**

Hegemony Toy Company constructs the following statement of cash flows using the indirect method:

Hegemony Toy Company
Statement of Cash Flows
For the year ended 12/31/20X1

| Cash flows from operating activities | | |
|---|---|---|
| Net income | | $3,000,000 |
| Adjustments for: | | |
| Depreciation and amortization | $125,000 | |
| Provision for losses on accounts receivable | 20,000 | |
| Gain on sale of facility | -65,000 | |
| | | 80,000 |
| Increase in trade receivables | -250,000 | |
| Decrease in inventories | 325,000 | |
| Decrease in trade payables | -50,000 | |
| | | 25,000 |
| Cash generated from operations | | 3,105,000 |
| | | |
| **Cash flows from investing activities** | | |
| Purchase of fixed assets | -500,000 | |
| Proceeds from sale of equipment | 35,000 | |
| Net cash used in investing activities | | -465,000 |
| | | |
| **Cash flows from financing activities** | | |
| Proceeds from issuance of common stock | 150,000 | |
| Proceeds from issuance of long-term debt | 175,000 | |
| Dividends paid | -45,000 | |
| Net cash used in financing activities | | 280,000 |
| | | |
| Net increase in cash and cash equivalents | | 2,920,000 |
| Cash and cash equivalents at beginning of period | | 2,080,000 |
| Cash and cash equivalents at end of period | | $5,000,000 |

---

The indirect method is very popular, because the information required for it is relatively easily assembled from the accounts that a business normally maintains.

The investor relations officer will receive fewer inquiries regarding the contents of the statement of cash flows. Nonetheless, you should be conversant in the reasons for any material changes listed in this report.

## The Statement of Retained Earnings

The statement of retained earnings reconciles changes in the retained earnings account during an accounting period. The statement starts with the beginning balance in the retained earnings account, and then adds or subtracts such items as profits and dividend payments to arrive at the ending retained earnings balance. The general calculation structure of the statement is:

Beginning retained earnings + Net income – Dividends +/- Other changes
= Ending retained earnings

The statement of retained earnings is most commonly presented as a separate statement, but can also be added to another financial statement. The following example shows a simplified format for the statement.

**EXAMPLE**

The controller of the Hegemony Toy Company assembles the following statement of retained earnings to accompany his issuance of the financial statements of the company:

Hegemony Toy Company
Statement of Retained Earnings
For the year ended 12/31/20X1

| | |
|---|---|
| Retained earnings at December 31, 20X0 | $150,000 |
| Net income for the year ended December 31, 20X1 | 40,000 |
| Dividends paid to shareholders | -25,000 |
| Retained earnings at December 31, 20X1 | $165,000 |

It is also possible to provide a greatly expanded version of the statement of retained earnings that discloses the various elements of retained earnings. For example, it could separately identify the par value of common stock, additional paid-in capital, retained earnings, and treasury stock, with all of these elements then rolling up into the total just noted in the last example. The following example shows what the format could look like.

## EXAMPLE

The controller of the Hegemony Toy Company creates an expanded version of the statement of retained earnings in order to provide more visibility into activities involving equity. The statement follows:

Hegemony Toy Company
Statement of Retained Earnings
For the year ended 12/31/20X1

| | Common Stock, $1 par | Additional Paid-in Capital | Retained Earnings | Total Shareholders' Equity |
|---|---|---|---|---|
| Retained earnings at December 31, 20X0 | $10,000 | $40,000 | $100,000 | $150,000 |
| Net income for the year ended December 31, 20X1 | | | 40,000 | 40,000 |
| Dividends paid to shareholders | | | -25,000 | -25,000 |
| Retained earnings at December 31, 20X1 | $10,000 | $40,000 | $115,000 | $165,000 |

# The Form 10-Q

A publicly held company is required to issue the Form 10-Q to report the results of its first, second, and third fiscal quarters. The Form 10-Q includes not just the financial statements, but also a number of disclosures. The following table itemizes the more common disclosures:

**Selection of Form 10-Q Disclosures**

| Item Header | Description |
|---|---|
| **Item 1A.** Risk factors | A thorough listing of all risks that the company may experience. It warns investors of what could reduce the value of their investments in the company. |
| **Item 3.** Legal proceedings | Describe any legal proceedings currently involving the company, and its estimate of the likely outcome of those proceedings. |
| **Item 4.** Submission of matters to a vote of security holders | Describe matters submitted to the shareholders for a vote during the most recent quarter of the fiscal year. |
| **Item 7.** Management's discussion and analysis (MD&A) | Describe opportunities, challenges, risks, trends, future plans, and key performance indicators, as well as changes in revenues, the cost of goods sold, other expenses, assets, and liabilities. |

| Item Header | Description |
|---|---|
| **Item 7A.** Quantitative and qualitative disclosures about market risk | Quantify the market risk at the end of the last fiscal year for the company's market risk-sensitive instruments. |
| **Item 8.** Financial statements and supplementary data | Make all disclosures required by GAAP, including descriptions of:<br>• Accrued liabilities<br>• Acquisitions<br>• Discontinued operations<br>• Fixed assets<br>• Income taxes<br>• Related party transactions<br>• Segment information<br>• Stock options |
| **Item 9A.** Controls and procedures | Generally describe the system of internal controls, testing of controls, changes in controls, and management's conclusions regarding the effectiveness of those controls. |
| **Item 15.** Exhibits and financial statement schedules | Item 601 of Regulation S-K requires that a business attach a number of exhibits to the Form 10-K, including (but not limited to):<br>• Code of ethics<br>• Material contracts<br>• Articles of incorporation<br>• Bylaws<br>• Acquisition purchase agreements |

> **Tip:** Maintain a record of the questions asked during earnings calls, and see if any of them could have been addressed within the MD&A section (Item 7). This can form the basis for an increased amount of MD&A material in the next Form 10-Q.

The Form 10-Q must be filed within 40 days of the end of the fiscal quarter if the company is either a large accelerated filer or an accelerated filer. If that is not the case, it must be filed within 45 days of the end of the fiscal quarter.

The investor relations officer should obtain and read the final draft of the Form 10-Q before it is filed, in order to be conversant with any questions that investors or analysts may raise about its contents.

## The Form 10-K

A publicly held company is required to issue the Form 10-K to report the results of its fiscal year. The Form 10-K includes not just the financial statements, but also a number of additional disclosures. The following table itemizes the more common disclosures:

**Selection of Form 10-K Disclosures**

| Item Header | Description |
|---|---|
| **Item 1.** Business | Provide a description of the company's purpose, history, operating segments, customers, suppliers, sales and marketing operations, customer support, intellectual property, competition, and employees. It should tell readers what the company does and describe its business environment. |
| **Item 1A.** Risk factors | A thorough listing of all risks that the company may experience. It warns investors of what could reduce the value of their investments in the company. |
| **Item 1B.** Unresolved staff comments | Disclose all unresolved comments received from the SEC if they are material. (only applies to written comments from the SEC received at least 180 days before the fiscal year-end by an accelerated or large accelerated filer) |
| **Item 2.** Properties | Describe the leased or owned facilities of the business, including square footage, lease termination dates, and lease amounts paid per month. |
| **Item 3.** Legal proceedings | Describe any legal proceedings currently involving the company, and its estimate of the likely outcome of those proceedings. |
| **Item 4.** Submission of matters to a vote of security holders | Describe matters submitted to the shareholders for a vote during the fourth quarter of the fiscal year. |
| **Item 5.** Market for company stock | Describe where the company's stock trades and the number of holders of record, as well as the high and low closing prices per share, by quarter. |
| **Item 6.** Selected financial data | For the last five years, state selected information from the company's income statement and balance sheet (should be in tabular comparative format). |
| **Item 7.** Management's discussion and analysis (MD&A) | Describe opportunities, challenges, risks, trends, future plans, and key performance indicators, as well as changes in revenues, the cost of goods sold, other expenses, assets, and liabilities. |
| **Item 7A.** Quantitative and qualitative disclosures about market risk | Quantify the market risk at the end of the last fiscal year for the company's market risk-sensitive instruments. |

| Item Header | Description |
|---|---|
| **Item 8.** Financial statements and supplementary data | Make all disclosures required by GAAP, including descriptions of:<br>• Accrued liabilities<br>• Acquisitions<br>• Discontinued operations<br>• Fixed assets<br>• Income taxes<br>• Related party transactions<br>• Segment information<br>• Stock options |
| **Item 9.** Changes in and disagreements with accountants on accounting and financial disclosure | Describe any disagreements with the auditors when management elects to account for or disclose transactions in a manner different from what the auditors want. |
| **Item 9A.** Controls and procedures | Generally describe the system of internal controls, testing of controls, changes in controls, and management's conclusions regarding the effectiveness of those controls. |
| **Item 10.** Directors, executive officers and corporate governance | Identify the executive officers, directors, promoters, and individuals classified as control persons. |
| **Item 11.** Executive compensation | Itemize the types of compensation paid to company executives. |
| **Item 12.** Security ownership of certain beneficial owners and management and related stockholder matters | State the number of shares of all types owned or controlled by certain individuals classified as beneficial owners and/or members of management. |
| **Item 13.** Certain relationships and related transactions, and director independence | If there were transactions with related parties during the past fiscal year, and the amounts involved exceeded $120,000, describe the transactions. |
| **Item 14.** Principal accountant fees and services | State the aggregate amount of any fees billed in each of the last two fiscal years for professional services rendered by the company's auditors for:<br>• Reviews and audits;<br>• Audit-related activities;<br>• Taxation work; and<br>• All other fees. |

| Item Header | Description |
|---|---|
| **Item 15.** Exhibits and financial statement schedules | Item 601 of Regulation S-K requires that a business attach a number of exhibits to the Form 10-K, including (but not limited to):<br>• Code of ethics<br>• Material contracts<br>• Articles of incorporation<br>• Bylaws<br>• Acquisition purchase agreements |

**Tip:** Maintain a record of the questions asked during earnings calls, and see if any of them could have been addressed within the MD&A section (Item 7). This can form the basis for an increased amount of MD&A material in the next Form 10-K.

The Form 10-K must be filed within 60 days of the end of the fiscal year if the company is a large accelerated filer or an accelerated filer, or within 75 days of the end of the fiscal year if the company is an accelerated filer. If the company does not have either designation, then the 10-K must be filed within 90 days of the end of the fiscal year.

The investor relations officer should obtain and read the final draft of the Form 10-K before it is filed, in order to be conversant with any questions that investors or analysts may raise about its contents.

## The Form 8-K

The Form 8-K is by far the most commonly-issued SEC filing. A public company uses it to disclose a broad range of material events that impact the business. The following table itemizes the types of disclosures that can appear in a Form 8-K.

**Types of Form 8-K Disclosures**

| Item Header | Description |
|---|---|
| **Item 1.101.** Entry into a material definitive agreement | Refers to an agreement not made in the ordinary course of business. Disclose the agreement date, the names of the parties, and the general terms of the agreement. |
| **Item 1.102.** Termination of a material definitive agreement | Refers to the non-standard termination of an agreement not made in the ordinary course of business. Disclose the termination date, the general terms of the agreement, the circumstances of the termination, and any termination penalties. |
| **Item 1.103.** Bankruptcy or receivership | If the business enters bankruptcy or receivership, identify the proceeding, the name of the court, the date when jurisdiction was assumed, and the identity of the receiver. There are additional disclosures regarding reorganization plans. |

| Item Header | Description |
|---|---|
| **Item 2.01.** Completion of acquisition or disposition of assets | Disclose the date of asset acquisition or disposition, describe the assets, and identify the counterparty. Also note the nature and amount of consideration involved. Further, note the source of funds for an acquisition, if there is a material relationship between the company and the source of funds. |
| **Item 2.02.** Results of operations and financial condition | Disclose material non-public information regarding the company's results of operations or financial condition if it was publicly announced or released by someone acting on behalf of the company. |
| **Item 2.03.** Creation of a direct financial obligation | If the company enters into a material, direct financial obligation, disclose the date when the obligation began, describe the transaction, note the amount and terms of the obligation, and other material issues. If the company becomes directly or contingently liable for a material amount under an off-balance sheet arrangement, disclose the same information, as well as the material terms whereby it may become a direct obligation, the nature of any recourse provisions, and the undiscounted maximum amount of any future payments. |
| **Item 2.04.** Triggering events that accelerate or increase a direct financial obligation | If there was a triggering event that altered a direct financial obligation and the effect is material, disclose the date of the event, describe it, note the amount of the obligation, and the payment terms. |
| **Item 2.05.** Costs associated with exit or disposal activities | If the company commits to an exit or disposal plan, disclose the date of the commitment, describe the course of action, and estimate the range of costs for each major type of costs and in total. |
| **Item 2.06.** Material impairments | If the company concludes that there is a material impairment charge, disclose the date of this conclusion, describe the impaired assets, and the facts and circumstances leading to the conclusion. Also note the estimated amount of the impairment charge. |
| **Item 3.01.** Notice of delisting or failure to satisfy a continued listing rule | If the company has received notice that it does not satisfy a rule for continued listing on an exchange, disclose the date when any notice was received, the applicable rule not being satisfied, and actions the company will take in response to the notice. If the company has submitted an application to delist from an exchange, disclose the action taken and the date of the action. |

| Item Header | Description |
|---|---|
| **Item 3.02.** Unregistered sales of equity securities | If the company sells unregistered securities, state the date of sale and the title and amount of the securities sold. Also name the principal underwriters and the names of the persons to whom the securities were sold. Also note the aggregate offering price and the amount of any discounts or commissions paid. Also describe any terms under which the securities are convertible into company stock. |
| **Item 3.03.** Material modifications to rights of security holders | If there has been a material modification to the rights of security holders, disclose the modification date, the name of the affected class of securities, and the effect on the rights of the security holders. |
| **Item 4.01.** Changes in registrant's certifying accountant | Disclose whether the company's existing independent accountant has resigned or been dismissed. Also disclose whether a new independent accountant has been engaged. |
| **Item 4.02.** Non-reliance on previously issued financial statements or a related audit report or completed interim review | If the company concludes that previously issued financial statements contain errors and so should not be relied upon, disclose the date when this conclusion was reached and identify the financial statements and periods that cannot be relied upon. Also note the facts underlying this conclusion, and state whether the issue has been discussed with the company's independent accountant. |
| **Item 5.01.** Changes in control of registrant | If there is a change in control of the company, disclose the identity of the persons who acquired control, the date of the change in control, the basis of the control, the amount of consideration used by the acquiring person, the sources of funds used, the identity of the persons from whom control was assumed, and any arrangements between the old and new control groups. |
| **Item 5.02.** Departure of directors or certain officers; election of directors; appointment of certain officers; compensatory arrangements of certain officers | If a director has resigned or will not stand for re-election due to a disagreement with the company, disclose the date of the resignation or refusal to stand for election, the positions held by the director, and describe the circumstances. If the director has sent written correspondence to the company concerning this matter, attach it to the 8-K. If a senior manager of the company resigns from the company or is terminated, disclose the date of the event. If a new senior manager is hired, disclose the person's name, position, and date of appointment, and compensation arrangements. |
| **Item 5.03.** Amendments to articles of incorporation or bylaws; change in fiscal year | If the company amends its articles of incorporation or bylaws, disclose the effective date of the amendment, and describe the alteration. If the company changes its fiscal year, disclose the change date, and the date of the new fiscal year end. |

| Item Header | Description |
| --- | --- |
| **Item 5.04.** Temporary suspension of trading under registrant's employee benefit plans | When a director or officer of the company is subject to a blackout period for an equity security, disclose the reasons for the blackout period, a description of those transactions to be suspended, the class of securities subject to the blackout, and the expected beginning and ending dates of the blackout period. |
| **Item 5.05.** Amendments to the registrant's code of ethics, or waiver of a provision of the code of ethics | If there has been an amendment to or waiver of the company's code of ethics, disclose the date and nature of the event. If a waiver is involved, also state the name of the person to whom the waiver was granted. |
| **Item 5.06.** Change in shell company status | If the company was a shell company (see the Initial Public Offering chapter), and has ceased being classified as a shell, disclose the material terms of the transaction. |
| **Item 5.07.** Submission of matters to a vote of security holders | If any matters have been submitted to shareholders for a vote, disclose the date of the meeting, whether it was a special or annual meeting, the names of directors elected, and a summarization of each matter voted upon at the meeting. Also state the number of votes cast for, against, and withheld on each voting matter, as well as by individual director (if there is a director election). |
| **Item 5.08.** Shareholder director nominations | If the company did not hold an annual meeting in the preceding year, or if the date of this year's meeting is more than 30 days from the date of the preceding year's meeting, disclose the date by which a nominating shareholder must submit notice on Schedule 14N, so that the company can include any director nominations by shareholders in its proxy materials. |
| **Item 6.01.** ABS informational and computational material | Disclose any informational and computational material for asset-backed securities. |
| **Item 6.02.** Change of servicer or trustee | If a servicer or trustee has resigned or been replaced, or if a new servicer has been appointed, disclose the date and nature of the event. For a new servicer, describe the material terms of the agreement and the servicer's duties. |
| **Item 6.03.** Change in credit enhancement or other external report | If the depositor becomes aware of any material enhancement or support that was previously applicable for any class of asset-backed securities, and which has been terminated other than by contract expiration or the completion by all parties of their obligations, disclose the date of termination, the identity of the parties providing enhancement or support, the terms and conditions of the enhancement or support, the circumstances of the termination, and any early termination penalties. |

| Item Header | Description |
|---|---|
| **Item 6.04.** Failure to make a required distribution | If distributions are not made to the holders of asset-backed securities by the required date, disclose the nature of the failure. |
| **Item 6.05.** Securities Act updating procedure | If any material pool characteristic of an offering of asset-backed securities differs by more than five percent from the prospectus description at the time of issuance, disclose the characteristics of the actual asset pool. |
| **Item 7.01.** Regulation FD disclosure | The company may disclose any information that it elects to disclose under the provisions of Regulation FD (see the Regulation FD chapter). |
| **Item 8.01.** Other events | The company can, at its option, disclose any information that is not specifically identified elsewhere in the Form 8-K. This is typically only done if the company believes that the information will be of importance to the holders of its securities. |
| **Item 9.01.** Financial statements and exhibits | Attach the financial statements, pro forma financial information, and any other exhibits filed along with the Form 8-K. |

Every Form 8-K must be filed within four business days of the event being disclosed. When a reportable event occurs on a weekend or holiday, the four-day rule begins on the next business day.

The investor relations officer should read the final draft of every Form 8-K. Investors and analysts may want to discuss the disclosed items, so this person must have a firm knowledge of each one, and the extent to which additional explanations can be made without requiring additional disclosure under Regulation FD (see the Regulation FD chapter).

## Forms 3, 4 and 5

Corporate insiders are considered to be those directors, officers, and shareholders who own more than 10 percent of a class of the securities issued by an entity. These insiders are required to file periodic reports with the Securities and Exchange Commission, disclosing their holdings in the company and any changes in that ownership. These forms are described in the following table.

The intent of these filings is to disclose to the public any changes in corporate ownership by insiders, which can be used to infer how insiders feel about the prospects of the business, based on their stock purchase and sale activity. The investor relations officer should be copied on all of these reports, in order to speak knowledgeably about their contents if asked by a third party.

**Corporate Insider Reporting Forms**

| Form Number | Form Title | Description |
|---|---|---|
| Form 3 | Initial Statement of Beneficial Ownership of Securities | File when the company is registering equity securities for the first time, or file within 10 days of a person becoming an officer, director, or beneficial owner. Lists company securities held. |
| Form 4 | Statement of Changes in Beneficial Ownership | File within two business days of a change in ownership. Lists changes in company securities held. |
| Form 5 | Annual Statement of Changes in Beneficial Ownership of Securities | File when reporting any transactions that should have been reported earlier on a Form 4. Due 45 days after the end of the fiscal year. |

**Note:** Corporate insiders are responsible for filing these forms, but the company frequently does so on their behalf, to ensure that the filings are made in a timely manner.

## The Disclosure of Non-GAAP Information

Some publicly held companies want to present the best possible version of their results to the investment community, and do so by selectively disclosing only the better portions of their actual financial results. The result can be misleading, when compared to the actual results reported under Generally Accepted Accounting Principles (GAAP). To mitigate the effects of this misleading information, the SEC's Regulation G requires certain additional disclosures. The following text is taken from the Regulation:

a. Whenever a registrant ... publicly discloses material information that includes a non-GAAP financial measure, the registrant must accompany that non-GAAP financial measure with:
   1. A presentation of the most directly comparable financial measure calculated and presented in accordance with GAAP; and
   2. A reconciliation ... of the differences between the non-GAAP financial measure disclosed or released with the most comparable financial measure or measures calculated and presented in accordance with GAAP.
b. A registrant, or a person acting on its behalf, shall not make public a non-GAAP financial measure that, taken together with the information accompanying that measure and any other accompanying discussion of that measure, contains an untrue statement of a material fact or omits to state a material fact necessary in order to make the presentation of the non-GAAP financial measure, in light of the circumstances under which it is presented, not misleading.

Regulation G also contains limited exemptions for certain foreign issuers of securities or in relation to proposed business combinations.

> **Tip:** To avoid the reconciliation requirements of Regulation G, it is easiest to adopt a policy of never issuing non-GAAP financial measures without the written approval of the company's disclosure committee.

An example of how Regulation G may be used to construct an information release is noted in the following example:

---

**EXAMPLE**

The reported net loss of Hegemony Toy Company was strongly impacted by the recognition of a $500,000 impairment charge against our goodwill asset. We believe that an adjusted net income measure more closely represents our actual performance, because it excludes the one-time, non-cash impairment charge. We define adjusted net income as the net income or loss of the company, less the impact of impairment charges.

Adjusted net income is not a financial performance measurement under GAAP. Adjusted net income has material limitations and should not be used as an alternative to such GAAP measurements as net income, cash flows from operations, investing, or financing activities, or other financial statement data contained within the financial statements. Because the adjusted net income figure is not defined by GAAP, and can be compiled in many ways, it may not be comparable to other similarly titled performance measurements issued by other companies.

The following table presents a reconciliation of Hegemony's adjusted net income to our net loss during fiscal year 201X.

|                      | For the Year Ended December 31, 201X |
| -------------------- | ------------------------------------ |
| Adjusted net income  | $400,000                             |
| Impairment charge    | (500,000)                            |
| Net loss             | $(100,000)                           |

---

In summary, the SEC requires that any non-GAAP information disclosed by a company must be accompanied by a reconciliation to a financial measurement that has been calculated using GAAP, and it should not be misleading. This means that non-GAAP information can still be released; it is up to the reader of the presented information to examine the accompanying reconciliation and decide if the non-GAAP information is relevant to his or her investing needs.

> **Tip:** The investor relations officer may make public a non-GAAP financial measure through a speech or other form of oral presentation. If this is intentional, prepare a reconciliation of the non-GAAP measure to a GAAP measure on the company's website, and mention the web page location during the presentation. Alternatively, issue a Form 8-K in advance that contains this information.

## Summary

The investor relations officer should be thoroughly familiar with the information issued by the company through its SEC filings. This knowledge should include a full understanding of all material components of the company's financial statements, which may require a briefing from the company controller regarding the larger line items or changes in those statements.

In particular, the investor relations officer should have an excellent knowledge of the management discussion and analysis (MD&A) section of the most recent Form 10-Q or 10-K, since investors and analysts will probably pay particular attention to the statements made in this section. If the company elects to include forward-looking information in the MD&A, this person should be fully briefed on the derivation of this information. Only by having a thorough understanding of SEC filings can one authoritatively interact with the investment community.

# Chapter 15
# Annual Meeting Planning and Voting

## Introduction

Corporate law requires that there be an annual shareholder meeting, when the shareholders assemble to vote a board of directors into office, and sometimes consider other motions as well. The trouble is that shareholders are typically widely dispersed, and so cannot attend the meeting. In many cases, it is impossible to convince *any* shareholders to attend. To resolve this issue, corporations engage in proxy solicitations, where shareholders are asked to give a designated representative the authority to vote their shares at the annual meeting. The investor relations officer is sometimes given responsibility for managing the proxy solicitation process, and may also coordinate some of the activities planned for the annual meeting.

In this chapter, we describe the types of shareholders, the structure of the annual shareholder meeting, and the complex process required to obtain proxies from those shareholders who do not plan to attend the shareholder meeting. We also note the problems caused by Rule 452 of the New York Stock Exchange, the notice access rule, electronic shareholder meetings, and related matters.

> **Related Podcast Episode:** Episode 120 of the Accounting Best Practices Podcast discusses how to obtain shareholder votes. You can listen to it at: **accounting-tools.com/podcasts** or **iTunes**

## Registered and Beneficial Shareholders

Before we begin a discussion of the annual shareholder meeting and the shareholder voting process, we will first address the two types of shareholders, since these two classifications have a significant impact on the paperwork and timelines associated with the annual meeting and the voting process.

A *registered shareholder* is a person or entity that holds the shares of a company in their own name on the company's stock register. The company or its stock transfer agent maintains a record of this ownership, and provides services directly to the shareholder for share transfers, dividend payments, and so forth. A registered shareholder is also known as a *shareholder of record*.

A *beneficial shareholder* is a person or entity that has an intermediary, such as a stockbroker or bank, hold their shares in a company. This approach is most common when shareholders want to consolidate their holdings of securities in one place to facilitate trading. Shares held in this manner are considered to be held in *street name*. Since most public companies are owned by shareholders who actively buy and sell ownership positions, it is likely that the majority of all shareholders in public companies are beneficial shareholders.

Within the beneficial shareholder classification are two further sub-classifications of shareholder – the non-objecting beneficial owner (NOBO) and the objecting beneficial owner (OBO). NOBOs allow the companies whose securities they own to obtain their contact information from the intermediaries that hold their securities. OBOs have elected to shield their identities, so companies must instead deal with the third party that holds their securities. When a person opens a brokerage account, they have the option to choose either the NOBO or OBO designation. If they do not make a selection, they may be given the OBO designation by default.

These differentiations are important when obtaining shareholder information for proxy voting, as will be described later in this chapter. The key point to remember from this discussion is that the company or its stock transfer agent maintains the ownership records for its registered shareholders, while the ownership records for beneficial owners are maintained by intermediaries.

## The Annual Shareholder Meeting

Corporations are required to have an annual shareholder meeting at which shareholders vote for the board of directors and other matters, as well as ask questions of management. Many private companies minimize this requirement by scheduling the meeting in out-of-the-way locations and presenting so little information that shareholders are discouraged from attending. Such cavalier treatment is possible for a public company, but there is an increasing trend toward making it a major event that can be used to solicit shareholder feedback and encourage greater shareholder identification with the firm. On the assumption that you prefer the latter approach, this section describes the planning for the annual shareholder meeting.

Depending on the size of an anticipated shareholder meeting, it may be necessary to begin planning for it shortly after the last annual meeting was concluded. The starting point of the planning process is the plan used for the preceding annual meeting, adjusted for any issues noted during the actual meeting. When revising this plan for the next event, consider the following factors:

- *Location*. The traditional location for an annual meeting is in the city where a company has its headquarters. However, there are alternatives, such as holding it in a city where the management team wants to conduct a road show, thereby tackling two issues on the same trip. Another option is to schedule the meeting near large concentrations of investors, with the intent of encouraging their participation. Yet a third option is to schedule it just before or after a major industry trade show, and in the same city *as* the trade show, in hopes of attracting analysts who will also be attending the show. If the meeting is scheduled away from the company headquarters, be particularly careful to reserve the meeting space well in advance, to avoid conflicts with other events.

**Tip:** Determine whether the rules of the state in which the company is incorporated mandates that an annual meeting be held at the company's principal office.

- *Director nominees.* Work with the chairperson of the board of directors to determine who will run for election for director positions at the annual meeting. The SEC requires that the following information be included in the proxy about each director nominee (as well as every existing director):
  - Age
  - Business experience
  - Five-year employment history
  - The specific experience, qualifications, attributes or skills that have caused the company to request that they serve on the board

  It is easiest to obtain this information through a questionnaire that is sent to the directors and nominees several months in advance.

- *Board resolutions.* Obtain from the board of directors the following resolutions:
  - Set the annual record date
  - Set the annual meeting date
  - Approve the slate of director nominees
  - Approve any other issues to be brought to a vote at the meeting
  - Approve the proxy statement and annual report that are sent to the shareholders
  - Appoint an inspector of elections

  In particular, the annual record date and meeting date should be settled well in advance of the annual meeting, since proxy mailing tasks are based on these dates.

- *Issue shareholder list.* If shareholders have a right to inspect the company's shareholder list (usually to solicit proxies for the upcoming meeting), provide the requested information.

- *Shareholder proposal cutoff.* Set the date by which shareholder proposals must be received for inclusion in the shareholder mailing.

- *Annual report.* Complete the audit of the financial statements, file the Form 10-K with the SEC, and prepare the annual report.

- *Meeting materials.* Prepare the agenda and management presentations for the meeting. Also, most state laws require that the list of shareholders of record be made available for shareholder perusal at the shareholder meeting.

- *Audio-visual.* Arrange for any audio or video recording equipment that will be used to record the meeting. It may be useful to post the resulting files in the investor relations section of the company web site.

- *Internet distribution.* To reach the widest possible audience, consider broadcasting the meeting over the Internet, and allowing viewers to post on-line questions for management to answer.

- *Security.* Notify building security of the date and time of the meeting. If there has been a history of disturbances at previous shareholder meetings, it may be prudent to also notify the closest police department of the meeting arrangements.

There is no legally-mandated order of business required for an annual meeting. The chairperson could establish whether a quorum is present, and then go straight to the results of the shareholder voting, ask for any shareholder questions, and terminate the meeting. The meeting can literally last just a few minutes. The agenda for such a meeting could be:

1. Call the meeting to order
2. Introduction of participants
3. Proof of notice of the meeting
4. Existence of a quorum
5. Election of directors
6. Results of voting
7. Adjournment

Alternatively, a company that is determined to provide more information to shareholders can schedule a number of additional presentations, such as:

- An overview of the company's results from the past year
- Question and answer sessions with the board of directors and senior company managers
- Presentations from company managers concerning certain areas of interest
- Demonstrations of new products

---

**Tip:** Prepare the chairperson for the more difficult questions that might be expected during the question and answer session.

---

**Tip:** Prepare for the chairperson a set of suggested responses to departures from the planned meeting agenda, such as how to deal with unruly shareholders, requests to depart from the stated agenda, and requests to bring a new motion before the meeting.

---

If the intent is to provide a more informative session for attending shareholders, encourage the entire board of directors to attend the meeting. There are three ways to do so:

- Make attendance at the shareholder meeting a requirement of being a director
- Schedule the next board of directors meeting to immediately follow the shareholder meeting, to encourage them to attend both meetings
- Pay directors an attendance fee for appearing at the shareholder meeting

Whatever the format of the meeting may be, always create a script for the chairperson to follow in administering the meeting. A script is based on the meeting agenda, but goes on to include the specific text to read during certain segments of the meeting. At a minimum, there should be an exact script for:

- *Announcing that a quorum has been established.* Whenever possible, determine in advance if there will be a quorum, based on proxies already received from shareholders. Also, schedule the establishment of a quorum at the *beginning* of the meeting, since any shareholder leaving the meeting thereafter is not considered to have invalidated the quorum for any actions taken after his or her departure.

- *Announcing the results of voting.* This depends on state law, but most allow an affirmative vote of the majority of those present at the meeting (including proxies) to approve most types of motions presented. However, some motions may require an absolute majority of all shares outstanding, or even a super-majority, so be sure of the voting requirements for each motion presented. Further, the stock exchanges sometimes require shareholder votes on certain issues, rather than just the approval of the board of directors.
- *Adjourning the meeting.* State law may require a certain procedure for adjourning a meeting.

**Tip:** Always schedule all legally-mandated items for the beginning of the shareholder meeting, in case a disruption requires that the meeting be terminated early.

The investor relations officer or corporate secretary should know how to handle any unexpected proposals coming from meeting attendees. It is usually possible to exclude these proposals based on provisions in the company's bylaws that require shareholders to submit proposals a certain number of days prior to the annual meeting. If so, the chairperson can ask the submitting shareholder to withdraw the motion and submit it for consideration at the next shareholder meeting.

**Tip:** Corporate counsel should attend the annual meeting if there is a possibility that motions will be presented by shareholders.

Consider issuing a press release after the annual meeting, noting the results of the voting at the meeting and any other information that might be of use to the investment community. The press release could contain a link to the company's archived video recording of the meeting.

## The Electronic Shareholder Meeting

Some states allow corporations to hold shareholder meetings entirely by electronic means – there is no physical meeting at all. The following extract from Section 211(a)(2) of the General Corporation Law of the state of Delaware is representative of how such meetings may be constructed:

Stockholders and proxy holders not physically present at a meeting of stockholders may, by means of remote communication participate in a meeting of stockholders; and be deemed present in person and vote at a meeting of stockholders, whether such meeting is to be held at a designated place or solely by means of remote communication, provided that:

(i) The corporation shall implement reasonable measures to verify that each person deemed present and permitted to vote at the meeting by means of remote communication is a stockholder or proxy holder,

(ii) The corporation shall implement reasonable measures to provide such stockholders and proxy holders a reasonable opportunity to participate in the meeting and to vote on matters submitted to the stockholders, including an opportunity to read or hear the proceedings of the meeting substantially concurrently with such proceedings, and

(iii) If any stockholder or proxy holder votes or takes other action at the meeting by means of remote communication, a record of such vote or other action shall be maintained by the corporation.

There are a number of advantages to holding an entirely electronic shareholder meeting, including:

- *Access*. Perhaps the largest benefit of the electronic meeting is making it accessible to any shareholder who has access to the Internet.
- *Reduced cost*. There is no cost associated with renting meeting space, flying directors to the meeting, staff time, and so forth. Offsetting these cost eliminations is the cost of hosting the electronic meeting.
- *Travel time*. The time required by the directors, senior managers, and other staff participants to travel to and from the annual meeting is eliminated.

---

**Tip:** Consult with corporate counsel before arranging for an electronic shareholder meeting, since this option is not yet permitted under some state laws. It may also not be allowed in the company's bylaws.

---

## The Shareholder Voting Process

A key element of the shareholder voting process is the concept of the proxy vote. If shareholders do not plan to attend a company's annual meeting, an alternative is to allow someone else to cast votes on their behalf, which is known as *voting by proxy*. In some companies, no shareholders attend the annual meeting at all, so *all* of the voting is by proxy.

The following steps show the approximate order in which a company handles the shareholder voting process. A key part of this process is obtaining proxy votes; it may even be considered the overriding goal of the process. The steps are:

1. *Notify stock transfer agent*. Contact the company's stock transfer agent with the meeting date, and work backwards from there to determine the record date and mailing date that the transfer agent needs to generate a shareholder list and conduct a broker search.

2. *Set record and meeting dates*. Establish well in advance the record date for the annual meeting, which is the date on which shareholders are recorded for inclusion in the proxy mailing. Also define the date of the meeting, as well as the voting cut-off date, which is typically the business day immediately preceding the meeting date. A large gap between the record and meeting dates gives more time for votes to be cast; a separation of at least 45 days

between the mail date (see next bullet point) and the meeting date is recommended. The annual meeting is usually held shortly after the company's audited annual financial statements have been completed.

> **Tip:** Determine whether the rules of the state in which the company is incorporated mandates that an annual meeting be held within a certain time period following its last annual meeting.

3. *Set mailing date.* The earliest that proxy and other materials can be mailed out to shareholders is one business day after the record date. However, a one or two week delay after the record date is customary, to allow for printing problems or a delayed approval of proxy materials by the SEC.
4. *NOBO notifications.* Send notices to stockbrokers and other entities that hold the company's shares on behalf of their clients (non-objecting beneficial owners). Federal rules require that the company contact these intermediaries (known as a *broker search* or *notice and inquiry*) at least 20 business days before the record date to inquire about how many packets of proxy materials to supply to them. Thus, if a broker search were initiated today, the record date could not be for at least 20 business days from today.
5. *Receive record date confirmation.* Broadridge Inc. sends the company a record date confirmation notice, on which is stated the unit quantity of the proxy materials package that should be printed for the beneficial shareholders. To this number is added the number of registered shareholders from the records of the stock transfer agent, to arrive at the total number of proxy material packages to create.
6. *Create proxy card.* Obtain from the corporate secretary the list of items to be voted upon at the annual meeting, and incorporate these items into the company's boilerplate version of the proxy card.
7. *Create proxy statement.* Assemble the information needed for the proxy statement, write the statement, and have it reviewed by the company's auditors and attorneys.
8. *Create annual report.* The Form 10-K is frequently used as the annual report, thereby eliminating the work that would otherwise be required to create yet another document for the annual meeting.
9. *Obtain board approval.* Obtain the formal approval of the board of directors for the record date, mailing date, proxy statement, and annual report, as well as for the appointment of an inspector of elections.
10. *Assemble proxy materials.* The full set of proxy materials to be sent to shareholders includes:
    o A proxy statement
    o A proxy card for registered shareholders or voting instructions for beneficial owners
    o The company's annual report
    o A notice of Internet availability

If the company plans to include any non-routine matters in proxy materials, the materials must be sent to the SEC at least 10 days before the final proxy materials are mailed to shareholders. If the SEC does not respond within 10 business days, the company can proceed with printing and distributing the proxy materials.

11. *Report printing.* Deliver the proxy materials and annual report to a financial printer, so that a sufficient number of copies can be made for the estimated number of shareholders.

12. *File proxy materials.* File the proxy materials with the SEC. If the company is listed on a stock exchange, these materials must also be submitted to the exchange.

13. *Distribute materials.* Coordinate with the company's financial printer and stock transfer agent to distribute proxy materials to the shareholders of record as of the record date. The mailing may be handled by a third party mailing service, in which case the stock transfer agent sends mailing labels to the mailing service. The materials intended for beneficial owners are sent to Broadridge, Inc., which forwards them to the intended parties.

14. *Post proxy materials.* Arrange with the company's webmaster to post the proxy materials to the company website.

15. *Engage proxy solicitor.* If it appears that there will be an insufficient number of votes cast (see the following NYSE Rule 452 section), hire a proxy solicitor to contact shareholders and ask them to vote before the cut-off date.

---

**Tip:** Vote totals may initially appear low, because the intermediaries that represent beneficial owners typically wait until 10 to 15 days before the annual meeting to electronically transmit their vote totals to the company's stock transfer agent. The need for a proxy solicitor will be apparent immediately after these votes are received.

---

16. *Obtain oath of inspectors of election.* If the company is having its stock transfer agent tabulate voting results, obtain the oath of the inspectors of election; this is a statement that the inspectors will observe strict impartiality and tabulate votes to the best of their ability.

17. *Tabulate votes.* The stock transfer agent keeps a running total of votes cast by shareholders. Shareholders may also be allowed to vote on-line, where they follow the instructions for on-line voting that were listed on their proxy ballots. If proxy materials were sent to the third parties that represent beneficial owners, then the third parties send voting instruction forms to the actual share owners, to find out how they want to vote their shares. The beneficial shareholders return the completed voting instruction forms to their intermediaries, who vote the shares on their behalf.

18. *Obtain report from inspectors of election.* The inspectors of election tabulate the proxy results, and then send to the company a report and certification of the inspector of election. This report states the voting results of the proxy,

and whether a quorum has been attained. This information is used as the basis for the voting results announced at the shareholder meeting.

Following the annual meeting, the corporate secretary creates the meeting minutes and files them along with the voting results and the report submitted by the inspector of elections. Also, the results of the voting are included in the company's next annual Form 10-K or quarterly Form 10-Q for the period in which the meeting was held.

## The Notice and Access Rule

The SEC requires that publicly held companies that are soliciting proxies from their shareholders also make available an electronic version of their package of proxy materials on the Internet. Companies must issue notice of the availability of these materials to their shareholders, and where to locate the materials. The notice must include the following information:

- Internet address at which the proxy materials are available for review, and a list of the materials available for review
- The date, time, and location of the shareholders' meeting
- Identification of each matter to be acted upon at the shareholders' meeting and the company's recommendations (if any) regarding these matters
- Contact information where shareholders can request a copy of the proxy materials
- The identification information needed for each shareholder to access a proxy card, along with instructions for how to access it
- Information about attending the shareholder meeting and voting in person

This *notice and access* rule presents the opportunity to significantly reduce the mailing costs associated with a proxy mailing. Instead of mailing the complete set of documents to shareholders, a company has the option of mailing a notice of where to find the materials on the Internet. If a shareholder receives this notice and still wants to have the complete set of proxy materials mailed to him, the company is required by the SEC to do so.

> **Tip:** Do not underestimate the number of shareholders who will want paper copies. Any additional copies that must be printed on demand will be much more expensive than would have been the case if the company had printed too many copies in a single one-time batch.

The SEC also requires that a company ask shareholders for their preferred mode of delivery in the future – by mail, e-mail, or Internet link. This means that companies must maintain records of these preferences for use in tailoring future communications to the requests of their shareholders.

There are certain situations, such as votes regarding business combinations, where the notice and access rule is not allowed. In these cases, a company must mail a complete set of proxy materials to its shareholders.

## The Householding Concept

The SEC allows public companies to reduce their mailing costs by sending a single annual report and proxy statement to a single address when several shareholders with the same last name live at the same address. This method, known as *householding*, can only be used if a company first issues a notification by mail to the affected shareholders at least 60 days prior to the proxy mailing date, stating the company's intent to consolidate proxy mailing materials. The notice must state how to contact the company's transfer agent to deny the recipient's consent to use householding.

A company only needs to send this notification once; it is not required for subsequent proxy mailings, unless the recipients have denied their consent for the company to use householding.

Note that every shareholder must still receive a proxy card or notice of how to vote – only the annual report and proxy statement can be consolidated with householding.

## NYSE Rule 452

The New York Stock Exchange (NYSE) has adopted Rule 452, which keeps brokers from voting for company directors on behalf of their customers – or at least, without specific instructions from those customers. This rule does not just apply to companies listed on the NYSE; it applies to *all* brokers, and they handle the shares of companies that list on other stock exchanges and in the over-the-counter market. Thus, the rule impacts *all* publicly held companies, no matter where their shares are listed.

In the past, investors almost always let their brokers vote for them, because it saved time and they could not be bothered to do so themselves. The result was a rough split of 30% of the votes being cast by shareholders, and 70% by their stockbrokers.

Rule 452 presents a major problem for any public company, because the reliable voters – stockbrokers – have been removed from voting, leaving the least reliable group to send in their votes on time. It is becoming all too common to not even receive the 50% of all votes needed to elect the board of directors. This is less of a problem in the larger firms that have a high proportion of institutional investors, since these investors have such large shareholdings that the submission of just a few ballots may bring the total number of votes cast past the 50% level. The issue is much more severe for smaller public companies, for they have few (if any) institutional investors, which leaves their shares spread among a larger group of individual shareholders.

The problems imposed by Rule 452 are difficult, but not impossible to surmount. Here are several options to consider:

- *Notice timing.* Create the longest possible gap between the mailing date for sending out proxy materials and the date of the shareholder meeting. By giving the shareholders a long time in which to submit their proxies, the company may receive a few additional votes. This is a minor improvement, since most shareholders either vote as soon as they receive their proxy materials, or throw them away.

- *Address cleaning.* Have the company's stock transfer agent hire a specialist to investigate bad shareholder addresses that have been returned by the postal service. The stock transfer agent handles this task, because it should be tracking the returned mail from prior proxy mailings, and also can immediately fix any issues found by the address cleaning specialist. Always review and adjust bad addresses just before the proxy mailing, to ensure that the largest possible number of shareholders actually receive their voting materials.

> **Tip:** It is much more difficult to update bad addresses when a shareholder is located in another country, which is an argument against obtaining an international shareholder base.

- *Stratified mailing.* Arrange with the mailing service handling the delivery of the company's proxy materials to send the materials by a faster delivery method, such as USPS priority mail, for the larger shareholders, and by a slower (and less expensive) method for all remaining shareholders. Doing so is both cost-effective (in aggregate) and rapidly gets voting materials into the hands of those larger shareholders whose votes will ensure that a quorum can be attained.

- *Follow up mailing.* If shareholders do not submit a vote by a certain trigger date, send them a reminder.

- *On-line voting.* Have the company's stock transfer agent set up an on-line voting system, so that shareholders can enter their votes on-line. This system eliminates mail float, so that votes can be tabulated a few days sooner than would be the case with mailed ballots. This is also an excellent way to obtain the votes of dilatory investors at the last minute, without paying for the overnight delivery charges needed for them to mail in a ballot.

- *Proxy solicitor.* A proxy solicitation firm reviews a company's shareholder base to determine the best way to contact them (typically from a call center), and then contacts as many as necessary to achieve a quorum. This is a labor-intensive process that requires a number of days to complete before votes are scheduled to be tallied. Also, this is an expensive option, since the proxy solicitor may need to obtain telephone contact information for shareholders, and spend time calling a large number of them.

- *Contact shareholders directly.* If there is little time left before votes are to be tallied, the only remaining approach will be to contact shareholders directly and badger them to submit their ballots. Since many will have thrown away their ballots, the best option is to encourage them to use an on-line voting system.

> **Tip:** The investor relations staff should maintain relations with the larger and more long-term shareholders, so it can contact them directly to solicit their votes.

The imposition of Rule 452 on all public companies is a serious problem that is not going away (unless the NYSE terminates the rule). Thus, the investor relations officer should be constantly aware of the proportion of votes cast in any shareholder vote, and be prepared to take early steps to solicit votes by a variety of means.

## Summary

The annual meeting can be dull and routine, or it can be one of the major shareholder outreach programs of the year. The management team and board of directors should jointly decide upon the level of emphasis that they want to place on the annual meeting. With sufficient funding and planning, this can be a major tool for increasing the level of commitment of shareholders to the company.

Irrespective of the amount of marketing to be integrated into the annual meeting, it is still a complicated process for which a procedure should be established, and for which planning should begin many months before the actual event. In particular, have corporate counsel review the meeting and proxy preparation plans to ensure that the company is in compliance with all applicable state laws, stock exchange rules, and bylaws.

# Chapter 16
# The Initial Public Offering

## Introduction

The beginning point of the investor relations officer's role with a company is the initial public offering (IPO). At the end of the IPO process, a company will have acquired a certain initial mix of investors that the investor relations department must deal with. Also, the company will have chosen a stock exchange on which its shares will be listed; the investor relations officer will likely have dealings with this exchange. Though this person does not play a large role in the IPO itself, it is still useful to understand the basic process by which a business goes public. The remainder of this chapter contains a high-level review of the IPO, notes the less well-known reverse merger into a public shell company, and describes the concept of blue sky laws.

> **Related Podcast Episode:** Episode 33 of the Accounting Best Practices Podcast discusses the acquisition of a public shell company. You can listen to it at: **accountingtools.com/podcasts** or **iTunes**

## Reasons for and Against an IPO

There are several reasons why the owners of a business may want to take it public through an IPO. The first is the perception that the owners can more easily sell their shares, or at least have the option to do so through a stock exchange. Second, being publicly held makes it easier to raise funds with which to operate the business or pay for acquisitions. Third, the absence of restrictions on the sale of shares tends to increase their price. Fourth, the increased ease with which a company can sell shares tends to reduce its proportion of debt to equity, which can reduce the risk of its financial structure. Another reason is prestige – taking a company public is considered by some to be the capstone of one's professional career. Also, the awarding of stock options has more meaning in a public company, since they can eventually be sold on a stock exchange. Finally, there is some evidence that the management team of a public company receives higher compensation than they would in a similar private company, so managers tend to be in favor of going public.

While these reasons may seem compelling, there are a number of other excellent reasons for *not* going public. First, it requires significant new expenditures for the services of auditors and securities attorneys, as well as additional in-house accounting, internal audit, and investor relations personnel. The cost of directors and officers liability insurance will also increase (possibly by several multiples of the prior amount). These incremental expenses may be large enough to eliminate the profits of a smaller company. Also, the multitude of public company activities will take up some of the time of the management team, such as attendance at shareholder meetings, analyst meetings, earnings calls, and road shows. Further, the new owners of the business may demand that the company focus more attention on the immediate generation of profits, rather than the pursuit of longer-term goals. Also, there is a risk that required public disclosures might shift some competitive advantage to other players in the industry. In addition, there is some risk that the original owner will be forced out as part of an unfriendly takeover, which would have been impossible if the company had remained private. Further, investment bankers charge a high fee for raising capital through stock offerings, which a smaller business might find exorbitant. Finally, there are always alternatives to selling stock on the open market to raise funds, and which may be less expensive than doing so through an initial or secondary stock issuance.

In addition to the problems just pointed out with being public, smaller firms may also suffer from stock manipulation. When there are few registered shares outstanding, it is relatively easy for dishonest shareholders to create transactions that rapidly alter the stock price and allow them to sell out at a profit.

In short, there are a number of arguments both in favor of and against going public. Smaller companies will likely find that the cost of compliance with securities laws will erase a large part of their profits, and so may elect to remain private. A larger firm with more revenues will probably find that these costs only reduce profits by a relatively small amount, so that the overall benefits of being public outweigh those of being private. It is in these larger and wealthier firms that we usually see a well-funded investor relations department.

## The Initial Public Offering

The following discussion of the IPO process represents the *approximate* flow of activities. In reality, there is some timing overlap between events. We have also clustered together some actions to improve the narrative flow. The intent is to give a sense of how the process works, rather than an exact series of perfectly sequenced steps.

When the board of directors believes that a company is ready to make the step from being a private company to a public company, it hires a legal firm that specializes in SEC filings to complete a registration statement. This form is mandated by the SEC, and contains a detailed review of the company's financial and operational condition, risk factors, and any other items that it believes investors should be aware of before they buy the company's stock. The primary categories of information in a registration statement are:

- Summary information and risk factors
- Use of proceeds
- Description of the business
- Financial statements
- Management's discussion and analysis of the business
- Compensation of key parties
- Related party transactions

There are a large number of additional categories of information, as well. As a result, the registration statement can be a massive document. Since the company's auditors and attorneys must review it several times, and in great detail, it is also a very expensive document to create.

Once the SEC receives the form, its staff has 30 days in which to review the document – which it will, and in excruciating detail. The SEC's in-house accountants and attorneys look for inconsistencies and errors in the registration statement, as well as unclear or overblown statements, and summarize these points in a comment letter, which it sends to the company. Some of the comments made by the SEC involve substantive issues, such as the nature of the revenue recognition methodology used by the company, and which may call for a restatement of the company's financial statements. Other comments may note minor typographical issues, such as a missing middle initial in the name of a board member. The SEC does not impose a materiality convention on its staff for reviews – all parts of the registration statement are subject to review, no matter how minor the resulting changes may be.

The company responds to all of the SEC's questions and updates its registration statement as well, and then sends back the documents via an amended filing for another review. The SEC is allowed 30 days for each iteration of its review process. The SEC staff is in absolutely no hurry to assist a company with its IPO; consequently, this question-and-answer process may require a number of iterations and more months than the management team would believe possible.

---

**Tip:** High-end securities attorneys are extremely expensive, and totally worth the money, since they can minimize the number of question-and-answer iterations with the SEC, thereby accelerating the process of going public.

---

While the registration statement is being reviewed and revised, the company is also negotiating with one or more underwriters to assist the company in going public. The choice of which investment bank to use as an underwriter depends upon a number of factors, such as the prestige of the bank, whether it has prior experience in the company's industry, the size of its contacts within the investor community, and its fee. A larger and more prestigious firm usually charges a higher fee, but also has a greater ability to sell the entire amount of a company's offering of securities.

---

**Tip:** Obtain references from candidate underwriters and call the CFOs of those companies to obtain an understanding of the actual level of support that each candidate provides, as well as its expertise and willingness to continue to support the company.

---

> **Tip:** It is better to hire the services of an underwriter that has previously been a *managing underwriter*, which means that it has experience in managing the IPO process. If a bank has only been part of an underwriting syndicate, it may lack the requisite amount of experience.

The company negotiates the terms of a letter of intent with its preferred underwriter. The following are among the key elements of the letter of intent:

- *Fee.* The primary fee of the underwriter is a percentage of the total amount of funds collected. In addition, there are a variety of legal, accounting, travel, and other costs that it may pass through to the company for reimbursement.
- *Firm commitment or best efforts.* The underwriter will either agree to a *firm commitment* or a *best efforts* arrangement. Under a firm commitment deal, the underwriter agrees to buy a certain number of shares from the company, irrespective of its ability to sell those shares to third parties. This is preferable if the company is targeting raising a certain amount of cash. Under a best efforts deal, the underwriter takes a commission on as many shares as it can sell. If an underwriter insists on a best efforts deal, it indicates that there is some risk of not being able to sell the targeted number of shares.
- *Overallotment.* The underwriter may want the option to purchase additional shares from the company at a certain price within a set time period after the IPO date, which it can then sell to investors at a profit.

The underwriter supervises the creation of a road show presentation, in which the senior management team is expected to present a summary of the company and its investment prospects to prospective investors. These investors are likely to be mostly institutional investors (see the Buy Side and Sell Side chapter). The bankers and management team will go through a number of iterations to polish the presentation.

The management team and its investment bank advisors embark on a road show, which spans several weeks and takes them to a number of cities to meet with investors. If investors are interested in buying the company's stock, they tell the banks how many shares they want to buy, and at what price.

> **Tip:** Do not sell fewer than one million shares during the initial public offering. Otherwise, there will not be a sufficient number of shares available to create an active market. Also, most stock exchanges require that at least one million registered shares be outstanding.

At this time, the company also files an application with the stock exchange on which it wants its stock to be listed. The stock exchange verifies that the company meets its listing requirements (see the Stock Exchanges chapter) and then assigns it a ticker symbol. In addition, if it does not already have one, the company hires a stock transfer agent to handle the transfer of shares between parties. The company's legal staff will also submit filings to the securities agencies of those states in which the company anticipates selling shares.

When the SEC is satisfied with the latest draft of the registration statement, it declares the filing to be "effective." The management team and its bankers then decide upon the price at which the company will sell its shares. A key determinant is the price at which institutional investors are most likely to buy shares, since they usually comprise a large part of the initial block of shares sold. Underwriters want to set the initial share price slightly low, so that there is more likely to be a run-up in the first trading day that they can publicize. Also, a slightly low price makes it easier to create an active aftermarket in the stock, since other investors will be interested in obtaining and holding the stock to realize additional gains.

---

**Tip:** The underpricing of shares is most common in an IPO. If management wants to obtain the highest price per share, consider selling fewer shares during the IPO and more shares in a secondary offering, when the amount of underpricing is less extensive.

---

The underwriter traditionally likes to set the initial price of a share at somewhere between $10 and $20. Doing so may require a stock split or reverse stock split, depending on the number of shares currently outstanding. For example:

- A company has an initial valuation of $100 million, and has one million shares outstanding. To offer shares at an initial price of $20, there must be a five-for-one stock split that brings the number of shares outstanding to five million shares. Thus, a $100 million valuation divided by five million shares equals $20 per share.
- A company has an initial valuation of $80 million, and has 20 million shares outstanding. To offer shares at an initial price of $16, there must be a four-for-one reverse stock split that brings the number of shares outstanding to five million. Thus, an $80 million valuation divided by five million shares equals $16 per share.

The company then sends the registration statement to a financial printer. The printer puts the final stock price in the document, and uploads it to the SEC.

In those cases where there is more demand for shares than are to be sold, the underwriter is forced to allocate shares among its customers. The bankers will likely allocate more shares to their best customers, and may be somewhat more inclined to reduce allocations to those customers who are less likely to hold the stock for a reasonable period of time.

The underwriter sells the shares to the investors that it has lined up. The underwriter collects cash from the investors, takes out its commission, and pays the remaining proceeds to the company at a closing meeting. The underwriter is typically paid about five percent of the amount of the total placement, though this can involve a sliding scale where a larger placement results in an aggregate fee that is substantially lower. Conversely, bankers may not be interested in handling a smaller placement without charging a correspondingly higher fee.

The company is now listed on a stock exchange, has registered shares that are being traded among investors, and has presumably just received a large amount of cash for its efforts. However, the IPO process is expensive, both in terms of costs and the time required by management to complete it. A simpler approach to going public is described in the next section.

## The Reverse Merger

A variation on the initial public offering concept is the reverse merger. A reverse merger occurs when a privately-held business acquires a controlling interest in a publicly held company and folds itself into the public company. This approach has the benefit of taking a company public at a much lower up-front cost than an IPO. It is most commonly used by smaller entities that do not have the robust cash reserves to pay for an IPO, or which have had operational or financial problems in their histories that repel underwriters and larger investors. A reverse merger can also be accomplished extremely quickly, sometimes in less than a month, because it does not require prior SEC approval.

Reverse mergers are nearly always completed with a *public shell company*, which is a public firm that has no operational activity and minimal assets. These firms are typically left alone for a number of years, to let all residual liabilities surface and be settled before being sold to a private company. They are usually administered by an attorney, who files all paperwork needed to keep a shell company compliant with all laws and taxing authorities during the holding period. An unusually "clean" shell company will attract a higher price from a private company that wants to avoid the risk of buying into undocumented liabilities.

When a private company buys a public shell company, the directors of the shell resign and are replaced by a new set of directors. The shell issues a new set of stock certificates to the shareholders of the old private company in exchange for their existing shares, so that these shareholders now have an ownership interest in the public company. The new ownership of the shell company (which is no longer a shell) files a Form 8-K with the SEC, in which it documents the new ownership arrangement. This Form 8-K is quite a long one, since it includes much of the information that is normally found in the annual Form 10-K. From this point forward, the company files the normal forms required by the SEC for any public company.

> **Tip:** The initial Form 8-K filing includes the audited financial statements of both the acquirer and the shell company, so the auditors of both entities should complete their audits of the required time periods well before the form must be filed.

There are several problems with reverse mergers into public shell companies that make them a less-than-stellar alternative for some companies. The issues are:
- *Liabilities.* Even shell companies that have been quiescent for a number of years may have lingering liability problems for which the new owner will be liable. This is a particular problem when creditors hear about the new owner

of a shell and assume the owner has bottomless cash reserves to be tapped through litigation.

- *No new funds.* A company that goes public through this route does not sell shares as part of the transaction, and so does not receive any cash for its efforts. A secondary offering is required to sell shares, which involves a protracted series of document reviews by the SEC that entails substantial legal fees.

- *No new registered stock.* The shares held by a company's original shareholders are not immediately registered as a result of a reverse merger. The company must register these shares with the SEC for them to be tradable, or encourage shareholders to use the SEC's Rule 144 exemption to sell their shares. Both options require the passage of time, and stock registration costs are substantial.

- *No large investors.* The investment rules of institutional investors do not allow them to buy the shares of the smaller firms that usually go public through a reverse merger, which significantly reduces the pool of potential investors.

- *Minimal float.* A shell company will have shareholders whose shares are registered for immediate trading, but the shares are unlikely to be actively traded. There also tend to be many small shareholders of a shell, of which quite a few may have forgotten that they own an interest in the company. It is difficult to establish an active trading environment with this base of investors.

- *Stock manipulation.* With the minimal float usually associated with a reverse merger situation, it is usually easy for a stock manipulator to create a considerable amount of share price volatility with very few trades. A high level of volatility tends to drive away more legitimate investors.

- *Reputation.* The investment community has found that there is a higher incidence of fraud and stock manipulation among reverse merger companies, so they are less likely to invest in these businesses.

---

**Tip:** A reverse merger is not a good idea if the company wants to issue shares to pay for an acquisition. The recipients of these shares will soon find, even after the shares are registered, that the float is so minimal that it may take them years to sell their holdings.

---

In short, the fund-raising, stock-selling, and float benefits of an IPO are not realized through a reverse merger into a public shell company. There is also a risk of buying into undocumented liabilities that could sap a company's cash reserves. If the management team still decides to proceed with a reverse merger, it can eventually raise funds, register shares, and broaden the float; however, it must be willing to spend a considerable amount of time and effort in doing so.

> **Tip:** Use a reverse-forward stock split to eliminate the clutter of small shareholders. This involves a reverse stock split to create share totals of less than one share for the smallest shareholders, which allows the company to cash them out. This transaction is immediately followed by a normal stock split to bring the share count back to its original state, minus the small shareholders.

## Blue Sky Laws

The state governments individually enacted blue sky laws to prevent securities dealers from committing fraud through the sale of fake securities to investors. The "blue sky" name is derived from being able to "sell the sky" to an investor without the restrictions of any regulations. In this article, we will describe the requirements of these laws, how they impact securities dealers, and how the laws can impact a business.

In essence, blue sky laws mandate that securities being offered for sale for the first time be qualified by the state regulatory commission, and registered with the state. Further, the terms and prices of the securities must follow the statutory guidelines imposed by the state. These guidelines are usually modeled on the Uniform Securities Act of 1956, for which the main provisions are:

- *Reason for existence.* The securities issuer is engaged in business. It is not bankrupt or in an organizational state, nor is it a blind pool, blank check, or shell company that has no purpose for being in existence.
- *Price.* The security is priced at a reasonable level in comparison to its current market price.
- *Unsold allotment.* The security is not related to any unsold allotments given to a securities dealer who has underwritten the security.
- *Asset base.* The issuer owns a minimum amount of assets.

Consequently, it is not possible for a securities dealer to market a company's stock for sale, unless the stock conforms to both state and SEC regulations. If a security is sold that does not conform to state blue sky laws, the following comment applies (as taken from section 410(a) of the 1956 Act):

> "Any person who offers or sells a security is liable to the person buying the security from him, who may sue... to recover the consideration paid for the security, together with interest at six percent per year from date of payment, [court] costs, and reasonable attorney's fees, less the amount of income received on the security, upon tender of the security, or for damages if he no longer owns the security."

The onerous penalties of the 1956 Act are a major concern for securities dealers, since its provisions may require them to buy securities back from investors. Since a buy back would only happen if securities had lost some or all of their value, the buyback could bankrupt a securities dealer. Given the ramifications of this penalty, securities dealers are very careful to ensure that blue sky laws are always followed.

An issuing entity is exempt from the blue sky laws if its securities are listed on a national stock exchange, such as the NASDAQ or New York Stock Exchange. For businesses listed in this manner, states issue a "manual exemption," which (despite the name) automatically allows securities to be sold within their borders. This exemption was initiated under the National Securities Markets Improvement Act of 1996.

The exemption is not so clear if an issuer's securities are only available for sale in the over the counter (OTC) market. If an issuer registers with one of the credit rating agencies and renews the registration each year, the majority of state governments will allow a registration exemption. This registration is a lengthy filing that includes the issuer's financial statements, the names of the executive officers of the business, and a description of what the entity does. Despite the presence of this registration facility, some states continue to require registration directly with them; these states are Alabama, California, Georgia, Illinois, Kentucky, Louisiana, New York, Pennsylvania, Tennessee, Virginia, and Wisconsin.

The content of blue sky laws vary by state. Consequently, if a company intends to sell its securities in a specific state, it should obtain legal advice in that state, to ensure that the local regulations are being followed. Also, anyone participating in a road show should be able to answer questions about the company's blue sky status, since this question is commonly asked by investors and brokers.

## The Role of Investor Relations in an IPO

The investor relations department must be constrained in its exuberance to issue information during the quiet period associated with an IPO. Specifically, it should not do anything to give the impression of trying to enhance the price at which a company's stock will initially sell. The SEC's Rule 135 allows a company to mention its IPO, but only in regard to the following items (taken from Rule 135):

a. An issuer ... that publishes through any medium a notice of a proposed offering ... will not be deemed to offer its securities for sale through that notice if:
  1. **Legend**. The notice includes a statement to the effect that it does not constitute an offer of any securities for sale; and
  2. **Limited notice content**. The notice otherwise includes no more than the following information:
     i. The name of the issuer;
     ii. The title, amount and basic terms of the securities offered;
     iii. The amount of the offering, if any, to be made by selling security holders;
     iv. The anticipated timing of the offering;
     v. A brief statement of the manner and the purpose of the offering, without naming the underwriters;
     vi. Whether the issuer is directing its offering to only a particular class of purchasers;
     vii. Any statements or legends required by the laws of any state or foreign country or administrative authority; and

       viii.  In the following offerings, the notice may contain additional information, as follows:

           A.  *Rights offering.* In a rights offering to existing security holders:

1. The class of security holders eligible to subscribe;
2. The subscription ratio and expected subscription price;
3. The proposed record date;
4. The anticipated issuance date of the rights; and
5. The subscription period or expiration date of the rights offering.

           B.  *Offering to employees.* In an offering to employees of the issuer or an affiliated company:

1. The name of the employer;
2. The class of employees being offered the securities;
3. The offering price; and
4. The duration of the offering period.

           C.  *Exchange offer.* In an exchange offer:

1. The basic terms of the exchange offer;
2. The name of the subject company;
3. The subject class of securities sought in the exchange offer.

           D.  *[omitted]*

   b.  [The issuer] may issue a notice that contains no more information than is necessary to correct inaccuracies published about the proposed offering.

The SEC also allows a business to release some factual information during the quiet period. Its Rule 169 states that such information can be disseminated if all of the following conditions are met:

1. The issuer has previously released or disseminated information of the type described ... in the ordinary course of its business;
2. The timing, manner, and form in which the information is released or disseminated is consistent in material respects with similar past releases or disseminations;
3. The information is released or disseminated for intended use by persons, such as customers and suppliers, other than in their capacities as investors or potential investors in the issuer's securities, by the issuer's employees or agents who historically have provided such information; and
4. The issuer is not an investment company ... or a business development company ...

For example, it should be acceptable to advertise products or issue financial results, as long as it is the type of information that the company has issued in the past. Conversely, a wide range of favorable comments about company sales, earnings, or business deals *cannot* be made. In particular, the company should not issue any projections about its future performance during the quiet period.

If there is a release of information that goes beyond a strictly factual statement, the issue must be noted in a Form 8-K disclosure to the SEC, and included in the prospectus that the company is using for its initial public offering.

---

**Tip:** To be safe, it is best to have corporate counsel approve the release of *all* types of public information – both within and outside of the quiet period.

---

In summary, the investor relations staff must be extremely circumspect in making public statements during a large part of the IPO process. During this period, the best use of investor relations time will probably be in preparing for the flood of information that it will start to release once the IPO has been completed.

It is more difficult to engage investor interest in a company that has used a reverse merger to go public, for several reasons. First, there is very little trading activity in the stock, which is probably trading in the penny stock range, and for which there has been no publicity to spark investor interest. Second, there tend to be a larger-than-usual proportion of very small and inactive shareholders, who are not likely to trade the stock; thus, the size of the active market may be even smaller than might initially be apparent. And third, there are no underwriters who would normally be pitching the company's stock to their networks of investors. Thus, the investor relations department is faced with an inordinately large amount of work to publicize the business and its prospects.

---

**Note:** There is no quiet period associated with a reverse merger, since no securities are being sold.

---

## Summary

This discussion of initial public offerings has been at a summary level, since the investor relations officer is not responsible for it, and is usually constrained from engaging in too many activities while the IPO process is being followed through to its conclusion. Once the IPO has been completed, the investor relations staff will be much more active, and will participate in many activities, as described elsewhere in this book.

# Chapter 17
# The Sale of Restricted Stock

## Introduction

At some point, a company will probably need to raise cash by selling its stock, or will pay employees with stock, or acquire other businesses with stock. These shares may be registered for sale through an initial public offering or secondary offering (see the Initial Public Offering chapter). However, the CFO may rebel against the massive paperwork requirements associated with issuing registered stock, and so will instead sell or otherwise issue unregistered stock. The investor relations officer should be familiar with the concept of unregistered stock, the methods by which it is issued, and how investors can convert it to registered stock. All of these issues are addressed in the following sections.

> **Related Podcast Episodes:** Episodes 89, 90, and 94 of the Accounting Best Practices Podcast discuss Regulation A, Regulation D, and Rule 144 stock sales, respectively. You can listen to them at: **accountingtools.com/podcasts** or **iTunes**

## Restricted and Unrestricted Stock

Restricted stock carries a restriction statement on the face or back of the certificate, stating that there are restrictions on its transfer, purchase, or resale. This restriction is usually because the issuing company has not yet registered the shares with the Securities and Exchange Commission (SEC). Such shares may have been issued through a private sale of stock to investors, as compensation, or for acquisitions. It can be quite difficult for the holder of restricted shares to move the shares to a different owner. An example of the restriction verbiage shown on a stock certificate is:

> "These securities may not be sold, offered for sale, or pledged in the absence of a registration statement."

Unrestricted stock does not contain a restriction legend, and so can be sold or transferred. However, there may still be restrictions on how *many* unrestricted shares can be sold. See the Rule 144 section for more information.

## The Accredited Investor

An accredited investor qualifies under SEC rules as being financially sophisticated. The SEC definition of an accredited investor is:

1. A bank, insurance company, registered investment company, business development company, or small business investment company;

2. An employee benefit plan, within the meaning of the Employee Retirement Income Security Act, if a bank, insurance company, or registered investment adviser makes the investment decisions, or if the plan has total assets in excess of $5 million;

3. A charitable organization, corporation, or partnership with assets exceeding $5 million;

4. A director, executive officer, or general partner of the company selling the securities;

5. A business in which all the equity owners are accredited investors;

6. A natural person who has individual net worth, or joint net worth with the person's spouse, that exceeds $1 million at the time of the purchase, excluding the value of the primary residence of such person;

7. A natural person with income exceeding $200,000 in each of the two most recent years or joint income with a spouse exceeding $300,000 for those years and a reasonable expectation of the same income level in the current year; or

8. A trust with assets in excess of $5 million, not formed to acquire the securities offered, whose purchases a sophisticated person makes.

This definition comes from Rule 501 of the SEC's Regulation D.

The accredited investor can be of considerable importance when a company is interested in the sale of unregistered securities, as described in the next section.

## Regulation D Stock Sales

Regulation D provides an exemption from the normal stock registration requirement, and is most useful when a company is still privately held. There are different rules and allowed funding amounts available under Regulation D, which are described in its Rules 504, 505, and 506. In general, to sell shares under Regulation D, a company must follow these rules:

- Only sell shares to accredited investors.
- Investors cannot be contacted through a general solicitation, such as advertising or free seminars open to the public.
- If shares are sold over a long time period, prove that all sales are covered by Regulation D. This can be proven by documenting a financing plan, selling the same type of stock to all investors, showing that all shares are sold for the same type of consideration, *and* by proving that the sales are being made for the same general purpose.

Because of the inability to advertise a stock sale, companies usually have to turn to investment bankers, who contact their clients to see who is interested in buying shares. The bankers impose a fee for this service, which is a percentage of the amount of funds generated.

If a prospective investor is interested in buying shares, the company sends them a boilerplate questionnaire to fill out, in which they state that they are accredited investors. This form provides the company with legal protection, in case the SEC questions whether the stock issuance is protected by Regulation D.

Investors then send their money to an escrow account that is maintained by a third party, until such time as the total amount of funding meets the minimum requirement set by the company. The investment banker then extracts its fee from the escrowed funds, the company collects its cash, and the company's stock transfer agent sends stock certificates to the investors.

Shares issued under Regulation D are not initially registered, which means that a restriction statement appears on the back of each certificate. This statement essentially prohibits the shareholder from selling to a third party.

This restriction on resale of the stock is usually a considerable concern for all but the most long-term investors. Accordingly, investors like to see one or more of the following guarantees being offered by a company:

- *Piggyback rights*. The company promises to include their shares in any stock registration statement that it may eventually file with the SEC. This is a near-universal inclusion in a Regulation D offering, since it does not impose an immediate obligation on the company.
- *Registration promise*. The company promises to file a registration statement with the SEC by a certain date. If the company is currently privately held, this promise essentially requires it to become publicly held, along with the various ongoing SEC filing requirements that are part of being a public company. A more onerous agreement will even require the company to issue additional stock if it does not obtain SEC approval of the registration statement by a certain date.

The downside of using a Registration D stock sale is that investors typically want something extra in exchange for buying unregistered stock. This may take the form of a reduced price per share. In addition, investors may demand warrants, which are a formal right to buy additional company stock at a certain exercise price.

---

**EXAMPLE**

Hegemony Toy Company sells 10,000 shares of its common stock for $10.00, along with 10,000 warrants to buy additional shares of the company for the next three years at $10.00 per share. The price of the company's stock later rises to $17.00, at which point the investor uses his warrant privileges to buy an additional 10,000 shares at $10.00 each. If he can then have the shares registered and sells them at the $17.00 market price, he will pocket a profit of $70,000 on his exercise of the warrants.

---

A company is paying a steep price if it issues warrants and then experiences a sharp increase in its stock price, since the recipient of the warrants will eventually buy shares from the company at what will then be an inordinately low price. If the company had not issued warrants, it would instead be able to later sell shares at the full market price.

If an investor wants one warrant for every share purchased, this is called 100% warrant coverage. If an investor agrees to one warrant for every two shares purchased, this is called 50% warrant coverage. These are the two most common warrant issuance terms, though any proportion of warrants to shares purchased may be agreed to.

An even more serious downside of using Regulation D is when prospective investors insist upon buying preferred stock, rather than common stock. Preferred stock may include a number of oppressive terms, such as favorable conversion rights into common stock, the payment of dividends, and perhaps even override voting privileges concerning the sale of the company or other matters.

Given the number of rights that investors may demand in a Regulation D stock sale, it is best to only use this approach when the company is operating from a position of strength, where it does not have an immediate need for cash.

## Regulation A Stock Sales

The preceding discussion of Regulation D was oriented toward stock sales to accredited investors. What if a company does not have access to this group of wealthy investors, or cannot find any who are willing to invest? An alternative is available under the Regulation A exemption.

Under Regulation A, a company is limited to raising no more than $5 million per year. Also, there is no limit to the number of investors who can buy the company's stock, and none of these investors need to be classified as accredited investors. Further, the company is not required to file any ongoing reports with the SEC. Finally, the shares sold under Regulation A are *not restricted*. The lack of a stock restriction should eliminate the need for any price discounts to investors, or the issuance of warrants. However, any company using this exemption is presumably so small that the market for its shares is microscopic, which means that investors will still have a difficult time selling their shares.

Of the maximum $5 million that can be raised, $1.5 million can be stock that is being sold by existing shareholders (though there are limitations on stock sales by company affiliates). Thus, Regulation A can be an avenue through which investors holding unregistered stock can sell their shares. The remaining allowable amount under the Regulation must be in the form of funds raised for use by the company.

There are some restrictions on the use of Regulation A. This exemption cannot be used under the following circumstances:

- The company has been investigated by the SEC for disclosure problems during the preceding five years
- The SEC is currently reviewing a registration statement filed by the company
- Any affiliates of the company, or its underwriter, have been convicted of a securities-related crime within the past 10 years

If a company qualifies for this exemption, the basic process flow is to issue an SEC-reviewed offering circular to attract investors, then file a Form 1-A with the SEC, then sell shares, and then file a Form 2-A at regular intervals until the offering has been completed. Though the filing requirements associated with this exemption are less than those required for an initial public offering, they are still substantial enough to require the services of an attorney and accountant. A company may find that the expense of using the Regulation A exemption is not sufficiently offset by the relatively minor amount of cash that can be raised with it.

In short, Regulation A is designed to be a moderately streamlined way to raise a small amount of cash. If there is a need to raise larger amounts of cash without going public, the Regulation D exemption is a better choice.

## Rule 144 Stock Sales

The investor relations department may not be directly involved in the sale of company stock. However, it will most definitely be on the receiving end of repeated inquiries concerning how investors can have the restrictions removed from their stock certificates. The most comprehensive way to do so is for a company to file a registration statement with the SEC. However, this filing is very expensive and can be prolonged. A possible alternative is the SEC's Rule 144.

Under Rule 144, someone who wants to sell his share holdings to the public must abide by these five conditions:

- *Holding period.* If the issuing company is a public company and is making its regularly-scheduled filings with the SEC, the shareholder must hold the shares for at least six months. The holding period begins when the shareholder bought and paid for the shares.
- *Adequate current information.* The issuing company must be currently fulfilling its filing obligations with the SEC.
- *Trading volume formula.* If the shareholder is an affiliate of the issuing company, the maximum number of shares that can be sold during any three-month period cannot exceed the greater of 1% of the outstanding shares of the same class being sold, or if the class is listed on a stock exchange, the greater of 1% or the average reported weekly trading volume during the four weeks preceding the filing of a notice of sale on Form 144. If shares are only listed over-the-counter, then they can only be sold using the 1% measurement.
- *Ordinary brokerage transactions.* If the seller is an affiliate of the company, all stock sales made by the seller must be handled as routine trading transactions. Brokers cannot receive more than a normal commission on these sales. The seller and broker are not allowed to solicit orders to buy the shares that are up for sale.
- *Notice of proposed sale.* If the seller is an affiliate of the company, the SEC must be informed of the proposed sale on Form 144 if the sale is for more than 5,000 shares or the aggregate dollar amount is greater than $50,000 in any three-month period. Further, the sale must take place within three months of filing the Form 144. If the shares are not sold, an amended notice must be filed.

If the seller is not an affiliate of the company, and has not been an affiliate for at least three months, the only applicable requirement is that the shares be held for one year from the purchase or receipt date.

Both affiliates and non-affiliates must first have the restriction statement removed from their share certificates before the certificates can be sold. To do this, the issuing company's attorney must send an opinion letter to the company's stock transfer agent, allowing the legend to be removed. To initiate this process, the investor should contact the company (not the attorney or the transfer agent) to inquire about the legend removal procedure. The paperwork that must eventually be sent to the stock transfer agent in order to complete a legend removal is:

- The original stock certificate
- Form 144
- Issuing company authorization letter to remove the restriction
- Legal opinion from the issuing company's attorney

---

**Tip:** If shareholders inquire about using Rule 144, remind them that the related legal opinion is only valid for 90 days, after which they will have to obtain a replacement opinion if any shares designated for sale have not yet been sold.

---

## Summary

At some point during its life, a privately held company will probably issue stock under Regulation D, which will result in the issuance of restricted stock. The filing requirements and low funding cap on the Regulation A exemption make it a less common alternative. It is also common for both privately and publicly held companies to issue restricted stock to employees or outsiders as payment for services rendered, or to the shareholders of acquired companies.

Once a company has gone public and there is an active market for its shares, the investor relations department should expect to be regularly dealing with investors who want to have the restrictions removed from their share certificates, so that they can sell the shares. Thus, it is *useful* for investor relations personnel to know about how restricted stock is sold or otherwise issued, but it is *essential* for them to know how stock restrictions are removed.

# Chapter 18
# The Road Show

## Introduction

A road show involves traveling to meet with a number of investors, in order to present an overview of the company to them. A road show may involve a general discussion of the business, or a more tightly-defined fund raising pitch. In either case, the road show is one of the key tasks of the investor relations department.

In this chapter, we describe the nature of the two main types of road shows, as well as how to create a presentation. We also note the many logistical aspects of road shows, and other related topics.

> **Related Podcast Episodes:** Episodes 99 and 102 of the Accounting Best Practices Podcast discuss road shows. You can listen to them at: **accounting-tools.com/podcasts** or **iTunes**

## The Fund Raising Road Show

As the name implies, a fund raising road show is a series of meetings with investors, with the specific intention of raising funds from them. During a road show, the presentation team will likely be accompanied by an investment banker, who has arranged all of the meetings with potential investors. These investors are likely to be fund managers, who are responsible for investing the funds with which they have been entrusted by clients. Because any one fund manager could potentially invest a very large amount in a company, each one deserves a private presentation.

### Road Show Routing

When a company plans to raise money through an investment banker, the banker typically issues a notification to his or her contacts throughout the country. If any investors are interested, the banker schedules them so that the presentation team can visit several investors in a row in one city, and then move on to the next city and present to the next cluster of interested parties. In some cities where there are large numbers of prospective investors, such as New York and Chicago, the presentation team will probably schedule an entire trip to just that one city, and then continue with their road show to other cities in the following week.

> **Tip:** If there are multiple visits scheduled in one city, it will be increasingly likely as the day goes by that the team will fall behind in its meeting schedule. If so, the investment banker should call ahead to the next scheduled investor to warn them of the delay. In addition, block out an open period in the schedule midway through the day, which allows the team to catch up on its schedule.

## The Presentation Team

The CEO should conduct the majority of the formal presentation, and respond to most of the questions from investors. This is because an investor who may be considering placing multiple millions of dollars with a business wants (and deserves to have) face time with the person responsible for that business. The chief financial officer will handle the more technical financial aspects of a presentation, but there should be no question that the CEO is delivering the bulk of the material. In those cases where a company competes based on its technology, it may be necessary to also include the company's chief technology officer in the presentation. The investor relations officer is typically present for this type of road show, but his or her presentation time is minimal.

## Presentation Format

The typical road show presentation is for about 90 minutes. A prospective investor may bring several associates or aides, but expect the total group size to be quite small. The investment banker attends all meetings, but mostly confines his or her comments to introductions at the beginning of a meeting, and inquiries about the investor's interest in the company at the end of a meeting. The typical meeting format is for the presentation team to walk through a handout that describes the company, its need for cash, and how it plans to use the cash (see the Presentation section for more information). The investor's team then peppers the presenters with questions. There is usually no need for a projector, since the group size is so small.

Before each meeting, the investment banker should brief the CEO and CFO about the types of investments that each investor prefers, so that they can tailor their presentations to address the issues that the investors want to learn about. Also, it is useful to determine at the start of each meeting how much an investor knows about the company's industry; it may be necessary to adapt the presentation to add or subtract information to make it match the knowledge of the investor.

Always assume that this meeting belongs to the investor, not the company. Therefore, if the investor wants to immediately ask questions, or set aside the formal presentation entirely, then go ahead and do whatever the investor wants. After all, the entire point of the meeting is for the investor to learn about the company and the safety of any investment made in it – so let the investor determine how to acquire that information.

> **Tip:** Consider sending a fact sheet to each investor in advance of the meeting. This gives the investor's team time to formulate questions for the presenters, and so improves the quality of the information they will glean from the meeting.

It is rather unusual for an investor to be rude in his questioning or general behavior. Most investors are simply trying to make a decision about whether to invest. If they decide that the company does not meet their investment parameters, they politely terminate the meeting and later tell the investment banker that they are declining participation in the funding round. They have no reason to lambast the CEO with pointed barbs about how to improve the company, since that is not the reason for the meeting.

Someone on the presentation team should write down the questions being asked. If the same questions keep coming up during multiple presentations, it is likely that the team needs to incorporate the topic into their standard presentation. At a minimum, the team should be prepared with a consistent response to the questions that keep arising.

> **Tip:** A good time to discuss investor questions is during the drive between presentation locations. This allows the team to continually enhance the content of their presentation from meeting to meeting.

### Summary

The fund raising road show is critical for obtaining debt and equity funding. Given its importance, the presentation team should be willing to customize its presentation for each investor meeting, as well as to meet wherever and whenever investors want. This is not the case for a non-deal road show, which we address next.

## The Non-Deal Road Show

As the name implies, a non-deal road show is one in which you are not attempting to raise money. Instead, the intent is to educate the investment community about the company. By doing so, they may be more inclined to investigate the company further, and perhaps buy its stock.

### Road Show Timing

A non-deal road show is normally conducted shortly after a company has released its quarterly results in a Form 10-Q or its annual results in a Form 10-K. By doing so, the presenters on the road show will be at little risk of disclosing any information that is not already public knowledge, since the most recent information should have just been issued to the SEC. Conversely, the longer the time interval between the public release of financial statements and a road show, the greater the risk that someone will make an inadvertent disclosure of material, non-public information (see the Regulation FD chapter for more information).

> **Tip:** If there are any residual facts that may come up in a road show that have not yet been disclosed, consider including them in a Form 8-K or press release just prior to the road show.

Conversely, road shows are never scheduled during the weeks immediately following the end of a reporting quarter, since the presenting team will likely know the details of how the company performed, and may let slip information about those results that has not yet been made available to the public (see the Regulation FD chapter).

As we will discuss shortly, there are a large number of attendees at non-deal road show presentations, so you should lock down meeting dates and times well in advance, so that most prospective attendees can block out the time to attend. Ideally, lock down road show dates at the beginning of the year, and do not alter them.

**Road Show Routing**

As just noted, the purpose of a non-deal road show is to educate the investment community. More specifically, it is about educating a *large proportion* of the investment community, and preferably people who have not come into contact with the company in the past. This means that the presentation team should continually target new geographic locations, to gain exposure to a larger number of new investors. Conversely, the team should avoid revisiting the same investor groups over and over again, since they already have an in-depth knowledge of the company, and are unlikely to invest in the company now if they had not already done so in the past.

> **Tip:** A recent survey reveals that the top road show destination is New York City, followed by London, Boston, and San Francisco.

The typical investor relations department does not have a sufficient number of contacts to set up its own non-deal road shows. Instead, rely upon an investment banker or an investor relations firm, which likely has an extensive contacts list. These firms make contacts on behalf of the company and arrange for meeting space, so that the management team only has to appear at the designated time and make its presentation. The exact routing of a road show will be driven to some extent by where the investment banker or investor relations firm has clients.

> **Tip:** If a road show is scheduled for just a single region, you can probably rely upon the contacts of a single investment banker or investor relations firm to fill the meetings calendar. However, a national tour may call for the services of several firms, with each one arranging for meetings in a separate region. If you want to expand the number of new attendees, it may be necessary to engage the services of different investor relations firms, since they all have different client lists.

Though we have just pointed out that you may rely upon the contact list of a third party to meet with investors, you should use a non-deal road show to compile your *own* list of contacts. This means collecting business cards during a road show, and entering them into an investor relations contacts database.

> **Tip:** Encourage attendees at each presentation to drop their business cards in a box in order to qualify for a door prize.

An interesting variation on routing a road show is to schedule one or more meetings near the site of an industry trade show. This is most efficient for the management team, which may already be attending the trade show. It may also work for those investors most interested in the industry in which the company operates, since they may also be attending the trade show. At a minimum, this approach is useful for meeting with any investors who live near the site of the trade show.

## Sell Side Participation

Sell side firms are interested in arranging road shows, since they will likely generate commissions on the purchase of company stock by their clients. Since their client lists undoubtedly include investors with whom the company does not currently have a relationship, the use of sell side firms for road shows is a win-win proposition for these firms and the company.

> **Tip:** A sell side firm may want to arrange an entire road show for a company, thereby locking up all prospective commissions for itself. From the company's perspective, it might be better to include multiple sell side firms in different portions of a road show, so that more of these firms are beholden to the company.

When a public company is too small to attract the attention of a sell side firm, hire an investor relations firm to arrange meetings with investors. Even though this is an out-of-pocket cost for the company, it still brings the company into contact with new investors, and so is a worthwhile expenditure.

## The Presentation Team

A non-deal road show does not always involve the company CEO. If the CEO can find the time for these presentations, that certainly makes a positive impression on the audience, but his or her presence is not always required or expected. If a company routinely engages in quarterly non-deal road shows, the presentation burden may be so great that it would be impossible for the CEO to attend every meeting without seriously detracting from his or her other tasks. It is entirely possible that the investor relations officer can handle a significant part of the presentation work, especially when the company schedules a large number of road show meetings per year. The CFO may be called upon to accompany the investor relations officer for at least part of a road show.

## Road Show Attendees

It is possible that some road show attendees will be individual investors. However, since you want to educate a large proportion of the investment community about the company, it is better to present to stockbrokers to a considerable extent. Stockbrokers advise many clients, so there is a multiplier effect when presenting to them. Ideally, presentations to a few hundred stockbrokers during a road show equates to putting your information into the hands of several thousand investors. However, the presentation needs to be a good one, or else that multiplier effect will work in reverse – the stockbroker will be more inclined to steer his clients *away* from your company.

Stockbrokers are among the least formal of all members of the investment community. A few have an extraordinarily relaxed dress code, so expect to see a few Hawaiian shirts in the audience. Also, they tend to wander into meetings late and leave early. This is not necessarily a sign of disrespect to the presentation team; instead, keep in mind that stockbrokers have to be available to their clients at all times, as well as monitor the markets, so they will only attend for those brief periods when they are not otherwise booked.

> **Tip:** The better stockbrokers are likely to be the ones who show up late and leave early, because they are so busy with their clients. It is most important to obtain their business cards for your mailing list, so have someone stationed by the door to request this information.

When dealing with stockbrokers, it is best to present to them during a lunch meeting, when they are most likely to be available. This means offering them a free meal (with drinks), and keeping the presentation short. If you can keep the presentation from exceeding 20 minutes, this gives them time for questions. Otherwise, if the team drones through a boring presentation, expect the stockbrokers to leave early. If you are presenting a massive hour-long presentation, there will probably not be many people left in the room by the end of it; and the people remaining are likely to be the least productive stockbrokers who have the fewest clients.

> **Tip:** Stockbrokers want to know how they will make money from your company, so make multiple references to the company's value as an investment opportunity throughout the presentation.

Stockbrokers rarely engage in any preliminary research about a company before attending a road show presentation, so expect a broad range of questions – some of them downright odd. Nonetheless, nearly all questions will be repeated as you proceed through a road show, so the team will eventually become comfortable with answering many types of questions.

> **Tip:** To ensure that everyone receives a copy of the company's handout, place one on each seat in the meeting room prior to the meeting, and also leave additional copies by the doors to the room.

### Presentation Format

Since a non-deal road show is intended to address a large audience, use a projector and projection screen. Given the size of some audiences, which may exceed 50, it is not workable to only issue a handout to participants. It is difficult to lead a large audience through a handout, and they will also be less attentive.

If the presentation team is comfortable with doing so, they can even turn off the projector, walk into the audience area, and make comments without notes. This can greatly increase audience interest in the presentation, but is only recommended when presenters are extremely comfortable with their material and have an engaging speaking style.

Though we do not recommend a handout as the primary form of presentation, there should be a brief handout that succinctly states the main points of the presentation. It should also prominently state the investor relations officer's contact information, as well as the name of the company and its ticker symbol.

> **Tip:** If the presentation team plans to meet with several hundred people, it is easiest to prepare handouts in advance and have them delivered to the hotel where the team plans to stay. In addition, always travel with enough handouts for the next presentation, in case the mailed versions are lost.

### Presentation Follow Up

After the presentation team completes the road show, the investor relations staff should use any attendance forms and business cards collected to create a contact list for everyone who attended a meeting. The staff should *immediately* issue a thank you note to all attendees, as well as a request to contact the investor relations department if they have any other questions about the company. Also include a fact sheet about the business, and other public relations materials that may seem appropriate.

If attendees indicate that they want to remain on the company's mailing list, send them a quarterly summary of the company's results, as well as copies of the more significant press releases. Do not abuse the mailing list privilege – if someone does not want to be on the company's mailing list, remove them from it at once.

> **Tip:** Ask attendees if there was anything about the company's presentation that could be improved. Though the response rate will be low, there may be a few pertinent comments that can be used to improve the presentation.

**Summary**

The non-deal road show is one of the most valuable tools of the investor relations department, for it allows them to interact with investors, and gives the investment community a chance to meet company managers and learn about the business. Accordingly, the investor relations officer should certainly schedule several non-deal road shows per year, and possibly substantially more.

The amount of work required for presentations may make it appear that a never-ending series of road shows will consume an inordinate amount of time. However, keep in mind that the presentation for a non-deal road show does not have to be completely overhauled every time the presentation team goes on the road. Instead, each new iteration usually only requires a few minor tweaks. If the presentation is relatively consistent, this means that the presentation team will eventually memorize most of it, and so will require a minimal amount of preparation time. Thus, advance preparation looks more like a refresher class than a full-blown dress rehearsal.

## The Reverse Road Show

On occasion, investors may come to the company premises, where the management team delivers a presentation to them. This approach can be useful to engage the interest of local investors who have a casual interest in the company. However, this pool of investors will soon become fully-educated about the company, which means that the use of reverse road shows will soon thereafter be confined to highly-interested investors who are willing to travel to the company. This latter group will not spend time on such a visit unless they are in the final stages of "kicking the tires" of a business, prior to making a large investment.

If a reverse road show is oriented toward this latter group of investors, the company should include as much of a facility tour as the investors want to see. A facility tour may include the local plant manager, since this person is the most knowledgeable about local operations, and can most thoroughly answer investor questions.

> **Tip:** An interesting variation on the reverse road show concept is available to those companies that have a large number of locations. You could arrange to hold road show meetings at local company locations, which essentially combines a facility tour with a presentation, and so maximizes the information given to participants.

## The Presentation

There must be a formal presentation document for any road show, both to ensure that the team covers all speaking points and to form the basis for a handout. The document is almost always created using PowerPoint, which is the standard presentation software. A road show presentation usually encompasses the following points:

- *Introduction.* State what the company does on a single slide.

- *The company as an investment*. State why the company is a good invest-ment.
- *Strategy*. In just a few points, describe the company's competitive strategy, such as franchising, expanding into new product lines, and so forth.
- *Competitive stance*. Describe how the company is competitively positioned within its industry, and how the company protects that position. Be sure to mention "hard" defenses, such as patents and regulatory approvals.
- *Market size*. Note the size of the market in which the company competes. Consider putting the source of this information in a handout, since investors may want to verify this information.
- *Customers*. If you have large, well-known customers, state who they are and the portion of the company's total business that they represent. Also, note the general types of customers.
- *Financial statements*. Include a condensed income statement and balance sheet that shows the company's results and financial position for the past few years.
- *Resumes*. On a single slide, note the names, titles, and areas of responsibility of the most senior company executives.
- *Summarization*. On one slide, note the key points about the company that will be of importance to a prospective investor.

When creating the presentation, consider the following points:
- *Minimize the number of slides*. Do not burden the audience with an over-whelming number of slides. Instead, tighten the message being presented to focus on only the most important aspects of the business. Otherwise, a pro-longed presentation will leave the audience so muddled that they will not have a clear idea of what the company does or how it creates value. A presentation that contains 100 slides is far too large; there is no perfect number of slides, but something closer to 20 slides will be more cogent.
- *Minimize the information on each slide*. As was the case with the number of slides, do not bury the audience with too much information on each slide. Try extending this concept to not just the number of words on a slide, but also to the length of the words. Ideally, the word count per slide should be short, as should the syllable count. Perhaps as few as a dozen words could be sufficient. Keep in mind that slides should contain only enough infor-mation to highlight the points being made by the presenter.
- *Minimize introductions*. Do not waste a great deal of time on introductions. Simply state the name and position of each presenter, without waxing lyrical about their accomplishments.

---

**Tip:** When there is too much information to present, presenters feel rushed and ask attendees to hold their questions until the end – which does not achieve the goal of having investors learn about the company on *their* terms.

---

The minimization recommendations noted here can be surprisingly difficult to implement. Everyone on the presentation team always has a favorite slide that they do not want to have removed or reduced, which leads to endless bickering over how the presentation can be pared down. In addition, those with larger egos will insist on spending too much time on their own accomplishments, which can probably only be completely resolved by excluding them from the presentation team. Ultimately, the final structure of the presentation will be based to a large extent on who wields the largest political club within the presentation team. The result is usually a presentation that is too long.

> **Tip:** If the company is using an investment banker or road show advisor, bring them into the presentation discussion. Their experience with what makes a good presentation may convince the team to alter their presentation.

## Road Show Preparation

A great many managers would rather lose a limb than make a presentation. Or, they may be comfortable in one-on-one meetings but not in making presentations to large groups (or vice versa). This can be a real problem, since a potential investor is more likely to invest in a company whose managers are capable of comfortably discussing their business in public.

It is possible to reduce road show jitters by engaging in an appropriate amount of prior preparation. Here are several suggestions:

1. *Individual preparation.* Encourage each participant to verbally go through his or her presentation several times, and adjust the presentation material as necessary. The author prefers to practice a presentation four times; by the end of the fourth iteration, the presentation is running smoothly enough to proceed to the next step.

2. *Group presentation.* Assemble the presentation team and walk through the entire presentation together. Try to simulate the actual presentation environment as closely as possible. Thus, if a presentation will involve standing at the head of a conference room table in a business suit, do the same in the group presentation.

3. *Obtain investment banker input.* Have the company's investment banker attend a dress rehearsal and suggest changes to the presentation. This may include adjusting the amount of time required to complete each slide, combining or separating slides, or reshuffling content.

4. *Adjust presentation incrementally.* During a presentation to a "real" audience, have anyone not actively presenting take notes on how the presentation can be improved, the questions asked, and the reaction of the audience to various points made. This information is extremely useful for adjusting the presentation through a series of iterations.

After a sufficient number of repetitions, there will be no need to make further adjustments to the presentation, and the presentation team should be thoroughly comfortable with their material (and less nervous).

> **Tip:** If a presenter still appears uncomfortable in making a presentation, despite the preparation tips noted here, consider shifting as much of that person's material to someone else, thereby minimizing the period during which they may suffer from stage fright.

In addition to the presentation itself, spend some time addressing questions that are likely to arise. If the company has had road shows in the past, this is simply a matter of looking back through the notes taken concerning questions asked by attendees. Common questions are likely to be in the general areas of:

- Threats to the business
- Barriers to entry
- Actions of competitors
- Trends in financial results

The team should agree upon the best response to each question. Also, it may make sense to designate someone to answer a certain group of questions, if that person has the best background for doing so. For example, the CFO usually handles all questions of a financial nature.

It is also extremely useful to gain some familiarity with the audience in advance. To do so, stand in the doorway to the meeting room, and greet everyone who comes in. You do not necessarily have to shake hands, but make eye contact and say something. It is even better to follow up with some small talk. Then, when you begin your speech, you will already have some familiarity with the audience. Also, because the audience has met you prior to the presentation, they will be more likely to be tolerant of any gaffes made during the presentation.

Conversely, and despite the undoubted inclinations of the presentation team, the presenters should not stand together in a group and ignore the audience. Doing so gives the impression that the presenters are aloof from their audience, and also does not give the presenters a chance to become familiar with their listeners.

> **Tip:** If the presentation team wants to work out the bugs in its presentation, consider presenting to a less-important audience first, so that the team can make changes before going in front of a more important group.

## Road Show Logistics and Other Meeting Issues

Road shows involve an immense amount of travel, as well as dozens of meetings that the presentation team wants to attend in a timely manner. In order to have a successful road show, be cognizant of a large number of logistical and other issues that can have a negative impact. These issues, along with improvement suggestions, include:

- *Air transport.* Given the state of the air traffic system, it is always best to fly the night before a presentation, or at least plan to arrive several hours in advance of the meeting. Jet maintenance problems, airline strikes, weather, and so forth can delay flights by many hours, so *do not* schedule a tight connection to a meeting.
- *Building access.* If meetings are being held in New York City, all of the major office buildings have rigid security requirements. Each member of the presentation team must show a driver's license to the security staff and receive a visitor's badge. Build a few extra minutes into the meeting schedule to allow for these security measures.
- *Car transport.* Whenever possible, arrange for a car and driver. Though this arrangement is certainly more expensive, it allows the team to concentrate solely upon its task of making great presentations, rather than worrying about how to find the next meeting location and where to park. Though the cost of a car and driver is much higher than for a simple car rental, the improved level of transport efficiency makes it nearly mandatory. Also, obtain the contact information for the driver at least one day in advance, to make it easier to coordinate pickup times and locations.

> **Tip:** If you are renting your own car, designate someone as the navigator. The navigator should have a GPS-equipped phone, as well as printed instructions for how to reach every address listed on the daily itinerary.

- *Cell phones.* The entire team should turn off their cell phones or set them to vibrate before a meeting begins. It is not only distracting, but also rude to have a cell phone ring during a presentation. If you turn on a phone between meetings to check for messages, there is a strong risk of forgetting to turn it off again for the next meeting. To be completely safe, consider turning off all phones for the entire day, or having them set to vibrate for the entire trip.
- *Clothing.* Every member of the presentation team should be dressed formally. Attendees will most certainly notice if a presenter appears in a polyester suit, or if the suit is rumpled. Accordingly, everyone on the team should pay fanatical attention to their clothes. This means bringing more shirts or blouses than you would normally think necessary, as well as ironing anything during the trip that appears to be even slightly wrinkled. Also, some presentations are held in poorly ventilated offices which can overheat quickly, so the team should invest in lightweight suits.

> **Tip:** If you are presenting in one city for several days, considering scheduling enough time partway through the day to return to the hotel, change clothes, and send out your wrinkled clothes for overnight dry cleaning.

- *Dinners.* A dutiful investment banker or investor relations consultant will stuff the team's day with an unending stream of meetings that may include breakfast and lunch meetings. By dinner time, the team will probably be exhausted. If possible, try to leave dinner open, so that the team can relax. Of course, throw out this advice at once if an investor requests a dinner meeting. If any team members are so tired that they would not be an asset during a dinner meeting with an investor, excuse them from attending.
- *Handouts.* When a company is trying to raise money, handouts will contain more material, and so will be heavier. Nonetheless, it would be catastrophic to lose them, so a junior person on the presentation team will probably be tasked with carrying around a large number of them. For non-deal road shows where handouts are given away in large numbers, consider traveling with a modest number of them, and mailing the bulk of the handouts forward to each city in which the team will be traveling.

---

**Tip:** Keep a sufficient number of handouts in carry-on luggage (*not* checked baggage) for the next scheduled meeting, so there is minimal risk of interfering with that meeting.

---

- *Itinerary.* As a road show progresses, there will be changes to the itinerary. Whoever is managing the team's travel arrangements is responsible for keeping the team apprised of any itinerary changes, preferably with a printed handout of the remaining schedule. In addition, the driver should receive a copy of the itinerary every day, so that he can plan the best routing from one location to the next. Be sure to supplement the itinerary with contact information, as well as driving instructions to reach each meeting location.

---

**Tip:** Have different people retain copies of the itinerary, to reduce the risk of losing it.

---

- *Meeting arrival.* Whenever possible, the team should arrive early, especially for non-deal road shows where they may need to adjust the presentation equipment in the room.
- *Projector.* The road show organizer is responsible for supplying a projector. However, it can be catastrophic if the presentation is heavily dependent on a projected image, and the projector then fails. Accordingly, consider bringing a smaller-size, high-resolution projector on every road show, strictly as a backup device.
- *Seating arrangements.* The presentation team always gets the worst seats. Individual investors, fund managers, and stockbrokers either have the money or access to it, so they always get the best seats. In particular, if there is a large amount of sunshine entering through a window, do not make the attendees stare into the sunlight and squint. Instead, the presentation team faces the window.

- *Spares*. A variety of items may fail during a road show, such as cables, cell phones, laptops, and laser pointers. Accordingly, always ensure that there is a backup for every device.

> **Tip:** During a road show, always have access to the electronic files for handouts and presentations, in case changes must be made during the trip.

All of the details noted here may indicate that the sheer volume of logistics associated with a protracted road show can make it one of the more annoying investor relations activities. To reduce the pressure, consider hiring a firm that specializes in managing road show logistics. They handle all meeting, housing, and transport arrangements.

After a road show has been completed, consider adding the presentation materials to the investor relations section of the company's web site. This could be as simple as posting the PowerPoint presentation from the road show, or it could even include a video of the presentation.

## Road Show Boredom

We cannot leave the road show topic without pointing out the extraordinary boredom of the process. Though we have pointed out that some presenters can suffer from nerves, this problem will vanish after the umpteenth repetition of a presentation. Instead, you will experience the following aspects of boredom:

- *Presentation volume*. There may be road show meetings over breakfast and lunch, and perhaps even dinner. In addition, expect several presentations in the morning, and even more in the afternoon. All of these meetings are essentially the same, so you may find yourself forgetting whether you made a point during the current presentation, or if you may have made it multiple times in a single presentation.
- *Repetitive questions*. After a certain number of presentations, you will find that you have answered every possible question. After that, there will be only a small number of outlier questions that are actually unique. Most of the time, you are responding to questions that you have heard dozens of times before.
- *CEO focus*. On any road show, investors want to meet with and listen to the CEO. Everyone else on the presentation team has a much smaller speaking role, which may devolve into answering just a few stray questions on specialty topics. This means that everyone but the CEO somehow has to stay awake through each meeting, which becomes progressively more difficult as the number of meetings piles up.

The basic problem is that investors want to meet with the presentation team in person, rather than talking to them on the phone or a video conference call, so there is no way to circumvent the road show. Boredom is an integral part of the road show, especially for those not centrally involved in actual presentations, and there is no way to avoid it.

## Summary

There is an enormous difference between the fund-raising orientation of a road show and the bulk presentation of information in a non-deal road show. When the orientation is on fund raising, road show meetings are longer and are one-on-one with specific investors, with meetings being held wherever investors want to meet. A non-deal road show is on an almost industrial scale, with each presentation designed to be an exact replica of the last presentation. In the latter case, meetings have far more attendees, and so are scheduled in larger meeting rooms. Thus, the information imparted, the number of attendees, and meeting locations are completely different, depending upon the type of road show.

No matter which type of road show you are engaged in, we cannot emphasize enough the need for a *short* presentation. Brevity makes it easier for someone to understand the business, so do not bury them with detail. A 15-minute presentation is quite acceptable. Anything longer than 30 minutes likely requires pruning.

Finally, the question of road show effectiveness persistently arises. Senior members of the management team must spend time preparing for road shows, as well as presenting the company to a large number of people. If a road show is designed to raise money directly from investors, it is quite easy to measure effectiveness – either the company raised money, or it did not. The effectiveness of a non-deal road show is nearly impossible to quantify, since it is more of a marketing activity than a fund-raising activity. In this case, the investor relations department should schedule as many road show meetings as its budget will allow, which will likely translate into a larger number of meetings for a larger and wealthier company.

# Chapter 19
# Third Party Investor Relations Services

## Introduction

There are a vast number of activities that the investor relations function might be responsible for – so many that it is nearly impossible to retain a sufficient level of in-house expertise to competently address them all. A responsible investor relations officer may find it necessary to hire the services of one or more outside firms to ensure that a company's investor relations goals are met. In this chapter, we address the types of third party investor relations services that are available.

> **Related Podcast Episode:** Episode 110 of the Accounting Best Practices Podcast discusses the National Investor Relations Institute. You can listen to it at: **accountingtools.com/podcasts** or **iTunes**

## The Investor Relations Consultant

Throughout this book, we allude to the special difficulties experienced by micro cap and nano cap companies in gaining attention in the investment community. Their tiny market capitalizations place them well beneath the notice of most (if not all) institutional investors, and most analysts. The result is a business that needs an alternative way to send its message to investors.

A possible option for these companies is to hire an investor relations consultant. The main value provided by this individual or business is a large number of contacts throughout the investment community, which they can provide in exchange for a monthly retainer and possibly company stock or warrants.

The usual result of hiring a consultant is an initial flurry of interest in the company's stock, which may increase its price for a short time. However, unless the company experiences fundamental improvements in its business, its stock price over the long term will probably revert back to where it was, simply because it is difficult to create an ongoing sense of excitement about a business that is, in essence, not changing. Thus, it is usually best to refrain from hiring a consultant until such time as the company actually has improved its financial performance to the point where it is worthwhile boosting public perception of why the company is now a better investment than had been the case in the past.

There are other situations where a consultant can be of use, especially where the level of in-house investor relations expertise is relatively low. All of the following are possible options:

- *Advisor to management.* The board of directors, CEO, or CFO may want the view of an outside expert on how the company is perceived in the marketplace, and on how its own operations are being run. This role tends to be on an occasional project-by-project basis.

- *Analyst contacts.* Many consultants have a large database of analysts who might be willing to provide coverage to a company. Consultants can provide introductions to these analysts.
- *Crisis intervention.* Some consultants specialize in how to deal with the public during such crisis situations as a catastrophic product failure or a hostile takeover attempt. This is more of a public relations activity than investor relations.
- *Event management.* The skill sets of some consulting firms are oriented towards the hands-on management of specific events, such as investor days, road shows, and annual meetings.
- *Regulatory knowledge.* A consultant may have detailed knowledge of the rules of the SEC and the various stock exchanges, and how they translate into requirements that a specific company must be aware of. Some consultants also monitor updates to regulations, and issue their interpretations of these updates to their clients.
- *Policies and procedures.* A consultant can use his knowledge of the investor relations policies, procedures, and forms used by other companies to construct systems that are tailored to the needs of a specific client.
- *Presentation skills.* Some consultants act as presentation coaches. They sit in on road show practice sessions and offer advice on presentation materials, speaking skills, and dress codes.
- *Writing skills.* Some consultants are expert writers, and can provide invaluable assistance in constructing press releases, scripts for earnings calls, and other presentation materials. They can also assist in the construction of fact sheets and annual reports. They may even have graphics departments that can provide the necessary visual enhancements to a key presentation.
- *In-house training.* If a company decides to promote someone into an investor relations position, it can retain the services of a consultant to provide initial and ongoing training to bring the employee up to the requisite knowledge level.
- *Web site construction and content.* A few consulting firms specialize in the construction and maintenance of the investor relations section of a company's website, including automatic feeds of some types of information into the site.
- *Surveys.* Consultants can run independent surveys of investors to determine their characteristics and how they view the company's value proposition and strategic direction.
- *Shareholder analysis.* Consultants can investigate the types of investors who buy the company's securities, and report back to management and the board of directors regarding how the proportions of different types of investors are changing over time, as well as changes in their geographic locations.

There is no such thing as a single investor relations consultant who can provide in-depth services in all of the areas just described. Instead, a consulting firm has a small number of areas in which it has deep knowledge, as well as more generic coverage of the other typical investor relations services. Thus, to obtain the best service, consider researching the skill levels of the various consultants in each of these fields, and hiring a small group of experts, each of which is assigned an area of specialization.

---

**Tip:** At a minimum, hire one firm that specializes in those activities associated with fund raising, and another firm to handle public relations – there tends to be a natural division between these two activities in the investor relations industry.

---

When evaluating investor relations firms, ask to see their list of current and recent clients. You may find that they have a large concentration of clients in a particular industry. This can be good if your business is also in that industry, since it implies that the firm has a deep knowledge of the investor relations nuances associated with a particular business area, such as oil exploration or biotechnology. The firm is also more likely to have extensive contacts within that industry. However, it could also mean that the firm does *not* have the expertise needed to provide services in a different industry.

If there is any question about where to cost-effectively invest cash in an investor relations consultant, always spend liberally for the initial public offering (IPO). An IPO may yield a massive influx of cash, so any assistance in creating a flawless road show and a superior investor presentation will have a handsome return on investment. The same logic applies to a secondary offering.

The prices charged by investor relations consultants can be quite high. The larger firms may insist on charging a monthly retainer for which only minimal billing detail is provided. Alternatively, smaller firms or individuals are more likely to agree to hourly billing rates and detailed explanations of the cost of each service provided. In a few cases, a consultant may be willing to provide services in exchange for company stock; this payment may be more palatable to a consultant if the company offers to include the shares in its next registration statement, so that the shares can be sold in the near future.

In summary, consultants can be used to supplement any area of investor relations weakness that a public company may have. If senior management wants a broad-based investor relations function, it will probably be necessary to budget for the ongoing services of a group of consultants.

## The Stock Transfer Agent

Publicly held companies use a stock transfer agent to maintain their shareholder records. This involves the following services:
- *Stock register*. The transfer agent maintains a current listing of who owns company shares. This listing is useful for determining the proportion of

ownership in the company by different types of investors, though this information can be obscured by the presence of *beneficial owners*, whose share holdings are hidden behind the name of their broker in the stock register.

- *Share issuance.* The transfer agent fills out and issues share certificates at the direction of the corporate secretary.
- *Share restriction removal.* Upon advice by counsel, the transfer agent can replace a share certificate with one that does not contain a trading restriction.
- *Proxy services.* Some transfer agents issue proxy notices to shareholders and tabulate their responses on behalf of the company.
- *Online voting.* Transfer agents may have an on-line voting option for shareholders, rather than the more traditional mail-in ballot.
- *Web reports.* Many stock transfer agents allow their client companies to directly access shareholder and proxy records, and download this information into electronic spreadsheets for further modeling.
- *Address cleanup.* Some transfer agents use a third party address cleanup service to correct the addresses of any shareholders for whom mailings have been returned as undeliverable by the postal service.
- *Dividend payment services.* A transfer agent can issue dividend payments to each shareholder of record, as well as stop payments and replace lost checks.

A stock transfer agent usually charges a monthly retainer for its services, as well as a charge for each individual transaction handled. These fees are kept relatively low, due to the number of competing services, so this is one of the lesser fees that a public company must deal with. Of more importance is transaction accuracy. For example, if a transfer agent has a history of issuing share certificates in the wrong amounts or to incorrect shareholder names, it is time to find a new transfer agent.

## The Proxy Solicitor

A company may want to contact its shareholders to obtain their votes for an upcoming director election or for a special election, such as a vote to be acquired by another company. In these cases, the investor relations officer may hire a proxy solicitor. A proxy solicitor contacts shareholders to obtain their proxy to vote in a certain direction on a ballot.

A proxy solicitor also maintains an ongoing record of who has voted and who has *not* voted, as well as which investors are opposed to or in favor of certain ballot issues. They can also establish whether a company has a known shareholder activist within the shareholder list, which can be useful for preparing for likely issues to be brought up by the activist.

Some institutional investors rely on proxy advisors for advice on how to vote on various company ballot issues. A proxy solicitor can delve into which institutional investors are using certain proxy advisors, and estimate how these investors will vote on certain issues, based on which proxy advisors they are using.

Proxy solicitors tend to bill on a monthly retainer basis, which can be expensive. They justify their worth based on their ability to influence shareholders to vote in the company's favor on ballot issues.

## Annual Meeting Voting

The voting process for the board of directors and other motions at the annual meeting is extremely clerical, and is routinely handled by a combination of a public company's stock transfer agent and a financial printing service. This topic is addressed in detail in the Annual Meeting Planning and Voting chapter.

## The Company-Paid Researcher

As noted in the Sell Side and Buy Side chapter, research reports about a company are usually created by independent analysts who either work for buy side or sell side firms. Their coverage is valued by many companies, since it makes investors more willing to invest in the company. Also, their third-party status earns them the trust of investors.

But what if a company is too small to attract the attention of an analyst? In this case, some companies resort to paying a researcher a set fee to write analysis reports about the company. A researcher may also have an investor following, who may be more inclined to invest in the company in the wake of a glowing research report. However, they will be *less* inclined to do so than if the researcher had been independent of the company, since there will be a perception that the researcher is biased.

A research report that a company pays for should be identified as such, including the exact relationship between the report writer and the company. Because the company's affiliation with the report is clearly stated, this means that the company is free to distribute it to anyone it wants. This is not the case with the reports created by independent analysts, since distributing their reports or posting them on the company's website would indicate a considerable amount of favoritism toward certain analysts over others.

> **Tip:** When selecting an outside research service, investigate its reputation for providing an independent viewpoint, rather than a slavish marketing promotion for a client company. The reports of those researchers with a more independent reputation are more likely to be accepted by the investment community.

> **Tip:** Pay for research reports in advance, which removes the temptation to pressure the report writer into creating an unfairly skewed report about the company in exchange for final payment.

In short, company-paid research may be a viable option for a smaller public company that is struggling to gain traction with investors.

## The Public Relations Firm

A publicly held company needs to continually send its message to the outside world – hence the inclusion of the word "public" in its designation as a public company. Many companies use a public relations firm to organize their communication efforts, as well as to ensure that a consistent message is sent. The best public relations firms already have extensive contacts with the business and general media, and so have a large edge over an in-house public relations staff in obtaining sweeping coverage of the company.

A public relations firm has an ongoing dialog with a public company's marketing and investor relations departments, as well as its CEO, outside auditors, lawyers, and attorneys to develop a complete picture of how the company wants to be presented to the outside world and how that picture coincides with its actual operations. The public relations firm then develops a message about the company and ensures that it is consistently issued to the outside world, which includes the media, investors, analysts, customers, local communities, and government entities. The firm may recommend certain communication channels over others, depending on the size of the company, its resources, and the intended recipients. The firm may also monitor the informational releases of a company's chief competitors, as well as conduct periodic surveys of the company's shareholders.

An alternative to a full-time relationship with a public relations firm is to only engage its services to deal with a specific event. For example, it might provide advice and handle the public relations for:

- An initial public offering
- A secondary offering
- An acquisition of another entity
- A hostile takeover bid from another company
- A crisis that could impact the company's reputation

Top-line public relations firms usually charge a monthly retainer fee, irrespective of the actual number of hours worked. Sole practitioners may be more amenable to working on an hourly basis. A typical progression is for a smaller public company to dabble in public relations with a close advisor, and then graduate to a larger firm once it validates the concept and allocates sufficient funding. It is generally best to eventually establish a long-term relationship with a public relations firm, which can then build up a solid knowledge base about how the company operates.

## Press Release Distribution Services

One of the most heavily used third party services is the press release distribution service. Depending on which service is used, press releases may be distributed to more than 1,000 daily newspapers, as well as radio and television stations and various types of Internet-based services. Users can elect to distribute internationally, or at much more refined levels, such as by region, industry, state, or city. Having a third party handle press release distribution is vastly easier and more comprehensive than attempting to manually send a press release to one recipient at a time. This can be a major time-saving service when the investor relations staff habitually issues a press release to coincide with the bulk of its Form 8-K issuances (see the SEC Filings chapter).

The two press release distribution services that work with the bulk of all public companies are Business Wire and PR Newswire. There are other distribution organizations, but these two offer such massive suites of additional services that most companies find it easier to work with one of them. Pricing is by individual press release.

Of the other services provided by these organizations, those that are of the most use to the investor relations department include:

- *SEC filings*. Conversion of SEC filings to the XBRL format and filing of the documents with the SEC.
- *Investor targeting*. Send press releases to lists of portfolio managers and financial analysts, sorting by such factors as geographic location, industry coverage, investment style, company market capitalization invested in, and rapidity of turnover within their portfolios.
- *Social responsibility*. Send press releases about the level of the company's social responsibility to funds, publications, universities, and national and television programs that deal with social responsibility issues.
- *Web site*. Construction and maintenance of the investor relations section of the company web site that incorporates instant posting of company press releases, interactive stock quotes and charts, investment calculators, all SEC filings, investor relations event calendars, and webcasting. These sites can also be configured for viewing on a mobile device.
- *Clipping service*. Monitoring of thousands of on-line news sources, television news, blogs, and social medial sites in multiple languages for any mention of the company, with clipped information sent to the investor relations staff every day and stored in an on-line database.

## NOBO Reporting

The investor relations staff may need to contact shareholders for such issues as proxy solicitations, surveys, and dividend reinvestment plans. This can be difficult, because the identities of a large proportion of shareholders are hidden behind their stockbrokers; their shares are held on a custodial basis by their brokerages. Thus, the shareholder list of a public company may include a small number of brokerages, each of which holds a large number of company shares which, in turn, are owned by their clients.

Most of these investors have signed paperwork with their stockbrokers to be *non-objecting beneficial owners*, or NOBOs. A NOBO permits the release of its name, mailing address, and share holdings to the companies whose stock it owns. To obtain NOBO contact information, a company must apply to Broadridge Financial Solutions, Inc. Broadridge can deliver a list of all NOBOs as of a given record date on paper, a CD-ROM, or peel and stick labels. E-mail addresses are not available.

> **Tip:** A NOBO report does not contain a listing of those shareholders who are registered directly with the company, nor will it list the names of any objecting beneficial owners who have not given permission for their names to be released.

Broadridge charges a mixed fee for this service that combines a minimum fee and a price per shareholder listed. A service request to Broadridge can be made directly, or through the company's stock transfer agent.

## Coordination of Third Party Services

If a public company were to engage the services of every entity just described in this chapter, it would soon pile up a noticeable additional monthly expense. Since many of the services just described are paid for with monthly retainers, a CEO might find it particularly disturbing that the company has taken on a substantial and recurring fixed cost.

It is only prudent to closely monitor this expense by appointing an employee to approve all invoices from third party service providers, as well as to oversee their activities. Since many of these third party services are doing work directly for the board of directors, CEO, or CFO, it is only reasonable to have the oversight person be at a fairly high responsibility level. Possible options are the investor relations officer, CFO, or vice president of sales and marketing, or dividing the oversight function for the various vendors among this group.

There are three areas in which third party services should be particularly well-coordinated with company operations and the designated supervisor. These areas are:

- *Reporting.* Each service provider should be required to prepare a monthly activities report, which can be useful in deciding whether the company is obtaining sufficient value for its payments.
- *Meeting scheduling.* Any service provider who needs inside knowledge of the company should literally be invited inside – that is, they should attend a number of regularly-scheduled meetings, which could include executive committee meetings and even board of directors meetings.
- *Policies and procedures.* The company and its service providers should agree upon a standard set of policies and procedures that all parties will observe, with the intent of having seamless transfers of information, with approvals in place for the release of information to the investment community, as well as proper document tracking to identify the paper trail for all public information releases.

## The National Investor Relations Institute

The National Investor Relations Institute (NIRI) is an association of those corporate officers and investor relations consultants who are "responsible for communication among corporate management, shareholders, securities analysts and other financial community constituents." It claims to be the largest professional investor relations association in the world, with more than 3,300 members who represent 1,600 publicly held companies.

From a collaboration perspective, NIRI operates more than 30 local chapters in the United States, plus a "virtual chapter" for those members located outside of the country or in areas within the United States that are not adjacent to a local chapter. NIRI also operates several online business roundtables where members can interact and share ideas.

For those wanting to learn more about investor relations, NIRI operates an annual conference, supports a series of webinar events, and presents seminars around the country on various topics. In all cases, training classes are hosted by experts in the investor relations field.

For more information about NIRI, access its web site at www.niri.org.

## Summary

The point of this chapter has been to provide you with knowledge of the supplemental investor relations services that are available. When deciding which services to buy from the outside, you should be particularly favorably inclined toward situations where a high level of skill is needed for a short period of time; retaining these services in-house is too expensive, so paying a consultant is more cost-effective. A consulting area to which these criteria apply particularly well is the services surrounding fund raising activities.

Another way to look at third party investor relations services is how their use varies over the ramp-up phases of a public company. A smaller business will have minimal investor relations expertise within the company, and so will have to outsource the bulk of its investor relations work. As the company expands, it will bring more investor relations work in-house, but then the increased heft of the company in the marketplace may call for the use of a variety of specialized services, such as event management, web site services, and proxy advice. Thus, the mix of third party services will likely change over time, but will always be needed in some form.

# Chapter 20
# Share Performance Measurements

## Introduction

A key concern of the investment community is whether to invest in the shares of a company, which involves multiple types of analysis. Investors are also interested in leading indicators of possible changes in the value of their shares, which they can use to decide whether to sell or hold the shares. The investor relations officer should routinely calculate these same measurements, in order to be able to respond to investor and analyst questions. In this chapter, we address a number of measurements that can assist in the investment decision, as well as other measures that can provide clues regarding future share prices.

## Overview of Share Performance Measurements

The decision to invest in a company is based on a wide array of factors, encompassing a number of measurements that can be used to interpret the operating and financial condition of an entity. In addition, an investor must evaluate the price of a company's stock, and whether that price fairly reflects the earnings power of the business.

In this chapter, we address several measurements that can be used to evaluate the price at which a share is currently selling. The price/earnings ratio compares the price of the stock to the most recently reported earnings of a business, while the capitalization rate derives the implied rate of return on share holdings. We also review the concept of total shareholder return, which compiles the total return for shareholders, based on dividends received and changes in the price of the stock.

We also look at the market value added concept, which calculates the difference between the market value of a business (i.e., the extended price at which all of its shares are currently selling) and the book value of invested capital. This measure provides a clue to the ability of management to generate value. A less-relevant (though common) measurement is the market to book ratio, which compares the market value of a business to its book value; the trouble is that book value is an accounting measure that may have little relevance when deriving the underlying value of a business.

We then turn to the prediction of the direction of a company's future stock price. One approach is the insider buy/sell ratio, under which the buying and selling activities of corporate insiders can be used to guesstimate whether insiders believe the current share price is too high or low. Another indicative measure is the options and warrants to common stock ratio; this ratio can be used to predict how many stock options and warrants may be converted to stock, which can in turn lead to a decline in the price of the stock, since more shares now have a claim on the residual value of a business. Yet another indicative measure is the short interest ratio, which quantifies the amount of interest by short sellers in a company's stock. Since short sellers usually conduct a considerable amount of investigation into the financial statements of a business, it is possible that a spike in short interest indicates problems that will lead to a stock price decline.

We conclude with the institutional holdings ratio, which measures the amount of a company's shares held by institutional investors in relation to the amount of trading volume. The outcome of this measurement is neither good nor bad; it merely reflects how large blocks of stock holdings can impact a variety of issues related to a business.

## Price / Earnings Ratio

The price/earnings ratio is the price currently paid on the open market for a share of a company's stock, divided by its earnings per share. The ratio reveals the multiple of earnings that the investment community is willing to pay to own the stock. A very high multiple indicates that investors believe the company's earnings will improve dramatically, while a low multiple indicates the reverse. If the ratio is already high, there is little chance for the stock price to climb even higher, so there is significant risk that the share price will slide lower in the future.

The investment community usually forces a stock price upward based on future expectations for such issues as new patents, new products, favorable changes in the laws impacting a company, and so forth.

To calculate the price/earnings ratio, divide the current market price per share by fully diluted earnings per share. The formula is:

$$\frac{\text{Current market price per share}}{\text{Fully diluted earnings per share}}$$

It is also possible to derive the ratio by dividing the total current company capitalization by net after-tax earnings. In this case, the formula is:

$$\frac{\text{Current company market capitalization}}{\text{Net after-tax earnings}}$$

Yet another variation is to build an expected price earnings ratio by dividing future earnings expectations per share into the current market price. This is not a firm indicator of where the ratio will actually be in the future, but is a good basis for deciding whether the stock is undervalued or overvalued.

There are several issues with the price/earnings ratio to be aware of. Consider the following problems:

- *Manipulation.* Earnings information can be manipulated by accelerating or deferring expense recognition, as well as through a variety of revenue recognition schemes. A more accurate measure of the value that the investment community is placing on a company's stock is the price to cash flow ratio. Cash flow is a good indicator of the results of operations.

214

- *Industry-wide effects*. Changes in the ratio tend to impact every company in an industry at the same time, because they are all subject to the same market forces, with slight differences between the various companies. Thus, a favorable change in the ratio may not be cause for excessive jubilation for a job well done, since the change may not be traceable to a company's performance at all, but rather to changes in its business environment.
- *Timing*. The price of a company's stock may fluctuate wildly in the short term, as such factors as takeover rumors and large customer orders excite investors and impact the price. Consequently, the ratio can be dramatically different if the timing of the measurement varies by just a few days.

**EXAMPLE**

The common stock of the Cupertino Beanery is currently selling for $15 per share on the open market. The company reported $3.00 of fully diluted earnings per share in its last annual report. Therefore, its price earnings ratio is:

$$\frac{\$15 \text{ Market price per share}}{\$3 \text{ Earnings per share}}$$

$$= 5:1 \text{ Price/earnings ratio}$$

## Capitalization Rate

It can be useful to derive the rate of return that investors expect on a company's stock, based on its current market price and the associated price/earnings ratio. We do this by simply reversing the price/earnings ratio, so that fully diluted earnings per share are divided by the current market price per share. The formula is:

$$\frac{\text{Fully diluted earnings per share}}{\text{Current market price per share}}$$

Since it contains the same information used for the price/earnings ratio noted in the last section, the capitalization rate should be considered to suffer from the same issues. Therefore, allow for possible manipulation of reported earnings, effects impacting the entire industry, and short-term variations in the price of the stock being examined.

**EXAMPLE**

A major institutional investor is interested in purchasing the shares of Atlas Machining Company, which has seen a major decline in its share price over the past year, due to concerns about its facilities in a country where there is a major ongoing insurgency. Despite the insurgency, Atlas has continued to report robust earnings of $3.50 per share in each of the last two years. The investor's target rate of return on its investments is 15%. The capitalization rate for Atlas for the past two years is as follows:

|  | Last Year | Current Date |
|---|---|---|
| Earnings per share | $3.50 | $3.50 |
| Market price per share | $43.75 | $21.88 |
| Capitalization rate | 8% | 16% |

The rapid drop in stock price has doubled the capitalization rate of Atlas over the past year, which makes this a reasonable investment opportunity that exceeds the investor's target rate of return.

## Total Shareholder Return

When an investor buys the shares of a company, the return generated by the purchase will be derived from a combination of the change in the share price over the measurement period, plus any dividends paid by the company in the interim. The formula (on an annual basis) is:

|  | Ending stock price – Beginning stock price |
|---|---|
| + | Sum of all dividends received during the measurement period |
| = | Total shareholder return |

The total return can then be divided by the initial purchase to arrive at a total shareholder return percentage.

This measurement can be skewed to a considerable extent if a shareholder has control over a business. If this is the case and the company is sold, then the shareholder will likely be paid a control premium in exchange for giving up control over the entity.

### EXAMPLE

An investor purchases shares of Albatross Flight Systems for $15.00 per share. One year later, the market value of the shares is $17.00, and the investor has received several dividends totaling $1.50. Based on this information, the total shareholder return is:

|  | $17.00 Ending stock price – $15.00 Beginning stock price |
|---|---|
| + | $1.50 Dividends received |
| = | $3.50 Total shareholder return |

Based on the initial $15.00 purchase price, this represents a 23.3% total shareholder return.

## Market Value Added

The market value added concept derives the difference between the market value of a business and its cost of invested capital. When market value is less than the cost of invested capital, this implies that management has not done a good job of creating value with the equity made available to it by investors. To derive market value added, follow these steps:

1. Multiply the total of all common shares outstanding by their market price.
2. Multiply the total of all preferred shares outstanding by their market price.
3. Combine these totals.
4. Subtract the amount of capital invested in the business.

The formula is:

| | |
|---|---|
| | (Number of common shares outstanding × Share price) |
| + | (Number of preferred shares outstanding × Share price) |
| - | Book value of invested capital |
| = | Market value added |

This measurement should only be used if a company's stock is robustly traded on an established stock exchange. Otherwise, a few occasional trades could trigger substantial changes in the market price of the stock. It may be possible to derive the market value of shares by engaging an appraiser to provide an estimate.

Also, be aware that the current stock price may be based on changes in investor confidence in the market or industry as a whole, and does not relate to the performance (or lack thereof) of management in running a business.

**EXAMPLE**

The investor relations officer of Cud Farms is preparing a press release that reveals the increase in market value added since the new management team was hired. The analysis is based on the following information:

| | Prior Year | Current Year |
|---|---|---|
| Number of common shares outstanding | 5,000,000 | 5,700,000 |
| Common stock price | $4.00 | $4.20 |
| Number of preferred shares outstanding | 400,000 | 375,000 |
| Preferred share price | $11.00 | $11.30 |
| Book value of invested capital | $18,000,000 | $20,625,000 |

The market value added for the prior year is calculated as follows:

| | |
|---|---|
| | (5,000,000 Common shares × $4.00 price) |
| + | (400,000 Preferred shares × $11.00 price) |
| - | $18,000,000 Equity book value |
| = | $6,400,000 Market value added |

The market value added for the current year is calculated as follows:

| | |
|---|---|
| | (5,700,000 Common shares × \$4.20 price) |
| + | (375,000 Preferred shares × \$11.30 price) |
| - | \$20,625,000 Equity book value |
| = | \$7,552,500 Market value added |

Based on this analysis, the investor relations officer can highlight an increase of \$1,152,500 in market value added since the new management team was hired.

## Market to Book Ratio

A common measure of the value of a company's shares is the market to book ratio, which compares the market price of a company' stock to its book value per share. If the market price is well above the book value, this is said to be an indicator of the additional value that the investment community is placing on the ability of a company to earn a profit.

To calculate the market to book ratio, divide the ending price of the company's stock by the book value per share on the same date. The formula is:

$$\frac{\text{Ending market price of stock}}{\text{Book value per share}}$$

There are numerous problems with this measurement that limit its practical use. Consider the following issues:

- The comparison is of the market value of a business to the historical costs at which assets were recorded. There is no realistic reason why an asset base of any particular size should relate to a particular multiple of market price.
- Accounting standards mandate that some quite valuable intangible assets may not be recorded in the accounting records. In businesses where intangibles are the chief competitive advantage, this means that the market to book ratio will be inordinately high.
- Accounting standards mandate the use of accruals, reserves, and depreciation that can artificially alter the value of assets, irrespective of their real market value.
- The market price of the stock used in the numerator is as of a specific point in time, which may not closely relate to the average price of the stock in the recent past.

**EXAMPLE**

An analyst is reviewing the share performance of Failsafe Containment, which manufactures reactor vessels. The current market price of the company's stock is \$20.00, and the book value per share is also \$20.00, resulting in a market to book ratio of 1:1. However, further investigation reveals that the company has substantial real estate holdings, for which the recorded book value is substantially lower than their likely resale prices. Consequently, the analyst assigns a buy rating to the company's stock, which also attracts the attention of several corporate raiders that subsequently purchase the company and sell off the real estate for significant gains.

## Insider Buy/Sell Ratio

In a publicly-held company, a large number of shares are typically held by corporate insiders. These insiders have the best access to information about the current and prospective performance of the business, and so are much more likely to sell their holdings when they believe the market price of the stock is likely peaking. Since these transactions must be reported to the Securities and Exchange Commission and are therefore public knowledge, it is not especially difficult for an outside investor to obtain and analyze stock transactions by insiders. The logic followed by an analyst is that a high proportion of insider sales of company stock to insider purchases of stock is indicative of an insider belief that the stock price will go no higher. This information can be used by an investor to decide when to alter holdings of a company's stock.

To calculate the insider buy/sell ratio, aggregate the number of insider purchases of company stock over the measurement period, and divide by the aggregate amount of insider sales of company stock over the same period. The formula is:

$$\frac{\text{Aggregate insider stock purchases}}{\text{Aggregate insider stock sales}}$$

A ratio of less than one indicates that insiders believe that the price of the stock is peaking, while a ratio of greater than one indicates the reverse.

This is not an easy ratio to interpret, for corporate insiders may have excellent reasons for purchasing and selling company stock that have nothing to do with their perceptions of the company's prospects. Consider the following situations:

- A company recently went public, and many employees holding shares must wait six months before they are allowed to sell their shares. They will undoubtedly do so in six months.
- A newly-hired CEO is required to purchase $1 million of company shares as a condition of her employment.
- A CFO wants to purchase a new house, and sells enough shares to cover the purchase price of the home.
- Employees have such lucrative stock options pending that it would be foolish not to buy shares, irrespective of the future direction of the company's performance.

If the ratio is to be used as a valid indicator of the future direction in which the price of a stock may turn, consider the following situations that may be most applicable:

- There is a broad sell-off or purchasing pattern among multiple employees.

- Employees are incurring debt in order to buy shares.
- Employees in the accounting department, which presumably have the best understanding of company performance, are showing a decided purchasing or selling trend.

## EXAMPLE

Six months have passed since Armadillo Industries went public. During the past week, Armadillo employees have finally had their shares registered, and have been actively liquidating their holdings in the company. An outside analyst reviews the following information to see if there is a discernible trend in insider activity:

| Employee Title | Transaction Type | Number of Shares | Transaction Date |
|---|---|---|---|
| Engineering manager | Sell | 300,000 | November 3 |
| Marketing director | Sell | 185,000 | November 3 |
| Chief financial officer | Buy | 25,000 | November 4 |
| Chief information officer | Sell | 160,000 | November 4 |
| Production manager | Sell | 325,000 | November 5 |
| Chief executive officer | Buy | 15,000 | November 6 |
| Controller | Buy | 5,000 | November 6 |

The information in the table results in an overwhelmingly negative insider buy/sell ratio of 0.046. However, the analyst also notes that every one of the stock sale transactions involved a mid-level manager who might have simply been cashing in for the first time. All of the managers most closely associated with the company's finances are quietly buying up small blocks of shares. Based on his analysis of the information, and despite the outcome of the ratio, the analyst believes that the company will report above-average results when its next quarterly results are released.

## Options and Warrants to Common Stock Ratio

A company may elect to pay third parties with warrants for various services, and compensate its employees with stock options. If the business does so extensively, this can create an inordinately large pool of options and warrants that could be converted to common stock in the near future, resulting in significantly reduced earnings per share, and therefore a possible reduction in the stock price. Because of this dilutive effect, outside analysts like to monitor the amount of outstanding options and warrants.

Analysts will not consider all options and warrants to be convertible into common stock. Instead, they will focus on just those instruments that are currently "in the money," which means that the designated exercise price is below the current market price of a company's common stock. In this case, someone could (for example) exercise a stock option at a designated price of $5.00 and immediately earn a profit of $1.00 if the market price is $6.00. Conversely, if the market price were $5.00 or less, no option or warrant holder would find it profitable to purchase common stock with their instruments, and so would let them expire unused.

Given the importance of being in the money, an analyst is only interested in these options and warrants, which may be far fewer than the total pool of options and warrants outstanding. Consequently, the calculation of options and warrants to common stock is to divide the grand total of in-the-money stock options and warrants by the total number of common shares currently outstanding. The formula is:

$$\frac{\text{Stock options in the money} + \text{Warrants in the money}}{\text{Total common shares outstanding}}$$

The measurement could be further refined to exclude those stock options that have not yet vested, since the holders of these options cannot yet exercise the options.

It may be useful to re-measure this ratio based on a modest prospective increase in the company's market price, rather than the current price. Doing so may significantly boost the number of shares beyond the level indicated by the initial measurement. This can warn outside investors that a run-up in the stock price could result in a large block of additional shares being issued.

## EXAMPLE

Creekside Industrial has recently gone public through an initial public offering. An analyst is reviewing the information submitted by Creekside to the Securities and Exchange Commission to ascertain the extent to which existing stock options and warrants may trigger the issuance of additional shares in the near future, thereby watering down the price of Creekside's stock. The analyst finds the following information:

| | |
|---|---|
| Common shares outstanding | 50,000,000 |
| Warrants in the money | 1,000,000 |
| Options in the money and vested | 3,500,000 |
| Options in the money and vesting in one year | 750,000 |
| Options in the money if price rises 20% | 2,750,000 |
| Options in the money if price rises 20%, and vesting in one year | 10,000,000 |

The analyst converts this information into a series of ratios that compare the options and warrants under various circumstances to common stock, which is noted in the following table:

| [cumulative] (000s) | In the Money Now | Vesting in One Year | In the Money with 20% Price Increase | In the Money with 20% Increase & Vesting in 1 Year |
|---|---|---|---|---|
| Options and warrants | 4,500 | 5,250 | 8,000 | 18,000 |
| Number of common shares | 50,000 | 50,000 | 50,000 | 50,000 |
| Ratio | 9% | 11% | 16% | 36% |

The analyst notes that the amount of stock outstanding is likely to increase to a modest extent in the near future and in one year, but that the real risk is associated with a 20% increase in the price of Creekside's stock. If that happens, an additional 18,000,000 stock options will be in the money, which could result in a cumulative total of 36% of the existing balance of shares being issued. The analyst concludes that any run-ups in the price of Creekside stock should be closely monitored.

## Short Interest Ratio

It can be useful to track the interest of short sellers in a company's stock, since this can presage an abrupt decline in the price of that stock, especially once the short sellers begin to publicize their findings in an effort to create bearish sentiments about the stock. The easiest way to track short seller interest is through the short interest ratio. To calculate it, obtain the aggregate amount of short interest (which is available from several websites) and divide by the average daily trading volume for the stock. Short interest is the number of shares that investors have sold short, and which they have not yet closed out. The formula is:

$$\frac{\text{Short interest}}{\text{Average daily trading volume}}$$

The outcome of this analysis is the number of days that it would take short sellers to cover their positions in the company's stock, which they would likely have to do if the price of the company's shares starts to rise (since an increase in price generates losses for a short seller).

There are several analyses that can be derived from the short interest ratio. Consider the following situations:

- A prolonged and significant short interest ratio reveals a great deal of downward pressure on a stock by short sellers; however,
- When the ratio exceeds 2:1, short sellers will likely need to start buying shares in order to cover their positions, which can create a short-term spike in the stock price.
- Also, the ratio can be applied to entire industries, to see if short sellers are bearish on the fundamentals of an industry. If so, this is a strong indicator that stock prices will be flat or fall across the sector.

## Institutional Holdings Ratio

The investors in a publicly-held company are typically comprised of a small number of institutional investors and a large number of retail investors. It is generally considered good to have a large proportion of institutional shareholders, for the following reasons:

- They indicate that a sophisticated investor is willing to buy into the company
- The investor relations department can more easily sell shares in large blocks to a small number of these investors

- The investor relations staff can more efficiently concentrate its publicity efforts on a small group of shareholders

There is no optimum level of institutional holdings to target. Instead, be aware of long-term trends in the activity ratio, and how this activity may impact the company's position in the public markets.

To calculate the institutional holdings ratio, divide the total trading volume by the period-end holdings of institutional investors. The measurement period is three months, since the holdings information comes from the Form 13F filings that institutional investors must file on a quarterly basis. The formula is:

$$\frac{\text{Total trading volume}}{\text{Institutional investor stockholdings}}$$

### EXAMPLE

The Excalibur Shaving Company recently went public, selling a massive number of its shares to a small group of institutional investors. The trouble is that there are so few remaining shares that retail investors are complaining of an inability to trade their shares. Accordingly, the investor relations department contacts several institutional investors to see if they will part with some of their holdings. The results appear in the following table:

|  | One Month After IPO | Six Months After IPO |
|---|---|---|
| Total trading volume | 2,500,000 | 10,000,000 |
| Institutional investor stockholdings | 50,000,000 | 30,000,000 |
| Institutional holdings ratio | 5% | 33% |

The table reveals that the investor relations department has succeeded in convincing some of the institutional investors to part with their shares, since the total holdings of this group have markedly declined. The change has resulted in a significant benefit, as activity in the company's stock has quadrupled.

## Management of Performance Measurements

The measurements noted in this chapter are among the more likely ones to be brought to the attention of the investor relations officer, but this will not be all. Some investors or analysts may place a particular emphasis on liquidity, profitability, cash flows, or other metrics. Consequently, the group of measurements with which one must be conversant will vary by company and the interests of the people making inquiries about investments.

As the investor relations officer becomes more familiar with the types of measurements that the investment community wants to discuss, it can make sense to devise a report that lists these measurements over time, perhaps by quarter, for the past few years. Doing so creates a useful basis for a discussion of long-term trends. Another option is to accumulate this information in comparison to the same measurements for the company's key competitors. If the company's measurements tend to lag behind those of the peer group, it may be time to investigate the issue and prepare talking points regarding any concerns that might be raised in an investor meeting.

As a company changes (both in terms of size and structure), so too must its measurements. For example, cash flow may be of great concern to a smaller business that has minimal cash reserves, but is of reduced interest to an established company that is more interested in grabbing a commanding share of its markets. Consequently, expect to slowly drop a small number of measurements that the company uses as part of its talking points, and transition to an equally small number of replacement measurements that better reflect the direction in which the company is headed. However, the core group of share performance measurements outlined in this chapter will probably not change over time, since they are applicable to all publicly-held companies.

> **Tip:** Only add a measurement to the group of "official" company measurements after considering the matter for some time. Once a measurement is added, it is quite difficult to terminate without raising suspicions that the company wants to hide the information that was formerly being presented.

It is of some importance to always use the same formula for each measurement presented. If the company modifies a formula, there will be a suspicion that the change was made in order to bolster the reported results of the business. To mitigate this concern, consider posting on the investor relations section of the company website the exact formula used for each measurement. If there is a realistic need to alter a formula, issue a notification of the change, and also reformulate the measurements for all comparative periods, so there are no instances of comparing "apples to oranges."

A final thought regarding performance measurements is that the company should, whenever possible, issue a complete set of measurements, rather than trickling out one or two measurements at a time. A complete package allows the investor relations officer to give a comprehensive and integrated view of company performance, which may head off any inquiries regarding poor performance that relate to just one or two measurements.

## Summary

The measurements addressed earliest in this chapter, such as the price/earnings ratio, can certainly give an investor a general feel for whether the shares of a company are over or undervalued. However, the decision to invest in a company should not be based on just the measurements noted in this chapter. Instead, investors are likely to conduct a comprehensive review of both the financial and operational condition of a business, as well as of the industry in which it operates, to arrive at a complete set of information that can be used as the basis for an investment decision. The investor relations officer should be aware of all the measurements that investors are likely to use, and can assist them in noting the strengths and shortcomings of each measurement.

# Glossary

## A

*Accelerated filer.* A company having an aggregate market value owned by investors who are not affiliated with the company of less than $700 million, but more than $75 million.

*Accredited investor.* An investor who is defined by the Securities and Exchange Commission as being financially sophisticated, and who therefore requires a reduced amount of financial disclosure.

*Accretive earnings.* An increase in earnings, usually assumed to be a net increase in earnings per share that is generated by an acquisition.

*Affiliate.* The officers, directors, and significant shareholders of a business.

*Analyst.* A person who engages in the evaluation of investments, and who develops buy, sell, or hold recommendations for securities.

*Annual meeting.* A gathering of company shareholders, at which the results and outlook of a business are discussed, and directors are elected.

*Annual report.* A report sent to a company's shareholders once a year, describing the operations and financial results and condition of the business.

*Average daily trading volume.* The average daily trading volume reported for a security during the preceding four calendar weeks.

## B

*Beneficial owner.* A shareholder whose share ownership is masked by a proxy arrangement with a stockbroker or other institution.

*Block.* A quantity of stock that either has a purchase price of $200,000 or more, or is at least 5,000 shares and has a purchase price of at least $50,000, or is at least 20 round lots of the security and totals 150 percent or more of the trading volume for that security.

*Broker search.* The process of contacting brokers, banks, and other intermediaries to determine how many annual reports and proxy statements will be needed for the beneficial holders in a company's proxy mailing. The search is performed by a company's proxy distribution or solicitation agent.

*Buy side.* The group of investing institutions, such as pension funds and mutual funds, that buys and sells large amounts of securities in their roles as money managers.

## C

*Cash equivalent.* A short-term, very liquid investment that is easily convertible into a known amount of cash, and which is so near its maturity that it presents an insignificant risk of a change in value because of changes in interest rates.

*Cautionary statement.* A statement made along with a forward-looking statement, noting factors that can cause actual results to differ from the information included in the forward-looking statement.

*Consensus earnings estimate.* The average earnings estimate for a business, as compiled from a group of analysts.

## D

*Dividend.* The distribution of cash or other assets to a class of company shareholders by the company in which they hold shares, as authorized by its board of directors.

## E

*Earnings call.* A conference call between the senior management team of a public company and the investment community, to discuss the company's financial results.

*Employee stock purchase plan.* A company program under which employees can buy company shares, usually at a discount, through ongoing payroll deductions.

## F

*Fact sheet.* A brief assemblage of information about a company, stating key points about its market positioning, operations, financial results, and financial position.

*Financial statements.* A collection of reports about an organization's financial condition, which typically include the income statement, balance sheet, and statement of cash flows.

*Float.* The number of shares in a public company that are currently available for trading by the public. This does not include restricted stock.

*Form 10-K.* A document filed annually with the SEC by a publicly held company, containing its audited financial statements and supporting commentary.

*Form 10-Q.* A document filed quarterly with the SEC by a publicly held company, containing its audited financial statements and supporting commentary.

*Form 8-K.* A document filed with the SEC by a publicly held company, to announce a variety of pre-defined significant changes impacting the company.

*Form S-8.* A document filed with the SEC by a publicly held company, to register shares issued to employees through benefit or incentive plans.

*Forward looking statement.* A statement that predicts results or suggests possible future results.

*Fund manager.* The person responsible for implementing the investment strategy for an investment fund.

## G

*GAAP.* A contraction of Generally Accepted Accounting Principles, which is an accounting framework used within the United States to construct financial statements.

*Guidance.* Estimates of future earnings that a business makes to the investment community.

## H

*Hedge fund.* An investment fund limited to accredited investors, which usually requires a lengthy investment period, and which can use many possible strategies to maximize returns.

*Householding.* The concept of grouping together the members of a household for the purposes of issuing a single annual report and proxy statement to a mailing address.

*Hypothecation.* The pledging of assets as loan collateral; usually refers to the debit balance in a margin account.

## I

*Initial public offering.* The first offering of the stock of a privately-held business to the investing public.

*Inspectors of election.* The persons appointed to tabulate shareholder votes, determine that ballots were properly cast, and announce the results of the voting.

*Institutional investor.* An entity that buys and sells securities in sufficiently large quantities to obtain reduced commissions and other preferential treatment.

*Intrinsic value.* The aggregated worth of a company's physical and intangible assets.

*Investment banker.* A person who raises capital on behalf of businesses, and who may also engage in brokering the sale of businesses.

*Investment club.* A group of individual investors that votes to buy or sell investments with their pooled funds.

*Investment community.* Everyone involved in the analysis or trading of company securities.

*Investor.* A person or entity that buys assets with the objective of eventually receiving a return on the purchased assets.

*Investor relations.* A functional area within a publicly held company that provides information about the financial and operational performance of the company to the investment community.

## K

*Key performance indicator.* A measurement used by a company to gauge its performance in certain operational and/or financial areas.

## L

*Large accelerated filer.* A company having an aggregate market value owned by investors who are not affiliated with the company of a minimum of $700 million.

*Large cap company.* A publicly traded company that has a market capitalization of more than $10 billion.

*Lockup agreement.* A legal agreement under which an individual (usually a company insider) cannot sell shares in a business for a specific period of time.

## M

*Market capitalization.* The total number of shares outstanding, multiplied by their current market price.

*Market maker.* A broker-dealer that facilitates trading in a security by displaying buy and sell quotations for the issuing company's shares, for which it may sell from its own inventory.

*Material non-public information.* Information not made available to the public generally, and for which there is a substantial likelihood that an investor would consider it important in deciding whether to buy, sell, or hold a company's securities.

*Micro cap company.* A publicly traded company that has a market capitalization of between $50 million and $300 million.

*Mid cap company.* A publicly traded company that has a market capitalization of between $2 billion and $10 billion.

*Mosaic theory.* The collection of a broad range of information about a company for use in determining the value of its securities.

## N

*Naked short selling.* The practice of selling shares short without first borrowing the shares that are being sold.

*Nano cap company.* A publicly traded company that has a market capitalization of less than $50 million.

*NASDAQ.* A computerized system that provides price quotations and facilitates the purchase and sale of securities.

*Non-deal road show.* One or more meetings with members of the investment community, where the management of a company educates potential investors about the business. There is no specific securities offering mentioned in these meetings.

*Non-objecting beneficial owner (NOBO)*. The owner of securities, who permits a financial intermediary to release the owner's contact information to the issuer of the securities. This information is used to contact the owner regarding proxies and other matters.

## O

*Objecting beneficial owner (OBO)*. An owner of securities that has elected to shield its identity, so companies must instead deal with the third party that holds its securities.

*Odd lot shareholder*. A shareholder who holds less than 100 shares of the stock of a company.

*Operating cycle*. The average time period required to acquire inventory, sell it, and obtain cash from the customer for the sale.

*Other comprehensive income*. All changes that are not permitted in the main part of the income statement. These items include unrealized gains and losses on available-for-sale securities, cash flow hedge gains and losses, foreign currency translation adjustments, and pension plan gains or losses.

*Over the counter bulletin board*. A stock listing service that shows real-time quotes, last-sale prices, and volume information for securities that are not listed on a stock exchange, but which are current in their SEC filings.

## P

*Penny stock*. A stock that trades at a price below $5. The resulting low capitalization of companies whose shares are classified as penny stock makes them speculative investments.

*Piggyback rights*. An investor's right to have his unregistered shares included in a share registration. The investor does not have the right to initiate the registration process.

*Pink sheets*. Bid and ask prices published by OTC Markets Group, Inc. for over the counter stocks. The name is derived from the pink color of the paper on which this information was originally printed.

*Preannouncement*. An announcement in advance of the date when earnings and guidance are normally issued, to adjust investor expectations.

*Press release*. A brief statement about a company event that is released for outside consumption.

*Pro forma*. The financial results of a business that reflect a proposed change, either for historical or projected results.

*Prospectus*. A document filed with the SEC, in which is stated the details of an offering of securities to the public.

*Proxy materials.* The proxy statement, proxy card, annual report, and notice of internet availability that are sent to shareholders of record in preparation for the annual shareholders' meeting.

*Proxy solicitor.* A person or entity that attempts to obtain the authorization of shareholders to vote on their behalf on a ballot.

## Q

*Quiet period.* The period immediately following the initial filing of a registration statement with the SEC, extending until the SEC staff declares the statement effective. During this time, company officials are constrained by SEC rules from making certain public statements.

## R

*Registration statement.* A detailed form that must be completed and filed with the SEC before the initial offering of securities to the investing public.

*Regulation A.* A regulation of the SEC, under which simplified filing documentation is allowed for offerings of $5 million or less.

*Regulation D.* A regulation of the SEC, under which a business can raise a limited amount of funds without registering the securities with the SEC.

*Regulation FD.* A regulation of the SEC, designed to prevent publicly-held companies from selectively disclosing certain information to the investment community.

*Restricted shares.* Shares in a company that cannot be traded without first being registered with the SEC or qualifying under an exemption.

*Retained earnings.* The accumulated earnings of a business since its inception, less any prior distributions to shareholders, and net of any prior period adjustments.

*Reverse road show.* A road show where investors come to the company for presentations.

*Reverse stock split.* A reduction in the number of outstanding shares of a company, usually in an effort to increase the earnings per share and/or market price per share.

*Reverse-forward stock split.* A two-step approach to eliminating the number of small shareholders, which begins with a reverse split in a sufficient amount to reduce some shareholders to less than one share, which allows the business to cash them out. The second step is a stock split that returns the remaining share counts to their original amounts.

*Road show.* A series of presentations by an issuer of securities to potential buyers, with the intent of creating interest in the securities it intends to sell.

*Round lot.* A grouping of 100 shares of a stock, or any grouping that can be evenly divided by 100.

*RSS feed.* A content delivery system, designed to syndicate news and other internet content.

## S

*Safe harbor statement.* A statement included in an information release that reduces or eliminates the liability associated with the information release, as long as the information was issued in good faith.

*Secondary offering.* New stock issued to the investing public by a company that is already publicly held.

*Securities.* Financing or investment instruments that can be traded, such as bonds, shares, options, and warrants.

*Securities and Exchange Commission.* A federal government entity that regulates the securities markets with the intent of protecting investors.

*Sell side.* The individuals and entities that assist the investing public in making investment decisions.

*Senior official.* Any director, executive officer, investor or public relations officer, or other person with similar functions.

*Shell company.* A business entity that has no substantial business activity or significant assets.

*Short interest.* The number of shares in a company that investors have sold short and not yet closed out.

*Short seller.* A person or entity that sells securities it does not own, using borrowed securities. The intent is to earn a profit if it buys back the securities at a lower price, which assumes that the price of the targeted security is declining.

*Short squeeze.* When those holding short positions must pay higher prices to acquire securities, in order to terminate their positions in those securities.

*Small cap stock.* The stock of a company that has a small market capitalization, usually considered to be in the range of $300 million to $2 billion.

*Stockbroker.* A person or business that executes the buy and sell orders of an investor in exchange for a commission.

*Stock exchange.* A physical or electronic financial market in which securities are bought and sold.

*Stock option.* The right to buy a stock at a predetermined price within a certain period of time, or on a specific date.

*Stock transfer agent.* An entity paid by a company to maintain its shareholder records, including account balances and share certificate issuances.

*Sovereign wealth fund.* An investment fund that manages cash on behalf of a government.

## T

*Ticker symbol.* A grouping of characters that uniquely identify a publicly-traded security. Investors use ticker symbols to place trade orders for securities.

## U

*Underwriter.* An entity that administers the issuance of securities by another business.

## V

*Value proposition.* The underlying intrinsic value that a company represents.

*Voting instruction form.* A ballot sent to a beneficial shareholder by its intermediary broker or bank, asking for voting instructions concerning a company's shareholder ballot.

## W

*Warrant.* The right to purchase an issuing company's securities from the issuer at a designated price and within a certain period of time.

*Wrap report.* A report issued to investors instead of a more elaborate annual report, containing a Form 10-K and supporting commentary.

# Index

Abandoned property laws ................... 135
Accredited investor ........................... 183
American Stock Exchange ................. 120
Analyst ............................................. 86
Analysts' day .................................... 91
Annual report .................................... 29
Annual shareholder meeting .............. 161

Balance sheet .................................... 140
Beneficial shareholder ....................... 160
Best efforts arrangement .................... 175
Bid-ask spread .................................. 117
Blue sky laws .................................... 179
Branding value basis .......................... 16
Broker search .................................... 166
Budget, investor relations .................... 5
Buy side ............................................ 96
Buy side analyst ................................ 98

Capitalization rate ............................. 215
Cautionary statement .......................... 70
Class certification .............................. 67
Clipping service ................................ 210
Closing out ....................................... 112
Communications calendar ................... 38
Communications review process .......... 37
Comparative balance sheet ................. 143
Conference presentations .................... 34
Consensus earnings estimate .............. 64
Consultant, investor relations ............. 204
Contagion effect ................................ 41
Customer credibility concept .............. 15

Delisting from a stock exchange ........ 124
Direct method ................................... 144
Direct stock purchase plan ................. 128
Disclosure form ................................ 47
Discovery process ............................. 67
Dividend payment service .................. 207
Dividend payments ............................ 130
Dividend reinvestment plan ............... 129

Earnings call
    Attendees ..................................... 49
    Bad behavior ................................ 53
    Logistics ...................................... 49
    Question and answer session ........... 51
    Structure ...................................... 50
    Variations on ................................ 53
Earnings press release ........................ 28
Electronic shareholder meeting ........... 164
Employee stock purchase plan ........... 128

Fact sheet ......................................... 31
Financial journalist ............................ 36
Firm commitment method ................... 175
Float management .............................. 126
Foreign investor ................................ 101
Form 10-K ........................................ 149
Form 10-Q ........................................ 148
Form 3 ............................................. 157
Form 4 ............................................. 157
Form 5 ............................................. 157
Form 8-K ......................................... 152
Forward-looking statement, legal basis
    for .............................................. 66

Green proposition .............................. 15
Growth strategy ................................ 104
Guidance
    Aggressiveness of ......................... 62
    Arguments in favor of .................... 55
    Consistency .................................. 60
    Guidelines ................................... 56
    Information issued ......................... 58
    Range .......................................... 59
    Schedule ...................................... 62
    Timing ......................................... 57
    When not to issue .......................... 64

Hedge fund ....................................... 99
Householding .................................... 169
Hyperlinks to other sites .................... 80

Income statement .............................. 137
Income strategy ................................ 105
Indirect method ................................ 146
Individual investor ............................ 99
Initial public offering
    Process flow ................................. 173
    Reasons for and against .................. 172

# Index

Insider buy/sell ratio ............................ 219
Inspectors of election........................... 167
Institutional holdings ratio................... 222
Institutional investor......................... 96
Intellectual property........................... 15
Investing strategies ............................ 104
Investment banker ........................... 95
Investment club ................................. 102
Investor relations
    Advantages of................................. 7
    Budget........................................... 5
    Consultant................................... 204
    Definition of ..................................... 1
    Interactions with public relations....... 8
    Officer........................................... 2
    Role in IPO ................................. 180
    Staff ............................................. 5
    Website ...................................... 73

Job description, investor relations .......... 2

Listing criteria
    Capital Market .............................. 122
    Global Market.............................. 121
    Global Select Market ..................... 120
    NYSE........................................... 119
    NYSE Amex ................................. 120
    Toronto Stock Exchange................ 122
Lock-up agreements ........................... 128
Low cost proposition .......................... 14

Mailing list ....................................... 38
Managing underwriter ....................... 175
Market maker ................................... 124
Market share, excess amount of .......... 18
Market to book value......................... 218
Market value added ........................... 216
Media relations ................................. 35
Merger arbitrage strategy ................... 105
Momentum monitoring....................... 111
Morning call ..................................... 87

Naked short selling............................ 111
NASDAQ ......................................... 120
NASDAQ Capital Market .................. 122
NASDAQ Global Market................... 121
NASDAQ Global Select Market ........ 120
National Investor Relations Institute .. 212
Negative news
    Early warning system ..................... 40

Response system ............................... 39
Negative reputation, impact of............. 20
New York Stock Exchange ................. 119
Newspaper articles ............................ 34
NOBO reporting................................ 210
Non-deal road show ........................... 191
Non-objecting beneficial owner.......... 161
Notice and access rule........................ 168
Notice and inquiry............................. 166
NYSE Rule 452................................. 169

Objecting beneficial owner ................ 161
Odd lot shareholders .......................... 134
Options to common stock ratio .......... 220
Over the Counter Bulletin Board ........ 124
Overallotment ................................... 175

Pacing concept ................................. 15
Piggyback rights................................ 185
Pink Sheets....................................... 125
Preannouncements ............................ 61
Presentation, contents of.................... 196
Press release ..................................... 25
Press release distribution service ........ 209
Price/earnings ratio ........................... 214
Private Securities Litigation Reform Act
    .............................................. 68
Proxy card ....................................... 166
Proxy solicitor.................... 167, 170, 207
Proxy statement................................. 166
Proxy voting..................................... 165
Public relations................................. 8
Public relations firm.......................... 209
Public shell company ......................... 177

Question and answer session................ 51
Quiet period ..................................... 45

Registered shareholder....................... 160
Regulation A stock sales .................... 186
Regulation D stock sales .................... 184
Regulation FD................................... 77
    Compliance with ............................ 45
    Essentials of .................................. 44
Regulation G .................................... 157
Researcher, company-paid.................. 208
Restricted stock ................................ 183
Reverse merger ................................. 177
Reverse road show ............................ 196
Reverse stock split ............................ 130

Reverse-forward stock split ............... 179
Risk mitigation ............................. 19, 42
Road show
    Attendees ..................................... 194
    Boredom ...................................... 202
    Fund raising ................................ 189
    International ................................. 101
    Logistics ..................................... 199
    Non-deal ..................................... 191
    Preparation ................................... 198
    Presentation follow up ................... 195
    Presentation format ....................... 190
    Presentation team .......................... 190
    Reverse ....................................... 196
    Routing ....................................... 189
    Sell side participation ................... 193
Roll up strategy ................................. 105
Round table discussions ...................... 34
Rule 144 stock sales ........................... 187

Safe harbor provision ................... 69, 133
Sales channels.................................... 16
Seasonality........................................ 19
Securities and Exchange Commission.... 9
Sell side ............................................ 86
Shell company ................................... 177
Short interest...................................... 112
Short interest ratio ............................. 112
Short seller
    Dealing with ................................ 113
    Passive dealings ........................... 115
    Strategy of.................................... 109
    Targets ........................................ 112
Short squeeze..................................... 113
Sovereign wealth fund......................... 99
Statement of cash flows...................... 144
Statement of retained earnings .......... 147
Steady income proposition ................. 14
Stock buybacks.................................. 132
Stock exchange
    Capital Market ............................ 122
    Delisting from.............................. 124
    Global Select Market .................... 120
    NASDAQ..................................... 120
    NASDAQ Global Market .............. 121
    NYSE.......................................... 119
    NYSE Amex ................................ 120
    Overview of................................. 117
    Toronto ....................................... 122
Stock index ....................................... 98

Stock monitoring................................111
Stock options.....................................106
Stock purchase plan ...........................107
Stock registration ..............................126
Stock split.........................................129
Stock transfer agent...........................206
Stockbroker........................................94
Stratified mailing ..............................170
Street name.......................................160

Technical analysis strategy .................105
Theme investment strategy .................106
Ticker symbol ...................................118
Toronto Stock Exchange .....................122
Total shareholder return .....................216

Unique product proposition..................16
Unrestricted stock ..............................183

Value drivers......................................17
Value proposition
    Branding based ..............................16
    Communication of..........................21
    Concept ........................................10
    Customer credibility .......................15
    Employee based.............................16
    Formulation ..................................12
    Green concept................................15
    Intellectual property .......................15
    Linkage to strategy ........................23
    Low cost .......................................14
    Pacing..........................................15
    Product based ................................16
    Research .......................................11
    Sales channel based.........................16
    Steady income ...............................14
Value strategy ...................................104

Warrants............................................185
Website
    Functionality .................................76
    Information removal........................83
    Interactive features .........................82
    Investor relations ...........................73
    Multi-language ..............................101
    Multimedia option .........................77
    Provided by third parties .................85
    Usage for IPO................................84
    Usage for Regulation FD.................77